Samantha Holland

"This is a timely and important book for the sports coaching community. Gender equality impacts upon all coaches and therefore all athletes. This accessible book will be of interest not only to academics, graduate students and undergraduates invested in redressing the gender imbalance across sports contexts, but also to coaches, coach educators and policy makers alike."

Dr Luke Jones, *University of Hull*

"This text should be a key point of reference for anyone wishing to gain more subject knowledge of the intersections of gender and sports coaching. Its strengths lie in its ability to unpack the complexity of the problem – the under-representation of women in sports coaching. It moves beyond homogenised notions of 'women' and 'sport' to look at different kinds of women's experiences in various sporting contexts. It explores the challenges posed by this under-representation, drawing from different theoretical and methodological approaches. Finally, its contributions lie in its ability to move beyond the 'problem' and 'challenge' to offer solutions for all those interested in addressing this imbalance."

Dr Annette Stride, *Principle Lecturer, Leeds Beckett University*

Improving Gender Equity in Sports Coaching

The sport coaching profession has historically been and continues to be a White male-dominated occupation and this remains a global issue. This imbalance persists despite an improvement in wider social attitudes and legislation towards equality and diversity within many societies, and despite the action by sporting organisations and national governing bodies. Within the research literature, the under-representation of women in sport coaching is a well-documented issue with a number of research studies highlighting the experiences and impact of being in the minority for women coaches. The issue of gender inequity in sport coaching is a long-standing one and shows little sign of changing significantly anytime soon. Therefore, a new approach is needed, one that draws on the knowledge and evidence we have to create actionable, sustainable, deep-rooting interventions that challenge the issue of gender equity at its very core. The overall purpose of *Improving Gender Equity in Sports Coaching* is to take an action or forward-thinking approach about what works, or could work, to improve the recruitment, development, or promotion of women sport coaches. The book brings together a global group of esteemed scholars working in this subject area. In this book, we have brought together not just the insight but also a collection of strategies and recommendations as to how this research could be or has been utilised to make our sport coaching environment places where all coaches feel as though they belong. As such, this ground-breaking book is a must read not just for students and researchers of gender equity in sport but also for policy and decision-makers working in sport.

Leanne Norman is Professor and Director of the Research Centre for Social Justice in Sport & Society within the Carnegie School of Sport at Leeds Beckett University, UK. Her research examines issues of gender equity related to sports coaching, sports leadership, and organisations. Her work is driven towards improving the participation, performance, and leadership pathways for diverse social groups, principally, different groups of women.

Women, Sport and Physical Activity
Edited by Elizabeth Pike, University of Hertfordshire, UK

The *Women, Sport and Physical Activity* series showcases work by leading international researchers and emerging scholars that offers new perspectives on the involvement of women in sport and physical activity. The series is interdisciplinary in scope, drawing on sociology, cultural studies, history, politics, gender studies, leisure studies, psychology, exercise science and coaching studies, and consists of two main strands: thematic volumes addressing key global issues in the study of women, sport and physical activity; and sport-specific volumes, each of which offers an overview of women's participation and leadership in a particular sport.

Available in this series:

Women's Artistic Gymnastics
Socio-cultural Perspectives
Edited by Roslyn Kerr, Natalie Barker-Ruchti, Carly Stewart and Gretchen Kerr

Women in Rugby
Edited by Helene Joncheray

Improving Gender Equity in Sports Coaching
Edited by Leanne Norman

For more information about this series, please visit: www.routledge.com/sport/series/WSPA

Improving Gender Equity in Sports Coaching

Edited by Leanne Norman

Routledge
Taylor & Francis Group
NEW YORK AND LONDON

First published 2022
by Routledge
52 Vanderbilt Avenue, New York, NY 10017

and by Routledge
2 Park Square, Milton Park, Abingdon, Oxon, OX14 4RN

Routledge is an imprint of the Taylor & Francis Group, an informa business

© 2022 Taylor & Francis

The right of Leanne Norman to be identified as the author of the editorial material, and of the authors for their individual chapters, has been asserted in accordance with sections 77 and 78 of the Copyright, Designs and Patents Act 1988.

All rights reserved. No part of this book may be reprinted or reproduced or utilised in any form or by any electronic, mechanical, or other means, now known or hereafter invented, including photocopying and recording, or in any information storage or retrieval system, without permission in writing from the publishers.

Trademark notice: Product or corporate names may be trademarks or registered trademarks and are used only for identification and explanation without intent to infringe.

Library of Congress Cataloging-in-Publication Data
A catalog record for this book has been requested

ISBN: 978-0-367-46413-4 (hbk)
ISBN: 978-1-032-04912-0 (pbk)
ISBN: 978-1-003-02864-2 (ebk)

Typeset in New Baskerville
by Apex CoVantage, LLC

Printed in the United Kingdom
by Henry Ling Limited

Contents

List of Figures   x
List of Tables   xi
About the Contributors   xii
Acknowledgements   xviii

Introduction: Bringing About Sustainable Change to Improving Gender Equity in Sport Coaching   1
LEANNE NORMAN

PART I
Setting the Scene: How Gender Inequity Manifests Itself in Sport Coaching Contexts and Why Change Is Needed   9

1 **The Glass Cliff, Gender, and Sport Leadership: A Narrative Review and Meta-Analysis**   11
GEORGE B. CUNNINGHAM

2 **Gender Stereotypes as Mechanisms of Social Exclusion of Women as Football Coaches**   30
TORSTEN SCHLESINGER, FLORIAN INGWERSEN AND YVONNE WEIGELT-SCHLESINGER

PART II
Strategies for Supporting a More Gender-Inclusive Sport Coaching Workforce   51

3 **Transformational Change: Creating a New Culture of Sport Coaching**   53
GUYLAINE DEMERS, CARI DIN AND PENNY WERTHNER

viii Contents

4 **Barriers and Supports in the Career Trajectories of Graduate-Level Female Sports Coaching Students**   70
STEPHEN HARVEY AND LETITIA PRICE

5 **Can Sex-Integrated Sport Provide a Gender-Equitable Coaching Environment?**   89
DONNA DE HAAN AND LUCY DUMBELL

6 **It's on Boys! University Coach Educators and the Production, Maintenance, and Disruption of Gender Structures**   104
NATALIE BARKER-RUCHTI, LAURA PURDY AND LOLITA DUDENIENE

7 **Gender-Equity Policies in Sport in Practice: From Words to Action**   121
SUSANNA SOLER, INGRID HINOJOSA-ALCALDE, PEDRONA SERRA AND ANA ANDRÉS

8 **Organisation-Level Practices to Support Women in Coaching**   138
LAURA BURTON AND AJHANAI NEWTON

PART III
From Research to Practice: Evidence of Impactful Research That Has Contributed to More Gender-Inclusive Sport Coaching Contexts   157

9 **Shared Experiences From the Margins: Culturally Diverse Women in Coaching in Aotearoa New Zealand, the United States, and the United Kingdom**   159
JULIA SYMONS

10 **Supporting and Developing Women in Sport Coaching: A Lifespan Career Approach**   177
NICOLE LAVOI AND COURTNEY J. BOUCHER

11 **An Evaluation of a Mentoring Programme to Support High-Performance Women Coaches**   198
LUKE NORRIS, NICOLA CLARKE AND LEANNE NORMAN

12 **Reflections on Career Development From Women Who Coach Canadian Elite Track and Field Athletes**   217
LARENA HOEBER AND LAURA DAHLSTROM

13 'If There Were More Women Coaches Around, I Think Things Would Be Different' Women Boxing Coaches: Struggles to Challenge and Change a Male-Dominated Sport Environment   234
JORID HOVDEN AND ANNE TJØNNDAL

Index   254

Figures

1.1	Glass cliff publications over time	20
2.1	Multilevel framework for explaining the impact of gender stereotypes on the exclusion of women from coaching education	35
7.1	Physical education textbook photographs reflecting leadership roles	131
10.1	Ecological Intersectional Model of Barriers and Supports for Women in Sport Coaching	179
10.2	Stages of Career Progression Model	179
10.3	Integration of stages of career progression within the Ecological Intersectional Model of Barriers and Supports for Women in Sport Coaching	180
11.1	Number of women involved in football worldwide from the Women's Football Member Association's Survey Report 2019	198
13.1	The Norway Female Box logo	236
13.2	A coach sparring with her athlete	240
13.3	Coaches and athletes posing for a group photo after training	241
13.4	Female coach and female cutman at work during a boxing tournament	245
13.5	Norway Female Box athletes walking home together from training	251

Tables

1.1	Glass cliff meta-analytic results	21
2.1	DFB licence holder in 2019, differentiated by male and female	30
2.2	Female graduates of German coaching education from 2015 to 2019	31
3.1	Numbers of accredited coaches at Olympic Games (including summer and winter)	55
3.2	Types of action taken to increase the number of female coaches/instructors and game officials/judges/umpires	56
3.3	Actions taken to increase the number of women in decision-making positions	57
4.1	Study's participant demographics	72
5.1	British Horse Society (BHS) qualifications	92
5.2	The representation of the sexes in the British Horse Society (BHS) register of accredited professional coaches and active fellows	93
7.1	Coach certification courses according to gender in Catalonia 2010–2017	123
7.2	Years experience as sport coaches according to gender	125
7.3	Current position in coaching according to gender	125
8.1	Six red flags: your organisation may not be ready to recruit	146
11.1	Coach characteristics	202
13.1	Description of the sample	238

About the Contributors

Ana Andrés is Lecturer at the Faculty of Psychology, Education and Sport Sciences Blanquerna at the Ramon Llull University, teaching subjects related to quantitative analyses and research methods both to undergraduate and postgraduate students. She has a PhD in Methodology for the Behavioural Sciences at the University of Barcelona. Her research is focused on assessment and quantitative analyses applied to health sciences, covering topics such as mental health and healthy lifestyle promotion.

Natalie Barker-Ruchti is Associate Professor at Örebro University, Sweden. Through her research on athlete learning and development in elite sport, as well as athlete safeguarding and welfare, she aims to inform sports coaching practice. As the previous programme director of the sports coaching education programme at the University of Gothenburg (2012–2019), she was able to shape the programme's curriculum content.

Courtney J. Boucher, MS, is Doctoral Student in the School of Kinesiology, and research assistant and two-time Borton Fellow for the Promotion of Girls and Women in Sport Leadership in the Tucker Centre for Girls & Women at the University of Minnesota, USA.

Laura J. Burton is Professor of sport management and department head in the Department of Educational Leadership within the Neag School of Education at the University of Connecticut, USA. Her research interests include understanding leadership in sport organisations and exploring development, access and success, and gender stereotypes in leadership. Her work has been published in the *Journal of Sport Management, Sport Management Review*, and *Harvard Education Review*, among other outlets. Laura co-edited Women in Sport Leadership: Research and Practice for Change (2019) and co-wrote the first organisational behaviour textbook specific to the field of sport management, Organizational Behavior in Sport Management (2018).

About the Contributors

Nicola J. Clarke, PhD, is Senior Lecturer in sports coaching at Leeds Beckett University, UK. Her research and teaching interests centre around understanding how the social context influences experiences and relationships in sport, with a focus on coaches, parents, and young athletes.

George B. Cunningham is Professor and Sr. Assistant Provost for Graduate and Professional Studies at Texas A&M University, USA. His research focus is on diversity and inclusion in sport and physical activity. He has published over 200 peer-reviewed journal articles and book chapters; has authored an award-winning book (*Diversity in Sport Organizations*); and has co-edited an award-winning book (*Routledge Handbook of Theory in Sport Management*). He is a member of the National Academy of Kinesiology.

Laura Dahlstrom is Policy Analyst with the Ministry of Parks, Culture and Sport for the Government of Saskatchewan. She recently represented the province on Federal Provincial Territorial Work Group on Advancing Women and Girls in Sport. She is a former U Sports and University of Regina Cougars track and field athlete and community coach. This chapter is based on findings from her master's thesis.

Donna de Haan, PhD, is Associate Professor at the Hague University of Applied Sciences in the Netherlands. Her expertise lies in the field of inclusion and diversity associated with issues of participation, coaching, and leadership in sport. Her work has been published in numerous peer reviewed journals including *Sports Coaching Review* and the *International Review for the Sociology of Sport*, and she has been awarded grants for her work on gender equity from the International Olympic Committee, UEFA and Erasmus.

Guylaine Demers is Professor at Laval University. She has promoted gender equality in sport for most of her life. Over the years, she has become the go-to leader, researcher and advocate on issues of gender equity in Canadian sport. She is a recipient of the IOC women and sport award for the Americas that acknowledge her tremendous contribution to the advancement of women in sport. Her most recent achievement was being awarded the first Canadian Gender+ Equity in Sport Research Hub.

Cari Din was Sport Coach for 25 years. She is an award-winning instructor teaching leadership and coaching at the University of Calgary in the Faculty of Kinesiology and a Canadian Centre for Advanced Leadership Fellow in the Haskayne School of Business. Cari is also a Taylor Institute for Teaching and Learning Scholar. Her keen interest in leadership learning, social learning spaces and advancing women in coaching are reflected in her contributions as an Alberta Women in Sport Leadership project mentor.

Lolita Dudeniene is Lecturer at Lithuania Sports University and Judo Coach at Kaunas Sport School Gaja. Her central areas of teaching and research pertain to monitoring training and performance, time-motion and coaching analysis, and long-term athlete development.

Lucy Dumbell is Academic Registrar at Hartpury University in the United Kingdom. Her fields of interest include participation and profiling of equestrian sport and understanding equestrian performance for leisure and sport. Her work has been published in peer-reviewed journals including the International Journal of the History of Sport and Sport in Society. She combines this expertise with work around quality, enhancement and regulation to improve student experiences of university learning.

Stephen Harvey is Professor of Coaching, Health and Physical Education in the Department of Recreation and Sports Pedagogy at Ohio University, USA, and a prominent figure in sport pedagogy research. Stephen is a licensed physical education teacher who has coached a collegiate national championship winning team in women's soccer as well as junior and master's level international field hockey teams. He has led coach development sessions for numerous organisations, including USA field hockey and the United States Olympic Committee. Stephen recently qualified as an International Council for Coach Education Coach Developer through participation in the Nippon Sport Science University Coach Developer Academy.

Ingrid Hinojosa-Alcalde is Lecturer at Institut Nacional d'Educació Física de Catalunya (INEFC), University of Barcelona (UB). She is a member of the research group Grup d'Investigació Social i Educativa de l'Activitat Física i l'Esport (GISEAFE). Her research is focused on the coaching profession from a gender and labour well-being perspective.

Larena Hoeber is Professor and Associate Dean for Graduate Studies, Research, and Special Projects in the Faculty of Kinesiology & Health Studies at the University of Regina. Her research focuses on women's roles and involvement in sport, contemporary qualitative research methods, and innovation in amateur sport organisations. Her work has been published in *Journal of Sport Management, Sport Management Review, European Sport Management Quarterly, Online Information Review, Sex Roles*, and *Gender, Work and Organization*.

Jorid Hovden is Professor at the Department of Sociology and Political Science at The Norwegian University of Science and Technology. She has published several international articles, edited books and book chapters in the area of gender relations and the gendering of sport organisations. She was a member of the extended board of the International Sociology of Sport Association and is the past president of the Association for Gender Research in Norway.

About the Contributors xv

Florian Ingwersen is PhD student at the Faculty of Sports Science of the Ruhr University of Bochum. He is doing research in the field of coaching with a focus on youth football and the influence of digital transformation on coaching. Furthermore, he has experience in coaching in a professional youth academy and is holding the Elite Youth Coach-licence of the DFB.

Nicole M. LaVoi, PhD, is Senior Lecturer in Kinesiology and Director of the Tucker Centre for Girls & Women at the University of Minnesota, USA. Her research pertains to gender and coaching, notably the longitudinal *Women in College Coaching and Report Card* research series, and the 2017 Routledge Outstanding Academic Title winning book *Women in Sports Coaching*.

Ajhanai (AJ) Channel Inez Newton is Doctoral Candidate in the Department of Educational Leadership within the Neag School of Education at the University of Connecticut, USA. Her research studies how institutions and organisations remain intact and modify around issues of diversity, inclusion, and equity. Ajhanai's research centres intersectional analyses of race and gender and studies the emergent trend of sport organisations hiring formalised diversity leadership positions. Her work has been published in the *Journal of Negro Education, Frontiers*, and the *Journal of Higher Education Athletics & Innovation*. Additionally, Ajhanai has presented at national and international sport-specific conferences.

Leanne Norman is Professor and Director of the Research Centre for Social Justice in Sport & Society within the Carnegie School of Sport at Leeds Beckett University in the UK. Her research examines issues of gender equity related to sports coaching, sports leadership, and organisations. Her work is driven towards improving the participation, performance, and leadership pathways for diverse social groups, principally, different groups of women.

Luke A. Norris, PhD, is Lecturer in Sport and Exercise Psychology in the School of Sports and Health Science at University of Exeter, UK. Luke's research focuses on coaches' experiences and perceptions of their social network structure, social support resources, and social support functions. Luke is also an active coach with over ten years' experience of coaching football.

Letitia Price is Doctoral Candidate conducting research on women in coaching and sport leadership. She is also Graduate Assistant for the Ohio University online master's degree in Soccer Coaching. In this role, she continues to provide coaching development support for the United Soccer Coaches Advocacy Coaches group. She previously coached international, professional, university and secondary school athletes within the areas of Strength & Conditioning, Football and Sport Performance

Lifestyle. Currently, Letitia is providing coaching support for the Ohio University Hockey varsity team to empower athlete-centred sport science support. She was recently included in the Equity, Inclusion and Diversity Committee for Ohio University intercollegiate athletics and coaches.

Laura Purdy works at Edge Hill University in the UK. Her research focuses on the careers and lives of sports workers in elite/professional sport. Her recent projects have examined the welfare, representation, and advocacy of sport workers in European contexts.

Torsten Schlesinger is Professor for Sport Management at the Faculty of Sports Science of the Ruhr University of Bochum. His research interests relate to sports club development, analysing decision-making processes in sport organisations, and human resource management in voluntary sports clubs.

Pedrona Serra is Lecturer at Institut Nacional d'Educació Física de Catalunya (INEFC), University of Barcelona (UB). Her research pertains to gender and sport and physical education. Pedrona's research focuses on under-representation of women in sport science and girls' career choices. She is a member of the research group Grup d'Investigació Social i Educativa de l'Activitat Física i l'Esport (GISEAFE).

Susanna Soler is Senior Lecturer at Institut Nacional d'Educació Física de Catalunya (INEFC), University of Barcelona (UB). She is the head of the research group "Grup d'Investigació Social I Educativa de l'Activitat Física i l'Esport" (GISEAFE). Her research focuses on gender equality in sport and physical education. She has received several grants for research on gender equity and the implementation of actions directed towards changing current gendered practices in sport by several sport institutions in Spain.

Julia Symons is based in Melbourne, Australia and has experienced the sports sector as an elite athlete, a sports administrator/practitioner and as a non-academic researcher through a Winston Churchill Trust Fellowship, investigating elite sports environments enabling culturally diverse women to thrive. Her work has focused on developing holistic sports strategies and programmes supporting the engagement of marginalised communities, whilst building organisational capacity to support this engagement respectfully and effectively. Julia advises sports and community organisations on creating inclusive sports environments in her capacity as a Director of the Centre for Multicultural Youth, a Panel of Expertise Member on the Victorian Women's Trust "Club Respect" initiative and a member of the Social Change Content Group for the 2022 International Working Group on Women & Sport World Conference.

Anne Tjønndal is Associate Professor and Head of the Research Group Sport and Society at the Faculty of Social Sciences, Nord University,

Bodø—Norway. In 2019, she was awarded the Celia Brackenridge International Research Award for her article "Girls Are Not Made of Glass!": Barriers Experienced by Women in Norwegian Olympic Boxing. She is a member of The Young Academy of Norway (AYF).

Yvonne Weigelt-Schlesinger, PhD, is Researcher in Sport and Gender Studies. She is holder of the UEFA B-licence for football coaching.

Penny Werthner is Dean and Professor, Faculty of Kinesiology, University of Calgary, Canada. She is a founding mother of the Canadian Association for the Advancement of Women and Sport and Physical Activity, now called Canadian Women & Sport. She has been an advocate for women's equality in sport for over 30 years. Her areas of research are sport psychology, women's leadership and coaching, and learning processes. She is the lead on women and leadership for the Gender+ Equity in Sport in Canada Research Hub.

Acknowledgements

Thank you to Georgia, Edward, and Dorothy for always being the lighthouses in the storm. This book is dedicated to you for your unwavering support, love, and patience. Thank you too to my colleagues at Leeds Beckett University for creating a collegial and inspiring environment in which to work. A tremendous thank you to all the authors who contributed to making this book happen. This book would not be possible without your brilliant minds, effort, and time. Finally, this book is for all the coaches whose stories are included in the following chapters. Keep knocking on doors, keep questioning, keep challenging and resisting, and remain visible. Sport needs you.

Introduction

Bringing About Sustainable Change to Improving Gender Equity in Sport Coaching

Leanne Norman

Sport is a prized and cherished part of our cultures. As a result of wider societal and legislative changes across many Westernised societies, we have seen an increase in sport participation and opportunities for a diversity of social groups. However, while sport can be a force for good, deeply embedded historical roots and ideas mean that it is not always an equitable and fair space for some. This book focuses on how sport shapes and in turn, is shaped by gender. Specifically, we address how gender relations and ideas are reflected in positions of power and responsibility: sport coaching. Gender equity, that is, to mean fairness of treatment for women and men according to their respective needs, in coaching is a long-standing issue and evidenced by the under-representation of different groups of women and reported poorer professional experiences. For example, in the UK, while the qualified base of coaches has improved over the last ten years and is now 70% of the total workforce (Sports Coach UK, 2016), the balance and representation within the coaching workforce have not radically changed. Approximately two-thirds of our coaching workforce are men, and this imbalance becomes more acute as the coaching pathway narrows. In high-performance coaching, such as Olympic level, 89% of Olympic coaches are men (Norman, 2017). On the issue of gender equity in coaching, we have a growing body of research literature that primarily focuses on women's experiences of the profession. In addition to the numerical imbalance, our research tells us that across the globe and in multiple contexts, women are outnumbered and often report feeling marginalised too.

But this is not just a book solely about the under-representation or the experiences of women as coaches. We have this insight and research which has raised great awareness of the lack of women in our coaching workforces. The time is now to move to a stance of action. For this, we need a different debate with different language, and more significantly, a different "lens" is required on the issue of the lack of diversity within our coaching workforces. The pace of change in the make-up of the coaching profession is slow because it is an issue of cultural change, of deeply embedded ideas and behaviours within sport that have been so long in the making, they have become normalised. Instead of focusing on increasing the numbers of women through ad-hoc initiatives or schemes, our work needs to be on shifting mindsets and changing behaviours. Ensuring fair treatment, representing all identities and differences, and building a culture of belonging are actions are needed and expected by coaches (existing and future), athletes, and participants. This book is intended to provide evidence-based ideas and inspirations for creating this mindset and behaviour shift. This is through sharing our research and examples of good practices that could or have worked. Diversity and inclusion amongst our coaches are not an add-on to the work we do in sport; they should form the basis of all the decisions and actions we make. By failing to challenge inequity amongst our coaches and within our sporting workplaces, we are weakening our ability to attract, retain, and nurture high-potential individuals. For existing coaches and athletes already in the system, our research has shown that this is also coming at a cost to their own well-being and sense of belonging in the sport.

Our work needs to move away from a focus on just "more women" or just an awareness of inequity. We cannot force change merely through technical or strategic approaches. We need to move to a state of action. To replace the biases and gendered assumptions within sport, we must create tools and actions that shape cultures and teams that are truly equitable, diverse, and inclusive (The Centre for Creative Leadership, 2020). Over recent years, globally and broadly, we have lived through turbulent times (the global health crisis, economic upheaval, digital and technological transformations to name a few). Now is the time to address organisational culture and build inclusive places to play, participate in, compete, coach, and lead sport. The voices you will read in this book are unanimous too in wanting to see change. The evidence from the research demonstrates that organisational culture is what will determine the level of organisational success in making sport fairer. The stories of the coaches from around the world contained within this book evidence the need for work to be done to "unlearn" and transform some of the current sport organisational culture which is largely metrics-based and performance-driven. Any strategising must consider culture, reward systems, and people, and prioritise equity in an organisation. Any diversity and inclusion strategy must be a central part of "what we do" and one that prioritises care and safety.

Making our coaching workforces fairer and equitable places to work will not happen quickly; culture does not change overnight. What the research in this book highlights is that deep-seated culture change is complex, long, but needed. The embedded nature of sporting cultures is so because sport is rooted firmly in beliefs and expectations of men and women which are then played out and reproduced by the social actors within that context (Kihl et al., 2013). Rather than just being about the marginal nature of women alongside men or problematic gender relations, gender, and organisational culture is also revealed through the organisation of men and women's sport itself, resistance and power between such programmes, political behaviours as based on gendered identities, and organisational identity that itself is based on gender as an organising principle (Kihl et al., 2013). Our (women) coaches are highly motivated, driven, and engaged members of our sporting systems. Accessing the full potential of this talent should be a strategic imperative. This book is a crucial collection of counter-stories that tell the ways in which inequity is experienced by our coaches and how we can use this evidence to remove barriers and change practices so that all coaches have a fair chance to the best coach they can be, whoever they are.

Overview of the Book

The 13 chapters have been grouped into three broad parts as follows: (1) setting the scene: how gender inequity manifests itself in sport coaching contexts and why change is needed, (2) strategies for supporting a more gender-inclusive sport coaching workforce, and (3) from research to practice: evidence of impactful research that has contributed to more gender-inclusive sport coaching contexts. All three parts speak to and inform each other. The purpose of presenting the structure in this way is to first provide a sense of context to the research and action that has occurred on the subject matter of gender equity in sports coaching. Context is crucial if we are to understand what issues lie at the heart of (in)equitable working environments. This improves the chances of creating more tailored and targeted approaches that are fit for the purpose and context, and for increasing credibility and buy-in from all the necessary stakeholders. The second part of the book presents suggested strategies for supporting a more inclusive and balanced sport coaching workforce, grounded in evidence and insight from some of the leading researchers in this field. Third, the final part of the book discusses examples of evidence-based practices from around the world that have made a difference to creating gender-equitable coaching environments. The strengths of all the chapters are that we have a collection of work from renowned authors in this subject area from a range of contexts (including sports and performance domains) and countries. There is no one-size-fits-all approach to improving gender equity. So, the book is intended to share insight from some of the good and proven practices that are making a difference to creating coaching workforces that are inclusive and representative.

Part I: Setting the Scene: How Gender Inequity Manifests Itself in Sport Coaching Contexts and Why Change Is Needed

Part I begins with George B. Cunningham's chapter *The Glass Cliff, Gender, and Sport Leadership: A Narrative Review and Meta-Analysis*. Cunningham presents his narrative review and meta-analysis of the extant scholarship in this subject area to shine a light on the how, why, and under what conditions women lack access to key coaching roles. Through this, it is found that the literature lacks an analysis of the consideration of the coaching positions women *do* obtain, the quality of those roles, and the subsequent outcomes. Therefore, Cunningham presents an overview of the glass cliff perspective: the notion that women are more likely than men to secure precarious and risky leadership positions. Women may have cracked the glass ceiling (or the real but invisible barrier prohibiting their ascension to top leadership roles), but in doing so, may have obtained an unenviable role that does not bode well for long-term success. Cunningham provides an overview of this perspective, including the primary tenets, possible antecedents, and potential outcomes to apply to and offer theoretical and implications for sport coaching contexts. Following this, in their chapter *Gender Stereotypes as Mechanisms of Social Exclusion of Women as Football Coaches*, Schlesinger, Ingwersen, and Weigelt-Schlesinger provide an overview of gender equity in football coaching workforces in Germany. They include data from the German Football Federation as well as from regional federations to show that women are significantly under-represented amongst football coaches, especially at the amateur level, despite no apparent formal barriers to the equality of coach education (CE). The authors argue that gender stereotypes, as social mechanisms, lie at the heart of the exclusion of women from football coaching positions and the CE system. They provide a multilevel approach to explain how such stereotypes function and influence the macro, meso, and micro levels of sports. The authors end the chapter with practical recommendations towards mitigating the influence of such gender stereotypes to allow women greater access to the coaching system.

Part II: Strategies for Supporting a More Gender-Inclusive Sport Coaching Workforce

The second part of the book focuses on using research evidence as the basis for suggested strategies and recommendations to improve gender equity within our global coaching workforces. This part presents research and strategies from scholars across the globe starting with Canadian authors, Demers, Din, and Werthner who make the case for 50/50 representation between male and female coaches at all levels of the system. The chapter details the historical and current statistics on women and coaching, noting that women remain seriously under-represented among elite-level employed coaches in all countries around the globe. The chapter also acknowledges a number of critical initiatives that have enabled change and discusses some of the individual, interpersonal, organisational, and sociocultural forces that influence women's experiences with sport coaching. The authors detail three specific strategies that, if implemented, will ensure gender equality for women coaches. North America also provides the context for Chapter 4 written by Harvey and Price. The authors make the case that while there continues to be a significant breadth of scholarly discourse in the coaching education literature to empirically legitimise the coaching profession, little is known about the impacts of a graduate-level coaching education degree on female coaches' career progression. Harvey and Price investigate the barriers and supports that the US-based female graduate-level sports coaching students face in pursuit of the sports coaching profession. They highlight effective opportunities that could positively influence female coaching career trajectories as well as present the factors that could reinforce the deeply entrenched barriers that exist in the coaching landscape. The chapter concludes with a discussion of various "calls to action" recommended for graduate-level coaching education programmes, embracing programmes of social responsibility to empower females in the coaching profession.

Following this chapter, in Chapter 5, de Haan and Dumbell provide a unique focus on equestrianism and explore the question of whether such a sex-integrated sport can provide a more gender-equitable coaching environment. The authors make the case that little is known about gender and coaching in such a sport and yet, it is a novel context for the way in which men and women compete alongside each other rather than in separate spaces. Using Bourdieu, de Haan and Dumbell review how the structures of equestrianism, including the CE system, may challenge (or indeed, reinforce) dominant ideologies of gender. The theme of disrupting gendered structures also forms the basis of Chapter 6 by Barker-Ruchti, Purdy, and Dudeniene. The authors focus on how coach education and coach educators produce, maintain, and disrupt gender inequalities in the university context. To do this, they have created a composite vignette from in-class discussions with year 1, 2, and 3 university CE students in Lithuania, Sweden, and the UK to demonstrate how students perceive and experience male and female coach educators and CE content. In this spirit of disruption, Barker-Ruchti et al. present the actionable recommendations to support universities in developing gender-equitable education. A European perspective on the issue of gender equity in sport coaching is continued in Chapter 7 from Spanish researchers, Soler, Hinojosa-Alcade, Serra, and Andrés. The authors analyse recently developed equity policies aimed at promoting the participation of women in coaching in Spain, and the analysis demonstrates that such strategies have often isolated and been strongly resisted by sports organisations. In this chapter, four actions implemented in a Spanish context focused on promoting access, progress, and retention of women coaches are presented and discussed. The actions are centred on engaging, recruiting, and retaining women. Soler et al. conclude their chapter with future directions for evaluating the impact of these measures to develop structural and permanent changes for ensuring gender equity in sport coaching. The theme of structural change also forms the basis of the final chapter (Chapter 8) within Part II by Burton and Newton. The authors offer strategies to make meaningful changes within sport organisations in support of women in sport coaching and highlight that any meaningful changes must first account for gender (intersectional) biases. Burton and Newton offer strategies for organisations to begin dealing with gender bias at the individual level and discuss organisational practices that can have an impact on mitigating bias and supporting the advancement of women in coaching.

Part III: From Research to Practice: Evidence of Impactful Research That Has Contributed to More Gender-Inclusive Sport Coaching Contexts

Parts I and II of the book present key evidence and recommendations for advancing gender equity within our sport coaching workforces. Building on this, Part III focuses primarily on how research has informed practice by evidencing impactful activities that have contributed to gender equity in particular coaching contexts. It begins with Julia Symon's collection of reflections and practices towards improving the representation and inclusion of culturally diverse women in coaching. Symons' global research focuses on three contexts: Aotearoa New Zealand, the United States, and the United Kingdom to centre and prioritise the experiences and insights of culturally diverse women in coaching. In doing so, Symons shares important perspectives and counter-stories. The chapter presents the importance of cultural safety in coaching, shares women's common experiences of "fitting in" versus "finding belonging", and explores the privilege, burden, and responsibility of representation for culturally diverse women in coaching. After investigating these themes of shared experience, it then provides practical recommendations and suggests key considerations for sports practitioners to explore and embed cultural safety in their coaching programme design and pathways, as well as their broader sporting organisations. In Chapter 10, the US scholars LaVoi and Boucher present their Stages of Career Progression Model (SCPM) which contains novel, nuanced, contextual, and specific ways of supporting women in sport coaching across their lifespan and career trajectory. Positioned within LaVoi's Ecological Intersectional Model of Barriers and Supports for Women Coaches, the SCPM aims to support decision-makers within sport organisations improve gender equity, change work environments, and better develop and support women coaches as they navigate challenges inevitable and inherent in work and life. The chapter adopts a "fix-the-system" approach in recognition that our coaching environments and places of work do not always adequately support women coaches. The SCPM from LaVoi and Boucher provides organisational sport leaders ideas for achieving gender equity across the career lifespan of women coaches. Working environments also form the focus of Norris, Clarke, and Norman's chapter (Chapter 11) in which the authors discuss their evaluation of The English Football Association's "Elite Coach Menteeship Programme". The chapter provides an evaluation of the programme and provides recommendations and implications to develop diversity and inclusion initiatives within other sporting organisations. Utilising interview-based evidence from a longitudinal, three-year study with coaches and a number of key programme stakeholders, Norris et al. discuss broader lessons learnt from the initiative, including a strong focus on purpose, intent, and expectations of programmes as well as how such change initiatives could be communicated or marketed to strengthen more inclusive organisational cultures. Moving from the UK to Canada for Chapter 12, scholars Hoeber and Dahlstrom shine a novel spotlight on the experiences of Canadian elite track and field women coaches who have navigated the coaching system to reach the highest echelons of their profession. In this chapter, Hoeber and Dahlstrom examine the career development of those women who have succeeded and stayed in coaching, sharing the coaches' reflections initiatives to support them as coaches at the system, organisational, and interpersonal levels of sport, and some of the personal strategies they used to remain coaching within the sport system. In Chapter 13, the Norwegian scholars Hovden and Tjønndal explore the impact of the national intervention, "Norway Female Box" on the support and empowerment of women boxing coaches. The chapter first presents the research that analysed the gendered, everyday challenges of the women boxing coaches including how they conceived and experienced their involvement in the intervention. Hovden and Tjønndal conclude with critical reflections on the "Norway Female Box" coaching programme as an example of best practice and provide recommendations for similar women-centred coaching programmes.

References

The Centre for Creative Leadership. (2020). *Unlearning your organisational culture.* The Centre for Creative Leadership.

Kihl, L., Shaw, S., & Schull, V. (2013). Fear, anxiety, and loss of control: Analyzing an athletic department merger as a gendered political process. *Journal of Sport Management,* 27(2), 146–157. http://ezproxy.leedsbeckett.ac.uk/login?url=http://search.ebscohost.com/login.aspx?direct=true&db=s3h&AN=85899067&site=ehost-live&scope=site

Norman, L. (2017, August 2017). *Gender in coaching report card for the Rio 2016 Olympic Games.* International council for coaching excellence annual conference, Liverpool, UK.

Sports Coach UK. (2016). *Coaching insights: Coaching statistics and analysis 2015/16.* Sports Coach UK.

Part I

Setting the Scene

How Gender Inequity Manifests Itself in Sport Coaching Contexts and Why Change Is Needed

1 The Glass Cliff, Gender, and Sport Leadership

A Narrative Review and Meta-Analysis

George B. Cunningham

Introduction

Although women constitute a major segment of workforces around the world, they are under-represented in key leadership positions. Consider, for example, that in 2019, 46% of all workers in the United States were women (World Bank, 2020). Nevertheless, they constituted just 22.5% of all board executives and 6.6% of all chief executive officers in Fortune 500 firms (Connley, 2019). In fact, the 33 women at the helm of the firms in 2019 constituted an all-time high (Connley, 2019), showing the persistent nature of inequality.

These trends are also evident in sport and physical activity. Among national sport organisations around the world, women constitute 16.3% of the chief executives (Adriaanse, 2016). In the United States, those figures are even lower, as just 5% of all chief executives of national governing bodies are women (Gaston et al., in press). At the Olympic level, women represented 45% of all athletes in 2016 (Crockett, 2016) but just 19.7% of the National Olympic Committee board positions (Ahn & Cunningham, 2017). These numbers mask the magnitude of inequality: one-in-twenty NOC boards had all men, while nearly one-in-five had fewer than 10% women. The under-representation of women in key leadership roles is also evident in other areas of sport, including the amateur ranks, such as intercollegiate athletics in the United States. Even though women represent 44% of nearly 500,000 intercollegiate athletes, they represent just 24% of all head coaches (Cunningham, 2019).

Collectively, these figures show that, even though they have better representation in other areas, such as employees or athletes, women sparsely occupy upper echelons, whether as coaches, board members, or chief executives. This lack of diversity is important for a number of reasons. First, the disparate numbers point to access discrimination (Greenhaus et al., 1990), or a form of bias that limits people's ability to obtain employment and that a number of researchers have identified in the coaching context (Darvin, 2020; Norman, 2010). Furthermore, the data seemingly suggest that key coaching roles in sport are suited best for men, thereby thwarting aspirations of current and future women leaders (Norman, 2014; Walker & Bopp, 2011). A lack of diversity also hurts team culture and all involved with the team. As evidence, LaVoi (2016; see also LaVoi & Dutove, 2012), in articulating her integrated framework, showed how women in leadership can serve as role models; lend support to other women in the sport industry; bring varied vantage points to discussions that historically men historically dominate; and are likely to behave in more civil, just ways than men. Furthermore, organisational strategies designed to enhance gender equality and inclusion are likely to benefit all people, women and men alike (LaVoi, 2016).

Consequently, a number of researchers have examined factors that influence women's representation in sport leadership roles, whether as coaches or administrators. Multilevel models offer one way of organising the burgeoning scholarship, with factors at the societal, organisational and intergroup, and personal levels (Burton, 2015; Cunningham, 2008, 2019; LaVoi & Dutove, 2012). Societal factors include laws and ordinances, institutional norms and expectations, and the influence of powerful actors; organisational and intergroup factors include bias among decision-makers, the culture of the team and sport organisation, socio-political and power dynamics, and diversity and inclusion strategies; and individual factors include people's investments in their human and social capital, and their self-limiting behaviours. In addition to coalescing the empirical research in the area, the multilevel approach captures the theories that scholars have used to understand women's career opportunities and experiences (Cunningham, 2016; Gearty et al., 2016).

A review of the extant scholarship shows a focus on how, why, and under what conditions women lack access to key coaching roles. Largely missing from this analysis, though, is consideration of the coaching positions women *do* obtain, the quality of those roles, and the subsequent outcomes. If, for example, women only have access to undesirable positions, then they are set up to fail, and the long-term prospects of their success in sport, whether as a coach or chief executive, are unfavourable. Therein rests the benefit of adopting a *glass cliff* perspective, or the notion that women are more likely than men to secure precarious and risky leadership positions (Ryan & Haslam, 2007; Ryan et al., 2016). In this case, women may have cracked the glass ceiling (or the real but invisible barrier prohibiting their ascension to top leadership roles; Norman et al., 2018), but in doing so, obtained an unenviable role that does not bode well for long-term success. In short, the glass cliff represents another form of gender bias, ultimately privileging men within the work context. The purposes of this chapter are as follows: (1) to overview the glass cliff perspective, including the primary tenets, possible antecedents, and potential outcomes; (2) to summarise the findings from a meta-analysis of glass cliff studies, including those in sport; (3) to apply the meta-analytic findings to the sport context; and (4) to offer theoretical and practical implications.

The Glass Cliff

Key Tenets

The primary premise undergirding the glass cliff is that women are most likely to secure leadership roles that are undesirable—those where there is a history of underperformance, chaos, or volatility. Ryan and Haslam (2005) initially uncovered evidence of the glass cliff in their analysis of the Financial Times Stock Exchange (FTSE) 100 firms listed on the London Stock Exchange. They found that women's appointment as chief executive was not related to subsequent company performance. Of particular interest were the additional findings: among companies that appointed men, the previous firm performance was stable, but those companies that chose a woman as the new chief executive experienced volatile, poor stock performance in the period leading up to that decision. Thus, the quality of the roles into which women and men stepped were markedly different. Subsequent work among Fortune 500 companies revealed similar trends: women were most likely to assume a chief executive position when the companies had experienced crises (Brady et al., 2011) or when the stocks had been performing poorly (Cook & Glass, 2014a). The patterns are evident outside of major corporations, too. In the world of UK politics, Ryan et al. (2010) found that women were most likely to run for seats that were difficult to win (based on the wide margin by which the incumbent had won in the previous election).

Of note, however, is the research evidence that points to another pattern of findings, thereby resulting in equivocal overall results. Adams et al. (2009) found no gender differences in the quality of appointment among Fortune 500 companies (see also Gupta et al., 2017). In a longitudinal study of Fortune 500 firms, Cook and Glass (2014b) observed that broad diversity was associated with the appointment of a woman as chief executive, but company performance was not. Hennessey et al. (2014) also failed to find support for the glass cliff in their analysis of Canadian businesses.

There are two studies in the sport realm that directly assessed these predictions. First, Ahn and Cunningham (2020) interviewed women who had completed FIFA's women's leadership development training. The programme started around the same time as FIFA's bribery scandal broke, and about half of the study participants drew parallels between the crisis-ridden status of the organisation and the decision to further develop women for leadership roles. In another study, Wicker et al. (2019) collected 11 years of archival data from NCAA women's soccer teams competing in the major athletic conferences, totalling 695 observations. They found that 59 head coaching changes took place over that time, and women took the helm in 15 of them (25.4%). In line with the glass cliff, women were more likely than men to secure a coaching position for a team with poor performance, as measured by wins and winning percentage. Thus, women were unlikely to guide the women's soccer teams, and when they were, they stepped into roles where the team was on a downward performance slide.

Antecedents

Additional researchers have examined why the glass cliff might occur, with considerable empirical support for stereotypes and the desire for organisations to signal change. On the other hand, there is less support for the notion that women are more willing to take precarious jobs than are men.

Stereotypes

As part of the cognitive domain of bias (Cuddy et al., 2008), stereotypes represent "the attitudes, beliefs, and behaviours people assign to others—that is, those characteristics they believe embody another individual or group of individuals" (Cunningham & Ahn, 2019, p. 84). They are socially constructed, and time bound, such that prevailing stereotypes in one context and at one point in time are likely to change. Stereotypes give rise to other forms of bias, including prejudice and discrimination.

In the leadership context, Schein (1973, 1975) showed how the stereotypes people have for managers align closely with those they hold for men in general. That connection, though, is not apparent for women. As a result, Schein noted the presence of the "think manager–think male" association, and it is present today (Koenig et al., 2011). Within the sport context, the "think manager–think male" connection influences how people rate women and men for athletic administrative positions in the United States (Burton et al., 2009), manager positions in Turkish sport organisations (Koca & Öztürk, 2015), and intercollegiate coaches (Walker et al., 2011).

The glass cliff extends this thinking to include also the "think crisis–think female" stereotype. According to Ryan et al. (2016), this association stems from the communal stereotypes that people frequently associate with women, including the belief that women are warm, understanding, caring, and so on. A number of authors have also shown these patterns exist in assessments of women coaches (Cunningham & Ahn, 2019; Madsen et al., 2017; Sartore & Cunningham, 2007). These are the very characteristics people seek when undergoing a stressful or chaotic time. In support of this connection, Ryan et al. (2011, Study 2) asked participants about the characteristics that leaders should possess when an organisation is *unsuccessful*, and they found these attributions corresponded with beliefs about women but not those people held for men. In other words, "the qualities that women are seen to possess are often also associated with companies that are failing" (Ryan et al., 2011, p. 482).

There are two important implications of the "think crisis–think female" stereotype. First, the "think manager–think male" stereotype is likely only applicable when the company is successful or has a history of steady performance. However, when the company is failing or in turmoil, the "think manager–think male" stereotype no longer applies; instead, people are likely to believe that women are well suited for the role. Second, these stereotypes give rise to subsequent prejudice and discrimination such that women are most likely to secure coaching positions that are precarious (Wicker et al., 2019).

Signal Change

Another antecedent of the glass cliff is the company's desire to signal to others that it is undergoing a radical change (Ryan & Haslam, 2007; Ryan et al., 2016). Organisations in precarious situations need to engage in change to right their course, and given the lack of women in top leadership roles, what better way to signal a commitment to transforming the workplace than to hire a woman? As Ryan and Haslam (2007) explained, decision-makers might surmise that "appointing a woman to a leadership role is a 'last resort' option that is attempted only when less drastic forms of change have been exhausted" (p. 560). In doing so, the organisation not only demonstrates a commitment to pursuing new paths, but also find themselves in a no-lose situation: if the woman is successful, then she has turned the organisation around and achieved the desired outcome; if not, then she has confirmed stereotypes about women and their ability to lead, and "the prior practice of appointing men can be justified and resurrected" (p. 560).

Kulich et al. (2015) demonstrated these dynamics through several experiments. In Study 1, they showed how participants selected women as a leader when poor performance was due to internal factors (e.g., poor previous leadership, thereby warranting organisational change) as opposed to external factors (e.g., a global economic downturn). In Study 2, they found that participants preferred women leaders when they wanted to signal change to outside entities, such as investors. Similarly, Ahn and Cunningham (2020) found that some of the women they interviewed attributed FIFA's women's leadership development programme to the desire to influence external perceptions. One participant suggested that the programme might "help to develop their [FIFA's] image and reputation building" following the bribery scandal (p. 127).

Women's Choices

Professional and career choices that women and men make could also explain the glass cliff. Indeed, a number of researchers have examined potential gender differences in advancement aspirations and the factors that prepare people for advancement, such as human capital and social capital investments. These studies suggest that women, relative to men, are more likely to have played collegiate sports (Cunningham & Sagas, 2002), earned accolades for the quality of their play (Cunningham & Sagas, 2002), and longer occupational tenures (Larsen & Clayton, 2019). Nevertheless, women also receive fewer returns for their capital investments (Cunningham & Sagas, 2005), report less leadership self-efficacy relative to men (Cunningham et al., 2007), and are less likely to pursue advancement opportunities (Machida-Kosuga et al., 2017).

If women are not more likely than men to pursue career advancement, is it possible that they are more willing to pursue precarious jobs? Such an explanation would lend credence to the glass cliff patterns highlighted so far. Whereas sport coaching researchers have not examined this question, the research outside of the sport setting does little to support this possibility. Rink et al. (2012) conducted two experiments with Dutch graduate students enrolled in business school. The participants reviewed job postings of organisations in crisis. Results showed that men evaluated the positions more favourably than women, and that women identified a lack of subordinate support as a key barrier. Thus, while stereotypes and the desire for the organisation in crisis to signal change likely lead to the glass cliff, the notion that women are more likely than men to accept precarious job roles lacks empirical support.

Outcomes of the Glass Cliff

There are a number of potential negative outcomes of the glass cliff, and researchers have shown some materialise but others generally do not. These include performance shortfalls, early exit from the organisation, and early exit from the occupation.

Performance

If women are more likely than men to obtain precarious leadership roles, it follows that the organisations they lead are also likely to perform poorly. The evidence to this point, however, is mixed. In their initial study on the glass cliff, Ryan and Haslam (2005) examined FTSE 100 companies on the London Stock Exchange. Even though women secure chief executive for poorly performing companies, the subsequent performance of companies led by women did not differ than those led by men. However, Hennessey et al. (2014), in their study of Canadian firms, observed that company performance declined after the appointment of a woman, as measured by stock market performance.

Within the sport world, Dawley et al. (2004), in a study conducted prior to Ryan and Haslam (2005, 2007) articulation of the glass cliff and thus not a direct test of their perspective, examined coaching changes in US intercollegiate athletics, as well as the performance prior to and after the transition. The gender of the new head coach was not associated with the team's previous performance or the performance that followed. Others have not focused on the performance following a change, but they have still illustrated that gender does not influence performance in amateur athletics (Darvin et al., 2018) or professional sport (Darvin et al., 2018; Gomez-Gonzalez et al., 2019; Smittick et al., 2019). In other words, hiring a woman as a coach is not related to poorer performance.

Whereas the appointment of a woman as leader has an equivocal effect on performance, the evidence related to stakeholder reactions and subjective evaluation of performance is more consistent. Haslam et al. (2010) found that the presence of women on firm boards corresponded with devaluation by investors (see also Lee & James, 2007), but these subjective actions did not align with objective measures of performance. In other words, the subjective ratings by investors were based on factors *other than* how the firm actually performed. Similarly, Gupta et al. (2017) found that women were more likely than men to encounter external activism when they secured a chief executive position. Gupta et al.'s work aligns closely with that from Schull et al. (2013) set in the context of US intercollegiate athletics. Though not focusing on the glass cliff, these authors observed that powerful external actors mobilised to ensure that a man secured the athletic director position (the chief executive in that context). These studies point to the role of prejudice and stereotypes in shaping stakeholder expectations—not the performance of the woman considered for the coaching position.

Turnover

Finally, gender differences in turnover rates are also possible outcomes of the glass cliff. Whereas there is considerable scholarship focusing on turnover in organisations, occupations, and sport (Cunningham et al., 2019; Reade et al., 2009; Rubenstein et al., 2018), scholarship focusing specifically on turnover following a glass cliff appointment is comparatively limited (Ryan et al., 2016).

In one study, Cook and Glass (2014a) examined Fortune 500 firms over a 15-year span. They found no gender differences in the tenures of the newly appointed chief executives. They did find, though, that when women and racial minorities secured leader positions and the firm performed poorly, they were likely to be replaced by a White man. The authors termed this dynamic the "saviour effect" (p. 1080). In an encompassing study of the 2,500 largest firms in the world, Davidson and Brest (2014) found that women were 40% more likely than men to be forced out of their chief executive position. In commenting on these findings, Ryan and Haslam concluded "Such findings present concrete evidence that, rather than simply being a matter of perceived or potential risk, the precariousness of glass cliffs manifests itself an increased incidence of career trauma" (p. 453).

Summary

Collectively, the research evidence suggests that the glass cliff could limit women's representation as leaders in sport organisations and, ultimately, thwart their career success. From this position, women are likely to secure precarious positions, a decision likely stemming from stereotypes and the organisation's desire to signal a change in the midst of poor performance. As a result, though performance might not suffer, the outcomes for women in leadership are not ideal. External actors are likely to devalue the organisation's performance, and women are more likely than men to exit the organisation.

Although Ryan and Haslam's (2007; Ryan et al., 2016) conceptual work and the associated empirical evidence both point to the existence of the glass cliff, the findings are, nevertheless, equivocal. The brief narrative review has highlighted the following: (1) instances where research findings did not align with conceptual predictions and (2) other examples where potentially conflicting patterns of evidence have emerged. As outlined in the following section, use of a statistical technique, meta-analysis, can help sort through these ambiguous findings.

Meta-Analysis of the Glass Cliff

The first purpose of this chapter was to overview the glass cliff perspective, including the primary tenets, possible antecedents, and potential outcomes. Having done so in the previous section, in this section, I move to achieve the second purpose: summarise the findings from a meta-analysis of glass cliff studies, including those in sport.

Meta-analysis represents an analytical technique that allows researchers to combine statistically the results from previous empirical studies to arrive at a common metric and summary effect size (Lipsey & Wilson, 2001; Schmidt & Hunter, 2015). Through meta-analysis, researchers can combine effect sizes, correct for sources of error, and determine overall patterns of findings that might be otherwise masked or ambiguous through other reviews. These advantages are consistent with Schmidt and Hunter's (2015) view that "the goal in any science is the production of cumulative knowledge" (p. 17). Lipsey and Wilson (2001) identified a number of benefits associated with meta-analysis, including a systematic approach, transparency, statistical accounting of sources of error, identification of the strength of associations, and the breadth of analysis. Researchers have used this data aggregation approach to understand other diversity-related phenomena, including the influence of group diversity on subsequent outcomes (Lee & Cunningham, 2018) and the occupational turnover of women in coaching (Cunningham et al., 2019).

Data Collection, Coding, and Analysis

The first step in meta-analysis is identifying studies. I conducted a computer search of Scopus, PsycINFO, Academic Source Complete, and Sport

Discuss. The search focused on documents that included "glass cliff" and combinations thereof included in the title or key words. I limited the search to 2005–2019, including papers that were in press, as 2005 was the first study Ryan and Haslam (2005) published on the topic. Research published in academic journals, book chapters, theses, and dissertations were all included, read, and analysed.

The search yielded 94 documents, and Figure 1.1 provides an overview of the documents per year. An upward trend, both linear and exponential, is evident, showing the increased interest in the glass cliff among scholars.

After the initial identification of documents, I applied the following exclusion criteria. First, as meta-analysis aggregates data from quantitative studies, I excluded articles that were reviews or only reported qualitative data. Second, I left out studies that did not provide the needed statistical information to compute an effect size. Specifically, this meta-analysis examines the association among variables, and thus, I used the correlation coefficient (r) as a measure of effect. The most straight-forward information gathered from the documents was the correlation and sample size. However, absent this information, it was possible to convert other data into an r-value, provided authors offered any of the following information: a frequency table; means, standard deviations, and cell sizes; a chi-square; a t-test with the sample size; or a t-test p-value with the associated sample size (see also Lipsey & Wilson, 2001).

I used a coding form (see Lipsey & Wilson, 2001) when reviewing the documents. The form included the full citation, the year published, context of the study (sport or not), design (experimental or cross-sectional), sample size, and measure(s) of effect. In some cases, it was possible to collect multiple effects from a single study, such as the performance prior to the appointment of a woman leader and the performance thereafter. As these are distinct variables associated with the glass cliff, I treated these effects as independent.

The analysis followed Cooper's (2010) guidelines. As a way of minimising potential bias, I transformed each correlation coefficient (r) to a z using Fisher's transformation (Fisher, 1970; Johnson & Eagly, 2000). The analysis then moved to a correction for sample size (Hedges & Olkin, 1985), calculation of the effect size, and the associated 95% confidence interval (Cooper, 2010). An effect size was significant if the confidence interval did not include the value of 0 (Cooper, 2010). I computed the Q statistic where possible to examine for potential moderators, or variables that influence the relationship between two other variables. A statistically significant Q value indicated that effect sizes in sub-groups significantly differ from one another (Cooper, 2010). Three moderators were of particular interest: publication type (published or not), setting (sport or not), and design (experimental or cross-sectional). Finally, in addition to reporting statistical significance, I followed Cohen's (1988) guidelines for reporting practical significance, with effect sizes of .10 considered small, .30 as moderate, and .50 as large.

20 *George B. Cunningham*

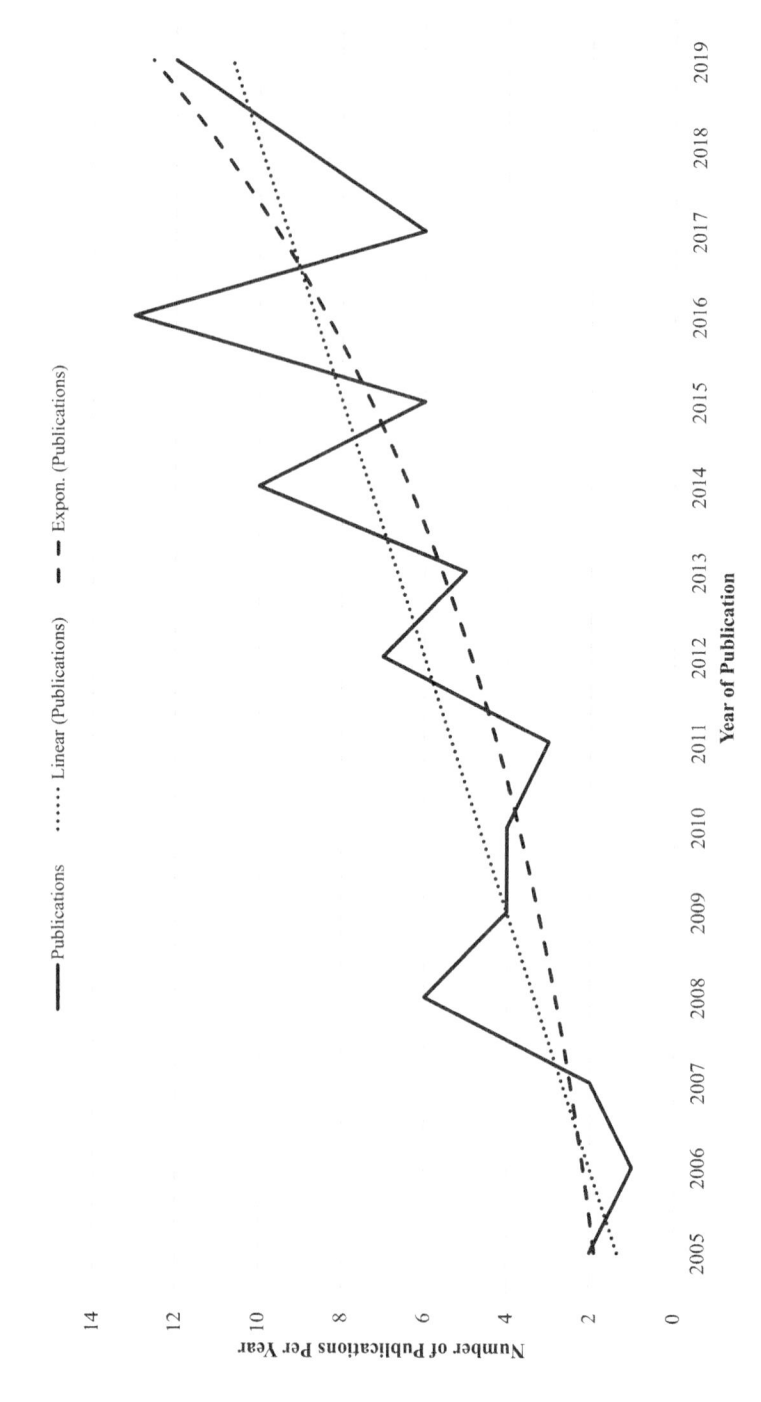

Figure 1.1 Glass cliff publications over time

Meta-Analysis Results

After applying the exclusion criteria, I retained 22 documents for the analysis, all of which appear in the References and denoted by asterisks. Because some of the papers reported on multiple studies, the final number of studies analysed was 27, which included an analysis of 55,757 individuals. As there is critical mass of studies needed to compute the corrected effect size, the analysis only included the results in which four or more studies were analysed.

All of the studies retained for the analysis appeared in academic journals and only one (Wicker et al., 2019) was set in the sport context. Thus, I was not able to compute moderator analyses for publication or setting. Even though most of the empirical glass cliff scholarship is set outside sport, understanding the overall effects can help inform subsequent analyses focusing on women in sport leadership. Table 1.1 provides the results.

Appointment to Precarious Positions

The first set of results focuses on evidence that women secure leadership roles in organisations with a history of poor performance or that were in crisis. The meta-analysis included results from 20 studies ($n = 4807$). Results from the meta-analysis indicated a statistically significant effect ($r_c = .070$, 95% CI: .041, .098), showing that women were likely to secure a leadership role in organisations in crisis. Thus, the central premise of the glass cliff was supported. It is worth noting, however, that the practical significance is low, according to Cohen's (1988) standards.

Additional analyses examined potential differences effect sizes reported in experimental studies ($r_c = .265$, 95% CI: .199, .332) and in cross-sectional studies ($r_c = .026$, 95% CI: −.005, .057). Results suggest the differences are statistically significant ($Q_b = 34.013$, $df = 2$, $p < .001$); thus, evidence of the glass cliff effect is stronger in experimental studies than it is in cross-sectional work.

Table 1.1 Glass cliff meta-analytic results

Relationship examined	K	N	r_c	95% CI
Woman appointed to failing company	20	4,807	.070	.041, .098
Experimental	9	894	.265	.199, .332
Cross-sectional	11	3,913	.026	−.005, .057
Think crisis–think female	7	754	.297	.224, .369
Performance following glass cliff appointment	4	411	−.011	−.023, .002
Turnover following glass cliff appointment	4	25,737	.082	.070, .094

Think Crisis–Think Female

The next set of analyses examined evidence for one of the primary antecedents, the "think crisis–think female" stereotype. The analysis included data from seven studies ($n = 754$). As illustrated in Table 1.1, results from the studies showed that there was a strong association between an organisation in crisis (resulting from poor performance, scandals, and the like) and the belief that women were well-suited for that job ($r_c = .297$, 95% CI: .224, .369). The effect size was moderate, according to Cohen's (1988) conventions. As the researchers conducted their studies in the laboratory, I did not compute moderator analyses.

Subsequent Performance

The next examination focused on evidence that women appointed to glass cliff positions had poor performance (see Table 1.1). Four studies ($n = 411$) provided the needed to conduct analyses. As illustrated in Table 1.1, the effects size was not significantly different from zero ($r_c = -.011$, 95% CI: -.023, .002); thus, organisational performance did not decline following women's appointment to glass cliff positions.

Turnover

Finally, the analysis investigated whether women experienced more turnover than men following their glass cliff appointment (see Table 1.1). This analysis included four studies ($n = 25,737$), with results showing that women did have significantly higher turnover rates, though the practical significance was small ($r_c = .082$, 95% CI: .070, .094).

Conclusions

The first two objectives of this chapter were as follows: (1) to overview the glass cliff perspective, including the primary tenets, possible antecedents, and potential outcomes and (2) to summarise the findings from a meta-analysis of glass cliff studies, including those in sport. Ryan and Haslam (2007) noted that:

> women are more likely than men to find themselves on a 'glass cliff' such that their positions of leadership are associated with greater risk of failure . . . If and when that failure occurs, it is then women (rather than men) who must face the consequences and who are singled out for criticism and blame.
>
> (p. 550)

Nearly 15 years since their writing, the review of glass cliff scholarship and subsequent meta-analysis supports this reasoning. Largely because of stereotypes and the organisations in crisis seeking to signal change, women are more likely than men to secure precarious leadership roles. When this occurs, organisations do not suffer (as there is no evidence that performance declines when a woman is leader), but women do. Subjective evaluations of performance formed by external stakeholders are likely to be negative (again, in spite of empirical evidence to the contrary), and women are likely to leave the organisation sooner than men.

Drawing from these findings, the next purposes of the chapter were as follows: (c) to apply the meta-analytic findings to the sport context and (d) to offer theoretical and practical implications. The results have many implications for women in sport coaching. Researchers continue to show that women face a glass ceiling, as they have limited opportunities to obtain head coaching positions and other leadership roles (Cunningham, 2019; Darvin, 2020; Norman, 2010; Wicker et al., 2019). The analysis offered in this chapter provides another, sobering layer: when women are able to obtain leadership positions, they are likely to be precarious ones. It is hardly any wonder, then, why many women report that sport is a toxic environment that privileges men (Darvin, 2020; Walker & Bopp, 2011), or why women across the sport industry leave the profession sooner than do men (Cunningham et al., 2019), oftentimes despite having more experiences and greater recognition for their sport-related accomplishments.

Despite the efficacy of the glass cliff in explaining women's opportunities and experiences, there were few studies set in the sport context. This represented a missed opportunity and curious omission. Many scholars outside of sport have focused on large, publicly traded firms, presumably because objective data are readily available. This is also true with sport, where coaching changes, performance measures, and other related factors are all within the researcher's grasp. Wicker et al.'s (2019) study of NCAA women's soccer teams illustrates as much. Other scholars could pursue similar courses of action. Focusing on sport could also provide scholars with the opportunity to examine whether the patterns observed among large, multinational corporations are also evident in sport.

Practical Implications

Sport organisations should ensure that all people have the chance to be successful and that they have the tools needed to do so. Promoting the glass cliff by hiring women to fill precarious positions does not attract top talent, nor does it serve the sport organisation well. People in glass cliff positions are likely to experience stress and the resultant disengagement from the workplace, including greater illnesses, absences, and ultimately withdrawal (Ryan et al., 2009). In short, the glass cliff hurts coaches, their teams, and the broader sport organisation.

Specific strategies are needed, then, to overcome the glass cliff phenomenon. The underlying theory and meta-analysis results offer several practical recommendations. The meta-analysis results showed that stereotypes are a key antecedent of the glass cliff. Given that stereotypes are bound by place and time (Cuddy et al., 2008), they are malleable. Exposure to powerful, successful women leading organisations with a history of success can help to reduce biases (Beaman et al., 2009). Work from Devine and colleagues also shows that people can overcome biases by treating them as a habit that they need to break (Devine, Forscher, Austin et al., 2012; Devine, Forscher, Cox et al., 2017). Devine et al. (2012) developed an intervention whereby people learned about their biases, how they negatively affected others, and steps they could take to reduce them. For example, they learned about stereotypical responses; the value of knowing people who counter stereotypes; thinking about people as individuals instead of as members of some large, homogeneous group; practicing empathy and perspective taking; and being around people who were different from them. People who went through this training saw a reduction in their bias, and the benefits lasted for up to two years in some cases.

Bruckmüller et al. (2014) identified other strategies for overcoming the glass cliff, and their recommendations have implications for coaching. They noted the primacy of transparency in the selection and evaluation process, as well as the value of gender quotas. Adriaanse and Schofield (2014) have also noted the value of gender quotas in sport, especially when operating alongside an emphasis on shared decision-making and power. Bruckmüller and colleagues also noted the importance of social resources in the way of networking and mentors (Bruckmüller & Branscombe, 2010; Bruckmüller et al., 2014). Structural, organisational, and interpersonal factors all limit women coaches' access to mentors (Cunningham & Sagas, 2005). Nevertheless, women coaches are likely to benefit from such individuals in their professional lives, and the support, advocacy, sponsorship, and advice that accompany mentoring relationships (see also Banwell et al., 2019).

Finally, Bruckmüller et al. (2014) note the importance of how managers frame interventions. A focus on women, their likelihood of being in precarious leadership positions, and stereotypes about women seemingly emphasises women, ignoring the role of men. In fact, a sole focus on women might only exacerbate preconceived notions, positioning women as "the other" in need of special training. Instead, sport organisations can focus on the importance of fairness and equality, ensuring that all people have a chance to be successful, the value of standardised, transparent selection processes, and the role of accountability for hiring managers and selection committees.

In short, these strategies offer steps for overcoming the glass cliff. Given the harmful effects of the glass cliff, such efforts are sorely warranted.

References

Adams, S. M., Gupta, A., & Leeth, J. D. (2009). Are female executives over-represented in precarious leadership positions? *British Journal of Management, 20*(1), 1–12. https://doi.org/10.1111/j.1467-8551.2007.00549.x

Adriaanse, J. (2016). Gender diversity in the governance of sport associations: The Sydney scoreboard global index of participation. *Journal of Business Ethics, 137*(1), 149–160. https://doi.org/10.1007/s10551-015-2550-3

Adriaanse, J., & Schofield, T. (2014). The impact of gender quotas on gender equality in sport governance. *Journal of Sport Management, 28*(5), 485–497. https://doi.org/10.1123/jsm.2013-0108

Ahn, N. Y., & Cunningham, G. B. (2017). Cultural values and gender equity on national Olympic committee boards. *International Journal of Exercise Science, 10*(6), 857–874.

Ahn, N. Y., & Cunningham, G. B. (2020). Standing on a glass cliff? A case study of FIFA's gender initiatives. *Managing Sport and Leisure, 25*(1–2), 114–137. https://doi.org/10.1080/23750472.2020.1727357

Banwell, J., Kerr, G., & Stirling, A. (2019). Key considerations for advancing women in coaching. *Women in Sport and Physical Activity Journal, 27*, 128–135. https://doi.org/10.1123/wspaj.2018-0069

Beaman, L., Chattopadhyay, R., Duflo, E., Pande, R., & Topalova, P. (2009). Powerful women: Does exposure reduce bias? *The Quarterly Journal of Economics, 124*(4), 1497–1540. https://doi.org/10.3386/w14198

Brady, D., Isaacs, K., Reeves, M., Burroway, R., & Reynolds, M. (2011). Sector, size, stability, and scandal. *Gender in Management: An International Journal, 26*(1), 84–104. https://doi.org/10.1108/17542411111109327

Bruckmüller, S., & Branscombe, N. R. (2010). The glass cliff: When and why women are selected as leaders in crisis contexts. *British Journal of Social Psychology, 49*(3), 433–451. https://doi.org/10.1348/014466609x466594

Bruckmüller, S., Ryan, M. K., Rink, F., & Haslam, S. A. (2014). Beyond the glass ceiling: The glass cliff and its lessons for organisational policy. *Social Issues and Policy Review, 8*(1), 202–232. https://doi.org/10.1111/sipr.12006

Burton, L. J. (2015). Underrepresentation of women in sport leadership: A review of research. *Sport Management Review, 18*(2), 155–165. https://doi.org/10.1016/j.smr.2014.02.004

Burton, L. J., Barr, C. A., Fink, J. S., & Bruening, J. E. (2009). "Think athletic director, think masculine?" Examination of the gender typing of managerial subroles within athletic administration positions. *Sex Roles, 61*(5–6), 416–426. https://doi.org/10.1007/s11199-009-9632-6

Cohen, J. (1988). *Statistical power analysis for the behavioral sciences* (2nd ed.). Lawrence Erlbaum. https://doi.org/10.1016/c2013-0-10517-x

Connley, C. (2019, May). *The number of women running Fortune 500 companies is at a record high.* www.cnbc.com/2019/05/16/the-number-of-women-running-fortune-500-companies-is-at-a-record-high.html

Cook, A., & Glass, C. (2014a). Above the glass ceiling: When are women and racial/ethnic minorities promoted to CEO? *Strategic Management Journal, 35*(7), 1080–1089. https://doi.org/10.1002/smj.2161

Cook, A., & Glass, C. (2014b). Women and top leadership positions: Towards an institutional analysis. *Gender, Work & Organisation, 21*(1), 91–103. https://doi.org/10.1111/gwao.12018

Cooper, H. (2010). *Research synthesis and meta-analysis: A step-by-step approach* (4th ed.). Sage.

Crockett, Z. (2016, August). More women will compete in Rio 2016 than in any other Olympics. *Vox.* www.vox.com/2016/8/5/12386612/rio-olympics-2016-women.

Cuddy, A. J., Fiske, S. T., & Glick, P. (2008). Warmth and competence as universal dimensions of social perception: The stereotype content model and the BIAS map. *Advances in Experimental Social Psychology, 40*, 61–149. https://doi.org/10.1016/s0065-2601(07)00002-0

Cunningham, G. B. (2008). Creating and sustaining gender diversity in sport organisations. *Sex Roles, 58*(1–2), 136–145. https://doi.org/10.1007/s11199-007-9312-3

Cunningham, G. B. (2016). Women in coaching: Theoretical underpinnings among quantitative analyses. In N. M. LaVoi (Ed.), *Women in sports coaching* (pp. 223–233). Routledge. https://doi.org/10.4324/9781315734651-13

Cunningham, G. B. (2019). *Diversity and inclusion in sport organisations: A multilevel perspective* (4th ed.). Routledge. https://doi.org/10.4324/9780429504310

Cunningham, G. B., & Ahn, N. Y. (2019). The role of bias in the under-representation of women in leadership positions. In N. L. Lough & A. N. Geurin (Eds.), *Routledge handbook of the business of women's sport* (pp. 83–94). Routledge. https://doi.org/10.4324/9780203702635-7

Cunningham, G. B., Ahn, N. Y., Anderson, A. J., & Dixon, M. A. (2019). Gender, coaching, and occupational turnover. *Women in Sport and Physical Activity Journal, 27*(2), 63–72. https://doi.org/10.1123/wspaj.2018-0038

Cunningham, G. B., Doherty, A. J., & Gregg, M. J. (2007). Using social cognitive career theory to understand head coaching intentions among assistant coaches of women's teams. *Sex Roles, 56*(5–6), 365–372. https://doi.org/10.1007/s11199-006-9175-z

Cunningham, G. B., & Sagas, M. (2002). The differential effects of human capital for male and female Division I basketball coaches. *Research Quarterly for Exercise and Sport, 73*, 489–495.

Cunningham, G. B., & Sagas, M. (2005). Access discrimination in intercollegiate athletics. *Journal of Sport and Social Issues, 29*, 148–163.

Darvin, L. (2020). Voluntary occupational turnover and the experiences of former intercollegiate women assistant coaches. *Journal of Vocational Behaviour, 116*, 103349. https://doi.org/10.1016/j.jvb.2019.103349

Darvin, L., Pegoraro, A., & Berri, D. (2018). Are men better leaders? An investigation of head coaches' gender and individual players' performance in amateur and professional women's basketball. *Sex Roles, 78*(7–8), 455–466. https://doi.org/10.1007/s11199-017-0815-2

Davidson, V., & Brest, L. (2014). *Trends in CEO succession in Australia's biggest public companies*. www.slideshare.net/strategyand/australian-chief-executive-study-2013-infographic

Dawley, D., Hoffman, J. J., & Smith, A. R. (2004). Leader succession: Does gender matter? *Leadership & Organisation Development Journal, 25*(8), 678–690. https://doi.org/10.1108/01437730410565004

Devine, P. G., Forscher, P. S., Austin, A. J., & Cox, W. T. (2012). Long-term reduction in implicit race bias: A prejudice habit-breaking intervention. *Journal of Experimental Social Psychology, 48*(6), 1267–1278. https://doi.org/10.1016/j.jesp.2012.06.003

Devine, P. G., Forscher, P. S., Cox, W. T., Kaatz, A., Sheridan, J., & Carnes, M. (2017). A gender bias habit-breaking intervention led to increased hiring of female faculty in STEMM departments. *Journal of Experimental Social Psychology, 73*, 211–215. https://doi.org/10.31234/osf.io/tdvy7

Fisher, R. A. (1970). *Statistical methods for research workers* (14th ed.). Collier-Macmillan.

Gaston, L., Blundell, M., & Fletcher, T. (in press). Gender diversity in sport leadership: An investigation of United States of America national governing bodies of sport. *Managing Sport and Leisure*. https://doi.org/10.1080/23750472.2020.1719189

Gearty, B. T., Mills, J. P., & Callary, B. (2016). Theoretical underpinnings among qualitative research. In N. M. LaVoi (Ed.), *Women in sports coaching* (pp. 234–254). Routledge.

Gomez-Gonzalez, C., Dietl, H., & Nesseler, C. (2019). Does performance justify the underrepresentation of women coaches? Evidence from professional women's soccer. *Sport Management Review*, *22*(5), 640–651. https://doi.org/10.1016/j.smr.2018.09.008

Greenhaus, J. H., Parasuraman, S., & Wormley, W. M. (1990). Effects of race on organizational experiences, job performance evaluations, and career outcomes. *Academy of Management Journal*, *33*, 64–86.

Gupta, A., Briscoe, F., & Hambrick, D. C. (2017). Red, blue, and purple firms: Organizational political ideology and corporate social responsibility. *Strategic Management Journal*, *38*, 1018–1040. https://doi.org/10.1002/smj.2550

Haslam, S. A., Ryan, M. K., Kulich, C., Trojanowski, G., & Atkins, C. (2010). Investing with prejudice: The relationship between women's presence on company boards and objective and subjective measures of company performance. *British Journal of Management*, *21*(2), 484–497. https://doi.org/10.1111/j.1467-8551.2009.00670.x

Hedges, L. V., & Olkin, I. (1985). *Statistical methods for meta-analysis*. Academic Press.

Hennessey, S. M., MacDonald, K., & Carroll, W. (2014). Is there a" glass cliff or a solid ledge for female appointees to the board of directors? *Journal of Organisational Culture, Communications and Conflict*, *18*(2), 125–140.

Johnson, B. T., & Eagly, A. H. (2000). Quantitative synthesis of social-psychological research. In H. T. Reis & C. M. Judd (Eds.), *Handbook of research: Methods in social personality psychology* (pp. 496–528). Cambridge University Press.

Koca, C., & Öztürk, P. (2015). Gendered perceptions about female managers in Turkish sport organisations. *European Sport Management Quarterly*, *15*(3), 381–406. https://doi.org/10.1080/16184742.2015.1040046

Koenig, A. M., Eagly, A. H., Mitchell, A. A., & Ristikari, T. (2011). Are leader stereotypes masculine? A meta-analysis of three research paradigms. *Psychological Bulletin*, *137*(4), 616–642. https://doi.org/10.1037/e617292010-001

Kulich, C., Lorenzi-Cioldi, F., Iacoviello, V., Faniko, K., & Ryan, M. K. (2015). Signalling change during a crisis: Refining conditions for the glass cliff. *Journal of Experimental Social Psychology*, *61*, 96–103. https://doi.org/10.1016/j.jesp.2015.07.002

Larsen, L. K., & Clayton, C. J. (2019). Career pathways to NCAA division I women's basketball head coach positions: Do race and gender matter? *Women in Sport and Physical Activity Journal*, *27*(2), 94–100. https://doi.org/10.1123/wspaj.2018-0068

LaVoi, N. M. (2016). A framework to understand experiences of women coaches around the globe: The ecological-intersectional model. In N. M. LaVoi (Ed.), *Women in sport coaching* (pp. 13–34). Routledge.

LaVoi, N. M., & Dutove, J. K. (2012). Barriers and supports for female coaches: An ecological model. *Sports Coaching Review*, *1*(1), 17–37. https://doi.org/10.1080/21640629.2012.695891

Lee, P. M., & James, E. H. (2007). She'-e-os: Gender effects and investor reactions to the announcements of top executive appointments. *Strategic Management Journal*, *28*(3), 227–241. https://doi.org/10.1002/smj.575

Lee, W., & Cunningham, G. B. (2019). Group diversity's influence on sport teams and organisations: A meta-analytic examination and identification of key moderators. *European Sport Management Quarterly, 19*(2), 139–159. https://doi.org/10.1080/16184742.2018.1478440

Lipsey, M. W., & Wilson, D. B. (2001). *Practical meta-analysis* (Applied Social Research Methods Series, Vol. 49). Sage.

Machida-Kosuga, M., Schaubroeck, J. M., Gould, D., Ewing, M., & Feltz, D. L. (2017). What influences collegiate coaches' intentions to advance their leadership careers? The roles of leader self-efficacy and outcome expectancies. *International Sport Coaching Journal, 4*(3), 265–278. https://doi.org/10.1123/iscj.2016-0120

Madsen, R. M., Burton, L. J., & Clark, B. S. (2017). Gender role expectations and the prevalence of women as assistant coaches. *Journal for the Study of Sports and Athletes in Education, 11*(2), 125–142. https://doi.org/10.1080/19357397.2017.1315994

Norman, L. (2010). Feeling second best: Elite women coaches' experiences. *Sociology of Sport Journal, 27*(1), 89–104. https://doi.org/10.1123/ssj.27.1.89

Norman, L. (2014). A crisis of confidence: Women coaches' responses to their engagement in resistance. *Sport, Education and Society, 19*(5), 532–551. https://doi.org/10.1080/13573322.2012.689975

Norman, L., Rankin-Wright, A. J., & Allison, W. (2018). "It's a concrete ceiling; It's not even glass": Understanding tenets of organisational culture that supports the progression of women as coaches and coach developers. *Journal of Sport and Social Issues, 42*(5), 393–414. https://doi.org/10.1177/0193723518790086

Reade, I., Rodgers, W., & Norman, L. (2009). The under-representation of women in coaching: A comparison of male and female Canadian coaches at low and high levels of coaching. *International Journal of Sports Science & Coaching, 4*(4), 505–520. https://doi.org/10.1260/174795409790291439

Rink, F., Ryan, M. K., & Stoker, J. I. (2012). Influence in times of crisis: How social and financial resources affect men's and women's evaluations of glass-cliff positions. *Psychological Science, 23*(11), 1306–1313. https://doi.org/10.1177/0956797612453115

Rubenstein, A. L., Eberly, M. B., Lee, T. W., & Mitchell, T. R. (2018). Surveying the forest: A meta-analysis, moderator investigation, and future-oriented discussion of the antecedents of voluntary employee turnover. *Personnel Psychology, 71*(1), 23–65. https://doi.org/10.1111/peps.12226

Ryan, M. K., & Haslam, S. A. (2005). The glass cliff: Evidence that women are over-represented in precarious leadership positions. *British Journal of Management, 16*(2), 81–90. https://doi.org/10.1111/j.1467-8551.2005.00433.x

Ryan, M. K., & Haslam, S. A. (2007). The glass cliff: Exploring the dynamics surrounding the appointment of women to precarious leadership positions. *Academy of Management Review, 32*(2), 549–572. https://doi.org/10.5465/amr.2007.24351856

Ryan, M. K., Haslam, S. A., Hersby, M. D., & Bongiorno, R. (2011). Think crisis—think female: The glass cliff and contextual variation in the think manager—think male stereotype. *Journal of Applied Psychology, 96*(3), 470–484. https://doi.org/10.1037/e633962013-515

Ryan, M. K., Haslam, S. A., Hersby, M. D., Kulich, C., & Wilson-Kovacs, M. D. (2009). The stress of working on the edge: Implications of glass cliffs for both women and organisations. In M. Barreto, M. K. Ryan, & M. T. Schmitt (Eds.), *Psychology of* women book series. *The glass ceiling in the 21st century: Understanding barriers to gender equality* (pp. 153–169). American Psychological Association.

Ryan, M. K., Haslam, S. A., & Kulich, C. (2010). Politics and the glass cliff: Evidence that women are preferentially selected to contest hard-to-win seats. *Psychology of Women Quarterly, 34*(1), 56–64. https://doi.org/10.1111/j.1471-6402.2009.01541.x

Ryan, M. K., Haslam, S. A., Morgenroth, T., Rink, F., Stoker, J., & Peters, K. (2016). Getting on top of the glass cliff: Reviewing a decade of evidence, explanations, and impact. *The Leadership Quarterly, 27*(3), 446–455. https://doi.org/10.1016/j.leaqua.2015.10.008

Sartore, M. L., & Cunningham, G. B. (2007). Explaining the under-representation of women in leadership positions of sport organisations: A symbolic interactionist perspective. *Quest, 59*(2), 244–265. https://doi.org/10.1080/00336297.2007.10483551

Schein, V. E. (1973). The relationship between sex role stereotypes and requisite management characteristics. *Journal of Applied Psychology, 57*(2), 95–100. https://doi.org/10.1007/bf00288030

Schein, V. E. (1975). Relationships between sex role stereotypes and requisite management characteristics among female managers. *Journal of Applied Psychology, 60*(3), 340–344. https://doi.org/10.1037/h0076637

Schmidt, F. L., & Hunter, J. E. (2015). *Methods of meta-analysis: Correcting error and bias in research findings* (3rd ed.). Sage.

Schull, V., Shaw, S., & Kihl, L. A. (2013). "If a woman came in . . . she would have been eaten up alive": Analysing gendered political processes in the search for an athletic director. *Gender & Society, 27*(1), 56–81. https://doi.org/10.1177/0891243212466289

Smittick, A. L., Miner, K. N., & Cunningham, G. B. (2019). The "I" in team: Coach incivility, coach gender, and team performance in women's basketball teams. *Sport Management Review, 22*(3), 419–433. https://doi.org/10.1016/j.smr.2018.06.002

Walker, N. A., & Bopp, T. (2011). The underrepresentation of women in the male-dominated sport workplace: Perspectives of female coaches. *Journal of Workplace Rights, 15*(1), 47–64. https://doi.org/10.2190/wr.15.1.d

Walker, N. A., Bopp, T., & Sagas, M. (2011). Gender bias in the perception of women as collegiate men's basketball coaches. *Journal for the Study of Sports and Athletes in Education, 5*(2), 157–176. https://doi.org/10.1179/ssa.2011.5.2.157

Wicker, P., Cunningham, G. B., & Fields, D. (2019). Head coach changes in women's college soccer: An investigation of women coaches through the lenses of gender stereotypes and the glass cliff. *Sex Roles, 81*(11–12), 797–807. https://doi.org/10.1007/s11199-019-01022-2

World Bank. (2020, March). *Labor force, female (% of total labor force)—United States.* https://data.worldbank.org/indicator/SL.TLF.TOTL.FE.ZS?locations=US

2 Gender Stereotypes as Mechanisms of Social Exclusion of Women as Football Coaches

Torsten Schlesinger, Florian Ingwersen and Yvonne Weigelt-Schlesinger

Introduction

In sport, female coaches, particularly at the elite level, are still a minority. In contrast, the situation in women's football seems to be at first glance a little different. The German women's national team has been successfully coached by female coaches for many years, and some regional associations of the DFB (umbrella association of German football) employ licensed female coaches on a full-time basis. However, a closer look leaves doubts about unrestricted access to coaching posts in football. Various statistics of the DFB and of regional federations indicate that women are clearly under-represented in the coaching position of girls' and women's teams. There was no woman coaching a team in the first division and only three women coaching in the second division of women's football in the 2019/2020 season.[1] This means that only 10% of elite women's teams (clubs) in Germany are coached by women. However, in this context, it must also be noted that 136 women hold the required licence[2] (Coach-A or Pro licence; Table 2.1).

Moreover, the DFB member and team statistics reveal that the number of female members of the DFB is over 1.1 million (800k over 16 years old) and over 10,000 girls and women teams were registered in 2019 (DFB, 2019). There has been a steadily growing number of girls and women who play

Table 2.1 DFB licence holder in 2019, differentiated by male and female

Licence	Male licence holder	Female licence holder	Percentage of women
UEFA Pro licence	884	30	3
Coach-A	4,994	106	2
Elite Youth Coach	6,351	164	3
Coach-B	27,321	833	3
Coach-C	43,719	3,274	7
Total	83,269	4,407	5

Source: DFB (2020)

Table 2.2 Female graduates of German coaching education from 2015 to 2019 (absolute number, in brackets percentage)

Licence	2015	2016	2017	2018	2019
UEFA Pro licence	1 (4)	2 (7.7)	1 (3.6)	0 (0)	1 (3.1)
Coach-A	2 (1.3)	4 (2.3)	9 (3.7)	9 (3.9)	10 (3.4)
Elite Youth Coach	16 (4.2)	14 (3.5)	6 (1.6)	16 (3.5)	13 (2.7)
Coach-B	64 (3.7)	64 (3.2)	67 (3.6)	81 (4.2)	52 (2.7)
Coach-C	455 (8.3)	471 (7.4)	426 (7.3)	469 (8.0)	506 (8.6)

Source: DFB (2020)

football in clubs and who would also be willing to become coaches during the last decade. Nevertheless, there is a clear mismatch between the number of teams and the number of licensed female coaches.[3] Furthermore, Table 2.2 shows that a comparatively small number of females participate in educational programmes for football coaches to obtain a coaching licence.

If women decide against participation in football coaching or to enter coaching education programmes, a great potential for innovation is lost, which besides being a better utilisation of human resources, could also enrich the coaching business by opening up new topics and fresh perspectives. As the statistics reveal, there are obviously mechanisms of social exclusion that significantly influence the access of women to coaching positions and educational programmes in football.

The marginalisation of women as coaches is a complex problem, and several studies have identified several factors and barriers operating at different levels (individual, interactional, organisational, and societal, or cultural), which explain the under-representation of female coaches. The effects of such mechanisms can be encountered wherever women attempt to enter a coaching position. Furthermore, there are several studies that reflect the situation of women and coaching in football at different performance levels (elite and grassroots level) and from different perspectives (e.g., Fasting & Pfister, 2000; Fasting et al., 2019; Lewis et al., 2018; Nesseler et al., 2020; Norman, 2019; Sinning, 2006; Weigelt-Schlesinger, 2008). However, in many countries as well as in Germany, there are hardly any formal barriers such as gender-specific participation rules or requirements in organisational statutes or educational programmes that would explain why women are significantly under-represented in coaching positions and education courses in football. Rather, there might be factors in football that are located more at an informal level, and therefore, often remain invisible but are nonetheless very effective in preventing women from striving for a coaching position and entering coaching education. In this context, gender stereotypes seem to be of importance. Within the field of gender research, there is a broad consensus that socially anchored gender stereotyping plays a crucial role when it comes to hindering or preventing women's careers in numerous areas of society (Cook & Cusac, 2010; Oakes et al., 1994), and are fundamental factors contributing to the exclusion of women from certain positions within organisations (Acker, 1990; Weinbach, 2004).

The aim of this article is to focus on gender stereotypes as an exclusionary mechanism keeping women from entering taking up coaching positions and education programmes in football. Our perspective taken here is sociologically oriented, which means that the under-representation of female coaches in football is focused on as a social circumstance. Accordingly, we conceptualise the phenomenon of social difference as the participation or non-participation of people in specific communicational contexts and describe this with the term "social exclusion". The term social exclusion refers to the fact that a person (or a population) is not considered or addressed in the communication processes of a certain social system (Stichweh, 2005). Here, differentiation must be made between external exclusion and self-exclusion: while external exclusion refers to direct or indirect conditions of belonging to a respective social area, self-exclusion is a conscious self-chosen non-participation (Cachay & Thiel, 2008). Accordingly, we want to analyse *the extent gender-related stereotypes are embedded in the specific social context of football at different levels and are associated with exclusionary effects on women as football coaches*. Based on this knowledge about the effect of stereotypes as a specific exclusion mechanism, strategies for promoting the inclusion of female coaches in football can be discussed in a more differentiated manner.

In order to discuss gender stereotypes regarding their exclusionary effects on women in terms of coaching positions and educational programmes in football, in a first step gender stereotypes and their social function should be basically framed.

Gender Stereotypes and Their Social Function

When dealing with the social function of gender stereotypes, it is first necessary to consider the underlying concept of gender. There is a shared view in sociological gender research that gender and subsequent gender differences are social constructions that are institutionally anchored in continually performed and internalised interactions (Hirschauer, 2001). This suggests that gender differences are not *natural* but acquired and enacted, and that they vary according to the particular social and gender order (Pfister, 2010; Wetterer, 2006). Thus, gender is a construct with profound relevance to social processes and structures that influence the order of all areas of life, such as roles in the family, work roles, and so on. However, the disadvantage of the gender construct is not that a difference is made between women and men, but that these differences are valued and stereotyped in order to legitimise an unequal hierarchy and balance of power (West & Fenstermaker, 1995).

Stereotypes can be understood as complexity-reducing summaries of properties or behaviour of certain groups of people and are based on processes of social categorisation and stigmatisation (Taylor, 1981). In addition to other characteristics such as age or ethnicity, gender is one of the most important characteristics of such categorisation processes. The gender-specific grouping (stereotyping) goes hand in hand with the typical assignment of characteristics and skills. Overlapping, socially divided and cognitively embedded knowledge structures of gender, that is, gender-stereotyped assumptions about "typical" characteristics of women and men, are essential elements to this construction process (Alfermann, 1996; Ridgeway, 2001). Thus, gender stereotypes are assumptions and simplistic generalisations about gender characteristics (e.g., biological sex) and the typical roles of men and women (e.g., Eckes, 1997; Schneider, 2005). Gender stereotypes can be viewed as collective shared structures of knowledge, which are not stored as lists of properties, but in a more structured way as clusters (or dimensions) such as strength/weakness or activity/passivity. We often characterise individuals differently or assign the same qualities to different degrees simply because they are male or female. While gender stereotypes are occasionally subject to changes, they are constantly reproduced in everyday speech so that the binary construction of gender is maintained (Goffman, 1977). However, it is important to emphasise that stereotyping should not be primarily understood as a superficial criticism. In social interaction, gender stereotypes serve as a means of orientation and organisation in order to reduce complexity, by assisting information processing and helping us to find a place within our social environment (e.g., Hirschauer, 2001; Oakes et al., 1994). Thus, stereotypes simplify the social world and help to act more efficiently in everyday life. Particularly, "gender" can be an orientation aid in order to observe male and female persons in a certain way and to adapt one's behaviour (Weinbach & Stichweh, 2001). The constructions created by stereotypes serve to distance us from others or to affiliate ourselves with them. However, such distance is never rigid or inaccessible to modification, nor does it concern every part of life (Hirschauer, 2001). Categorisation processes based on gender stereotypes are particularly problematic because they offer an orientation grid that seems comparatively easy to handle. On the one hand, such categorisation processes reinforce the need for clear gender affiliation. On the other hand, they catalyse differences by providing opportunities to play up the gender divide (Weinbach & Stichweh, 2001). Therefore, stereotypical constructions contribute to a situation where individuals exclude themselves or are externally excluded based on gender-related (self-) positioning. Accordingly, gender-based modes of interpretation and perception also become relevant to an individual's career opportunities (Acker, 1990).

Multilevel Approach Explaining the Impact of Gender Stereotypes on the Exclusion of Women From Coaching Education

Gender stereotypes can be analysed both at the social level as well as at the individual level. At social level, it is about the generalisation of gender-related behavioural expectations (Borggrefe et al., 2018). Accordingly, the question arises to what extent the requirements and expectations regarding the role of a football coach are gender-specific connoted as "male or female" at different social levels. Thus, we will look at a societal level the extent that football can be seen as masculine, which is associated with (stereotyped) expectations to the coaching role. At an organisational level, we will consider the extent of gender stereotypes becoming relevant as premises of coach recruitment and supporting, or with the self-understanding in the club culture. Finally, at the interactional level, we will analyse the extent to which the acceptance of female coaches with their competencies are stereotyped within interactive situations, for example, within the clubs with colleagues, players, board members, or with other participants at coach education programmes.

On the other hand, at individual level it must also be considered whether and how a person themselves internalises gender-related stereotypic expectations through participation in certain social situations and uses this as a basis for their own behaviour and self-positioning. Therefore, the question arises how do (potential) female coaches relate themselves regarding gender-related expectations in football, and to what extent do they align their actions and decisions accordingly?

In the following, by linking the different levels as pointed out in Figure 2.1, the influence of gender stereotypes as complex social mechanism of the exclusion of women from coaching positions and education programmes in football will be discussed in more detail.

Stereotypical Expectations of Coaching Role in Football at Societal Level

A central assumption is that although gender differences become less important in modern society, they are still utilised to make decisive distinctions between men and women (Weinbach, 2004). In the following, we consider gender as the respective functional addressing of systems-specific communication (Luhmann, 1988). But it should be noted that gender stereotypes do not formally present exclusion criteria of social systems (at societal level) because the inclusion conditions are not directly associated with the qualities assigned to an individual. Rather, gender stereotypes can be communicated perpetually in indirect ways and influence both the expectations as well as the actions of people in a wide range of social areas.

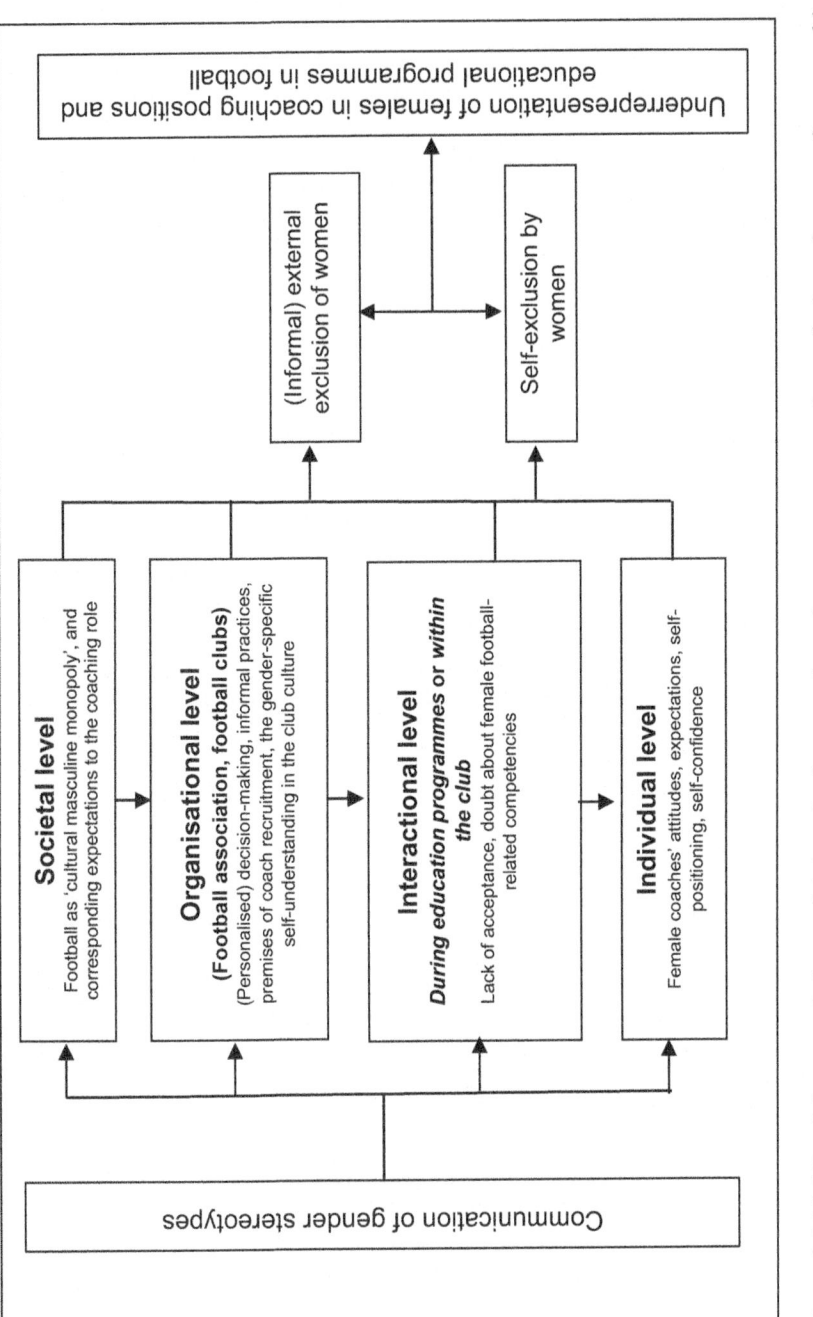

Figure 2.1 Multilevel framework for explaining the impact of gender stereotypes on the exclusion of women from coaching education

In general, sport is a social area with a focus on physical abilities and communication of bodies, and gender can therefore be easily maintained as a pattern of social order, since gender-specific attributes can be ascribed to biological differences between males and females (e.g., Pfister, 2010; Theberge, 2000). Accordingly, even today certain types of sport construct and demonstrate masculinity. Therefore, if sport is constructed by gender-specific abilities (as other social practices too), it cannot be a gender-neutral medium. For football, it is assumed—at least in the still male-dominated Western world—that gender barriers are more tightly and more frequently constructed than in other sports (e.g., Scraton et al., 1999; Sülzle, 2011). Despite the latest developments in women's football, this kind of sport still serves as a means of producing and staging masculinity (Meuser, 2008), and becomes still an "arena for masculinity" (Kreisky & Spitaler, 2006). Therefore, strategies can be expected on part of the men in order to ensure the hegemonic power of masculinity in football, particularly regarding positions of responsibility, such as the coaching role, with the result that the clear lines drawn between genders persist.[4]

Against this background, it becomes clear that also generalised behaviour towards and expectations of specific functional roles, such as the role of coach, will become relevant, which are closely related to the respective functional logic of a social context. Accordingly, gender-specific requirements related to the coach's role in football and corresponding stereotypic attributions should be considered. References that the coach's role in football can be seen as a sex-typing position that requires certain personality traits, which are often stereotyped as masculine, can be found in various studies (e.g., Fasting & Pfister, 2000; Fasting et al., 2019; Murray et al., 2020; Scraton et al., 1999; Sinning, 2006; Weigelt-Schlesinger, 2008; see for female referees, e.g., Reid & Dallaire, 2019). This corresponds with expectations towards the actions and competences of football coaches, which are often related to gender-specific connotations (Lewis et al., 2018; Murray et al., 2020). Many so-called female characteristics are biased by gender stereotypes, such as being even-tempered, socially competent and empathic. Women as coaches are more likely to be described in terms of attributes such as their capacity for teamwork, communicative competence, and fairness, while male coaches are said to display confidence, assertiveness, and leadership qualities. Hence, in the field of coaching, qualities associated with leadership or task orientation are closely related to male coaches, while pedagogical skills, communicative qualities traditionally correspond to female gender role stereotypes (Sinning, 2006; Weigelt-Schlesinger, 2008). It should be noted that such stigmatisation is often not meant to be explicitly degrading, but is usually phrased in a hidden, positive way: female coaches are assigned a high degree of team or social skills and characterised as supportive, cooperative, and striving for harmony. However, such stereotypical constructions also indirectly imply that in positions of responsibility women are unassertive, too soft, and indecisive in their interaction with players or colleagues. Accordingly, the focus on success and achievement is also more stereotypically assigned to men (Bahlke et al., 2003). It is also important to note that this does not mean that women cannot be coaches, but that a female coach should have the characteristics of a man.

Furthermore, the stereotypical perception of behaviour can also vary when, for example, the same behaviour is described for a male coach as being dynamic and for a female coach as aggressive. Football is continuously related to toughness and aggressiveness, so that it is common for women who are actively involved in football (as players or coaches) to be viewed as not being "real" women (Pfister & Fasting, 2003). Also, female football players see the behaviour of male coaches more clearly shaped by aggressiveness, directness, authority but also football-related competence, that is, as typically male (Fasting & Pfister, 2000; Haselwood et al., 2005), and this leads to players' preferences for a male coach (e.g., Bahlke et al., 2003; Weigelt-Schlesinger, 2008). Coaches need to be aware that gender-based stereotypes may influence how others perceive their competency (Murray et al., 2020). In order to be accepted as a football coach, a woman must first be a coach and then a woman. If women are self-confident, ambitious, and demonstrate strong leadership skills, this is often interpreted as deviating from the feminine norm and downgraded as typical "male behaviour" or stigmatised as "unfeminine". Female coaches with such behaviour are often perceived as arrogant and even impertinent, whereas the same behaviour in male coaches is interpreted as confident and competent. A way out of this dilemma may be to trivialise one's strengths in interaction, in order not to be stigmatised as being too ambitious and forceful, as quasi-unfeminine (Pfister & Fasting, 2003). Therefore, female coaches sometimes refuse to orient themselves towards stereotypical feminine traits in order to satisfy common notions about the leadership style of a coach.

It must also be considered whether women and men are assessed differently in coaching positions. On the one hand, women are evaluated more negatively if they work in a male domain. On the other hand, a leadership style for women and men that is congruent with gender stereotypes leads to better ratings. Accordingly, acceptance problems could arise both for women with a more directive (masculine) leadership style and for men with a more feminised oriented leadership style.

Moreover, the assessment of coaches regarding football-related skills and competencies is often related to gender stereotypes that assign to men a greater football-related competence than women. Consequently, football-specific competencies of women are also continually called into question and women's qualifications for coaching positions are often underestimated (Weigelt-Schlesinger, 2008). Moreover, the legitimacy of having a woman in the role of a football coach is questioned because it is suspected that the responsibilities of the coaching position (such as leading a team) can be undermined by further typical (external) gender-specific responsibilities, such as caring for the family (Bahlke et al., 2003).

In sum, it becomes clear that the evaluation of the coaching role in football is still linked to male stereotypes and women who want to become football coaches must deal with such stereotypical ideas about the fit of women and football.

Gender Stereotypes Within Organisational Structures of Football

Gender stereotypes, communicated at the societal level, also enter the organisational structures of football (e.g., clubs or federations), which also develop specific mechanism to (re)produce gender relations. Therefore, we should reflect how gender stereotypes and organisational structures interact and influence processes of recruiting and promoting female coaches.

According to Luhmann (2006), organisations can be viewed as social systems consisting of and reproduced through (communicated) decisions. Therefore, all observable organisational features in sport clubs, such as aims, hierarchy, filling positions, or supportive measures for specific groups, are the results of preceding organisational decisions (Thiel & Mayer, 2009). The recruitment process is particularly relevant in organisations, since suitable and interested applicants do not find vacant positions automatically. How and on what basis recruiting decisions are made, and who makes these decisions, is equally relevant. Recruitment processes are linked to the uncertainty of matching the right person to the job, a task that not only depends on measurable and evidential expertise but also on the personality of the jobholder. Their performance is significantly related to other life references, experiences, and personality traits (Schreiner & Thiel, 2011). In order to minimise the recruitment risk, certain procedures and practices are applied in the recruitment process. Before the recruitment starts, it is necessary to define the coach's tasks and the requirements to be met by the candidates who may be suitable for a coaching position. The matter of who has the power to define the requirements of the coaching position within the club is crucial to the process of coach recruitment.

Sport clubs are characterised on a structural level by personalised decision programmes (Thiel & Mayer, 2009). That means, decisions are delegated to single persons or exclusive networks, such as the members of the club board. Furthermore, recruitment processes are often shaped by informal procedures and practices (Combrink, 2004; Hovden, 2000). Personalised and informal recruitment practices in sports clubs permit a greater scope of individual preferences on the part of the decision-maker. This may complicate the handling of gender-related neutrality, because those who are in hiring positions and networks (mostly men) prefer individuals similar to themselves, as a means of reducing organisational uncertainty (Schlesinger & Weigelt-Schlesinger, 2013). Existing studies in sport organisations show that decision-making bodies with a higher proportion of women have fewer expectations of masculine stereotypes compared with those including few or no women (Hartmann-Tews & Combrink, 2005).

The relevance of stereotyped orientation in recruitment processes is particularly revealed by gender stereotype-based assessments of function and expectations of competences by the decision-maker. At the same time, those actors participating in the recruitment process can determine stereotypical expectations and preferences in criteria, which are viewed as being relevant to coach recruitment, criteria that are considered negotiable and the practical constraints that are considered to be non-negotiable (Bahlke et al., 2003). This implies that the recruitment of women as coaches is clearly related to what extent the coaching position within the club is associated with specific masculine-connoted role expectations (Aicher & Sagas, 2010). As a result, the question is not whether and how male and female coaches differ, but how the decision-makers believe them to differ on account of gender-specific attributions. It appears that in clubs where masculine-connoted role expectations exist, women are rarely considered in the recruitment process for a coaching position, and also the acceptance of women in coaching positions and the willingness and interest in working together with women may be limited (Hovden, 1999). Furthermore, masculine-connoted stereotypes can determine to what extent the promotion of female coaches is considered as relevant, for example, how the club coordinates and applies programmes for promoting women, and how women are inspired and supported to become a football coach (Schlesinger & Weigelt-Schlesinger, 2013).

Moreover, the culture of a sports organisation defines its approach towards the way that certain gender-related values and norms are construed and internally communicated (Shaw & Slack, 2002). Accordingly, gender stereotypes can be deeply rooted in the culture and collective shared thinking of a football club (Norman, 2019; Schlesinger & Weigelt-Schlesinger, 2013). Gender stereotypes often work as a form of "guidance" that encourages men and women in clubs to perceive and reflect things in a particular way based on established gender-specific patterns. Consequently, gender stereotypes can be used as reference points to reinforce gender differences and to legitimise processes of external exclusion. At the same time, this makes it difficult to remove established gender-specific patterns of action in football clubs, since all the decisions can be linked to the collectively shared value of beliefs in a subliminal manner. The stronger of the identification of the club members is linked to a more cultural self-image within the club (as this is often masculine in the case in football), the more difficult it will be for members to understand why changes should be encouraged that contradict to these cultural dispositions. Therefore, the gender-specific self-image within the club culture, as well as the capability to distance (masculine-connoted) self-images, determines the "innovative ability" of a club regarding the promotion of women as coaches.

A look at the club structures indicates that (1) (personalised) decision-making programmes, (2) informal practices, (3) male-related premises in coach recruitment, and (4) the gender-specific self-understanding anchored in the club culture can promote the selective influence of gender stereotypes. Since these mechanisms mostly do not work separately, but rather are closely linked with each other, football clubs can develop an effective system for maintaining gender differences. This also explains why measures to promote female coaches in the club are difficult to enforce. Furthermore, external guidelines and programmes sometimes cannot prevent gender stereotypes from acting as selection mechanisms at the informal level, even before formal structures of the club take effect. In some cases, making inequality and discrimination visible by certain equality or gender mainstream measures could have counterproductive effects by systematically undermining the measures at the informal level.

Reproducing of Gender Stereotypes Within Interactional Situations of Football

Especially in interaction situations where individuals can perceive each other directly and face to face (Kieserling, 1999), the behaviours and activities of a person play a vital part in the performance of gender and can be "read" by the recipient as a sign of their assumed gender. Therefore, gender differences are constantly reproduced, replicated, changed, or evened out at interactional level (Hirschauer, 2001). However, it should be emphasised that gender as a social category is not made relevant in every interactional situation, rather gender affiliation can also be covered by other social characteristics (e.g., age and ethnicity) or neutralised (Weinbach & Stichweh, 2001). Nevertheless, in various formal and informal interactional constellations between other coaches, players, club functionaries, or course instructors in the masculine-dominated area of football, women are always present with the characteristics of their person, of which gender represents a very important one.

Often mechanisms at interactional level exist that prevent women from starting coaching education at club level. In interactional constellations, women are directly confronted with the underlying gender-related beliefs and expectations. Thus, female coaches are mainly attributed with "female" qualities and they are often not accepted or trusted to be technically competent coaches. As a result, obvious femininity in the field of football coaching is associated with unprofessionalism and incompetence. It becomes apparent that female players and coaches often perceive their football club as being discouraging, because women are accepted less in technical respects by the male functionaries. This environment often appears to persuade women not to seek a coaching position in the club in the first place.

Furthermore, if women participate in educational programmes to get a football coaching licence, they can be confronted with the gender stereotypical beliefs and expectations of both the predominantly male instructors as well as the (mostly) male course participants. Male participants emphasise during courses that female coaches are incompetent as far as football is concerned and they often feel confirmed in their assumption that a woman has only limited practical football skills (Schlesinger & Weigelt-Schlesinger, 2012). Therefore, in coach education, women are only accepted by the other course participants if they can play football "properly". Women who do well in the practical parts of the course tend to be accepted more easily by their fellow participants than other women. Also, the (mostly) male course instructors do not place much trust in the skills of the female coaches. They often presuppose that the women's abilities and theoretical knowledge regarding football are rather limited. A course instructor club describes this as follows in an empirical study (Weigelt-Schlesinger, 2008):

> Very often the women's experience in playing is just not enough to lead a team. None of those we have educated so far has really been able to do it. There hasn't really been any woman who could practically demonstrate it. Well, a woman who understands the game, who can read the game as it needs to be read – so far, we haven't had a woman like that with us.
>
> (int. 1)

However, such stereotypic perspectives are often not necessarily expressed in a directly discriminating way but are covered by seemingly objective facts, for example, the hint that prospective female coaches have clearly less expertise in the theory and practice of football. Therefore, women are often confronted with interaction situations during their educational programmes where their presence is questioned and they feel pushed into a special role. At the same time, it becomes clear, also in interactions during education courses that female coaches have to demonstrate their football-specific analytical abilities over and over again and always need to perform twice as well as men in order to receive the same level of acceptance as a coach, while their male colleagues are accepted from the beginning (Weigelt-Schlesinger, 2008). This could explain why the proportion of women as C licence holders is higher than in the subsequent higher licence levels (see Table 2.2). If the women have had such experience, it is obvious that the inhibition threshold for acquiring further licence levels is quite high.

Self-Exclusion of Women From Football Coaching due to Stereotypic Expectations

It should be taken into account that the (informal) definition and communication of the coaching role and male-connoted expectations towards a football coach do not only have an influence on the decision-maker in a club, but also always have an influence on the potential female coaches. Entering a coaching position or participating in educational programmes in football can also be related to the process of self-exclusion, because potential female coaches must be willing to meet the requirements and expectations of the coach position, and will thus be interested in and apply for the position or not. Therefore, we should look at the reasons for self-exclusion of women from coaching in football, and to what extent self-exclusion is associated with assumed or constructed unequal treatment or injustice.

In particular, the consideration of the more informally formulated requirements for the coaching position reveals that women's football-specific competencies are repeatedly doubted, particularly by male colleagues and functionaries in clubs or educational courses. Against this background, it should be noted that women themselves can also develop gender stereotypes in relation to coaching practices due to their suggestions that male functionaries or coaches have a lower acceptance of women in football and that masculine expectations regarding the coaching role exist. This is further reinforced by the fact that many of the women themselves are mainly coached by men. Such stereotyped pictures, ideas, and expectations, which women develop regarding the coaching position, lead to the consequence that women estimate themselves as unsuitable or inappropriate for a coaching position in football. This is related to the fact that both men as well as women strive to carry out and interpret the coaching role and activities in a way that aims to present gender affiliation and coaching activities in a congruent manner. The perceived discrepancies can be influenced by women's own stereotypical expectations and suggestions concerning the coaching position in football. Here, it should be noted that stereotypic attribution always affects the addressed female coach as an essential part of her personality, namely that of their gender role identity. This means that not only in the role of the coach is she doubted but also as a woman, and thus, the whole of the person. Therefore, women do not find the coaching role attractive, or do not view themselves as being suitable, based on male-connoted role expectations, as pointed out in several studies (e.g., Bahlke et al., 2003; Cunningham et al., 2007; Lewis et al., 2018; Norman, 2010a, 2010b; Weigelt-Schlesinger, 2008). Thus, many women decide against engaging in coaching or entering coach education programmes to avoid the social pressure resulting from a lack of acceptance and latent mistrust towards their football-specific competencies as a coach. This may have the effect of excluding them, particularly if women rely strongly on the feedback and acceptance of their male colleagues for self-rating and behaviour. A female coach of a football club describes this as follows in an empirical study (Weigelt-Schlesinger, 2008):

> Most women think: I'm the only woman and have to deal with the men. They have different expectations and have more experience in football. It's a kind of uncertainty that just keeps many women from doing it.
> (int. 4)

However, whether self-exclusion takes place depends on to what extent a woman commits herself to such (negative) gender-specific assumptions (Weigelt-Schlesinger, 2008). If there are common constructed and established ideas and images among women, who construe the role as football coach as masculine or assume discriminatory attitudes from (male) colleagues and functionaries, women can feel strengthened in their assumption that they are not being accepted or welcomed to be a football coach or as a participant in educational courses. To do this, women must not have had any real (discriminatory) experiences themselves; rather for validation of such constructions simply the presumption is enough for other women to also share this idea. The presumption that other women feel the same way becomes circular to each other, and thus, has a reinforcing effect. As a result, such collectively shared realities can solidify and contribute to the perpetuation of gender stereotypes in football by women themselves. This, in turn, creates a horizon of legitimation that lets women's behaviours regarding their self-exclusion from coaching positions and educational programmes appear as usual and reasonable. Therefore, we can conclude that women must overcome the higher (informal) selection thresholds in masculine-connoted sports areas such as football (Pfister, 2004; Weigelt-Schlesinger, 2008). Potential female coaches do not only need an expertise in football but also great resilience to overcome this hurdle and enter coaching positions and participate in educational programmes. This means, although an outsider will not see any formal reasons for exclusion, women exclude themselves from the beginning due to their individual gender-specific patterns of perception and interpretation towards the coaching role in football.

How Can We Deal With the Effect of Gender Stereotypes as Mechanisms of Social Exclusion of Women as Football Coaches?

This chapter focuses on gender stereotypes as social mechanisms on the exclusion of females from coaching positions in football clubs and the coaching education system. The reflection of different levels makes it clear that gender stereotypes aim not to exclude women in a direct manner, rather they appear subliminal as exclusionary mechanisms, but are still very effective. Due to this complexity and their subliminal impacts, the influence of gender stereotypes in football cannot be eliminated entirely, but it can at least be mitigated to some extent. However, it should be mentioned that within the DFB as an umbrella organisation there are no specific measures or programmes available yet that support women in football coaching. In the following, we will discuss three main thoughts at different levels regarding, how the exclusionary effects of gender stereotypes in football could be addressed.

Depersonalisation of Recruitment and Promotion Practices for Women as Coaches in Football Clubs

The personalised and informal conditions underlying the recruitment process in football clubs allow single decision-makers to repeatedly dominate the clubs' communication and decision-making processes through their stereotypical opinions against female coaches. To reduce such a personalised influence, precise arrangements are needed that formalise the search process and define criteria for assigning coaches, and the structures for promoting female coaches need to be institutionalised. Only then can individuals and exclusive (male-dominated) networks be effectively prevented from systematically enforcing their stereotypic preferences during the recruitment processes and avoiding the support of female coaches entering "through the back door". To address gender inequity in football, the DFB as umbrella federation should supply guidelines to adjust recruitment practices more gender-sensitive. Furthermore, the federation should provide advisory services to deal with structural and cultural changes that empower clubs to improve their gender balancing and to develop incentives (material and non-material) for initiatives with the aim to encourage females to become coaches.

Nevertheless, it must be noted that formalisation of recruitment practices and structural changes will not automatically reduce the gender imbalance of female coaches in football. Nevertheless, it could lead to more visible recruitment processes, which may support women in football coaching positions.

Gendering Coaching Education Programmes in Football

In order to deal with gender in a constructive manner, an increased sensitivity for the issue is required from those individuals who are responsible for coaching education. Above all, their awareness of gender-specific differences in general and women's different self-concepts and identities is needed. First, it seems essential to train the course instructors and offer specific courses to promote the integration of women in the specific education programmes of the association. Gender-specific topics need to be addressed in much greater detail than they have been in the training of the instructors thus far. Second, in this context, the involvement of female coaches in the education programmes should be promoted because they are the ones who have experience of discrimination during their work in this space and are able to report on their own coping strategies. Furthermore, in educational programmes, there were often no specific contents of women's football available and there were no images of women coaches in much of the material. Therefore, certain subjects that are specific to women's football need to be integrated into coaching education. Accordingly, both separate programmes for female and for male coaches of girls' and women's teams might be an option worth considering as well as to develop more inclusive contents of programmes per se. Furthermore, special courses for potential high performers (e.g., for former national or Bundesliga players) similar to male former national players could be another mean to promote women at the elite level.

Addressing the Risk of Self-Exclusion Through the Mentoring of Female Football Coaches

Our reflection indicates that low acceptance based on the masculine connotations of the expectations of the position of coaches in football prevents potential female coaches from entering a position as a coach. As a result, some women tend to question their own skills and competences as a coach in response to gender-specific attributions of competence. Hence, some women themselves contribute to perpetuating gender stereotypes and consequently have less interest in a coaching position. To reduce the risk of self-exclusion, potential female coaches need to break away from their usual thought patterns and learn how to become more resistant to the evaluations of male colleagues, instructors, and functionaries. Therefore, it is necessary for women to regard their own skills and competences as self-evident, rather than as discriminatory elements of their femininity. Mentoring programmes and individual coaching would assist with this, since they facilitate the entry of potential coaches into a coaching job, accompany them during their work, and provide (emotional) support when acceptance problems arise (Pfister, 2004).

Conclusion

Based on a multilevel approach, the article reflected the complexity, how gender stereotypes as social mechanisms determine the exclusion of females from coach positions in football clubs and the coaching education system. Since gender stereotypes in football appear on different levels and usually appear more informal and subliminal, dealing with them is difficult and cannot be reduced to some single measures. Furthermore, it is generally known that gender stereotypes change only slowly, particularly in the football milieu. Therefore, the recommendations offered here should be incorporated into a long-term process, which might lead to changes that will not immediately become evident but could have a lasting effect in the future. However, much will depend on to what extent it is possible to implement "women's football-specific thinking" in the leadership structures of the clubs. Only then, it can be expected that supporting intentions will no longer be lip service but will be reflected in specific initiatives and also in the increasing number of active female coaches (with the appropriate licenses).

Notes

1. In men's football one team in the 4th division is coached by a woman. In history of German Football, no woman has ever coached in any of the three professional leagues.
2. The German coaching education system has five levels. The lowest level is Coach-C (UEFA Grassroots), but it is possible to start after a selection test the education at the second level Coach-B (UEFA B level). These both licences are awarded by the regional associations of the DFB. The next level is the Elite Youth Licence (UEFA B level), followed by Coach-A (UEFA A level). The highest license in German football is the so called 'Fußball-Lehrer license' (UEFA Pro license). Elite Youth Licence, Coach-A and Pro licence are conducted by the DFB.
3. However, it should be noted that it is not necessary to hold a coaching license for coaching a grassroots team.
4. Wherever women enter predominantly male areas, this corresponds with loss of an important basis of identification, because social prestige and identity is still related to there being a high proportion of men in positions of responsibility (Rustemeyer & Thrien, 1989). Consequently, social prestige decreases as soon as the proportion of women in male-dominated areas such as football coaching increases.

References

Acker, J. (1990). Hierarchies, jobs, bodies. A theory of gendered organisations. *Gender & Society*, 4, 139–158.

Aicher, T. J., & Sagas, M. (2010). Are head coaches in intercollegiate athletics perceived as masculine? An evaluation of gender stereotypes and the effect of sexism on intercollegiate coaches. *Gender Issues*, 27, 165–174.

Alfermann, D. (1996). *Geschlechterrollen und geschlechtstypisches Verhalten* [Gender roles and gendertypic behaviour]. Kohlhammer.

Bahlke, S., Benning, A., & Cachay, K. (2003). *"Trainer . . . das ist halt einfach Männersache." Eine Studie zur Unterrepräsentanz von Trainerinnen im Spitzensport* ['Coach . . . is a men's job.' A study of underrepresentation of female coaches in elite sports]. Sport und Buch Strauss.

Borggrefe, C., Cachay, K., Bahlke, S., & Dölling, R. (2018). 'Das ist ja Mädchhandball'—zur Problematik geschlechtsbezogener Kommunikation im Sport ['But that's girls' handball!'—The problem of gender-related communication in elite sport]. *Sport und Gesellschaft*, 15, 191–223.

Cachay, K., & Thiel, A. (2008). Soziale Ungleichheit im Sport [Social inequality in sport]. In K. Weis & R. Gugutzer (Eds.), *Handbuch Sportsoziologie* (pp. 189–199). Hofmann.

Combrink, C. (2004). *Relevanz und Irrelevanz von Geschlecht in ehrenamtlichen Führungsgremien von Sportjugendverbänden* [Relevance and irrelevance of gender in leadership executives of sport youth associations]. Lit.

Cook, R. J., & Cusac, S. (2010). *Gender stereotyping: Transnational legal perspectives*. University of Pennsylvania Press.

Cunningham, G. B., Doherty, A. J., & Gregg, M. J. (2007). Using social cognitive career theory to understand head coaching intentions among assistant coaches of women's teams. *Sex Roles*, 56, 365–372.

DFB. (2019). *Mitgliederstatistik 2019.* [Member statistics 2019]. 07.02.2020 via www.dfb.de/fileadmin/_dfbdam/202541-bestandserhebung.pdf

DFB. (2020). *Statistik Trainerlizenzen* [Statistics coach licenses]. (Internal working paper).

Eckes, T. (1997). *Geschlechtsstereotype: Frau und Mann in sozialpsychologischer Sicht* [Gender stereotypes: Woman and man in sociopsycholocigal perspective]. Centaurus Verlag.

Fasting, K., & Pfister, G. (2000). Female and male coaches in the eyes of female soccer players. *European Physical Education Review, 6,* 91–110.

Fasting, K., Sand, T. S., & Nordstrand, H. R. (2019). One of the few: The experiences of female elite-level coaches in Norwegian football. *Soccer & Society, 20,* 454–470.

Goffman, E. (1977). The arrangement between the sexes. *Theory and Society, 4,* 301–331.

Hartmann-Tews, I., & Combrink, C. (2005). Under-representation of women in governing bodies of sport: The significance of recruitment procedures and affirmative action. In G. Doll-Tepper, G. Pfister, D. Scoretz, & C. Bilan (Eds.), *Sport, women & leadership* (pp. 71–78). Sport und Buch Strauss.

Haselwood, D., Joyner, A. B., Burke, K. L., Geyerman, C. B., Czech, D. R., Munkasy, B. A., & Zwald, A. D. (2005). Female athletes' perception of head coaches' communication competence. *Journal of Sport Behavior, 28,* 216–230.

Hirschauer, A. (2001). Forgetting sex. A praxeology of a membership category. *Kölner Zeitschrift für Soziologie und Sozialpsychologie, 41,* 208–235.

Hovden, J. (1999). Is it worth the price? Women's involvement in leadership and coaching in sports organizations in Norway. *Women Sport and Physical Activity Journal, 8,* 23–45.

Hovden, J. (2000). Gender and leadership selection process in Norwegian sporting organizations. *International Review for the Sociology of Sport, 35,* 75–82.

Kieserling, A. (1999). *Kommunikation unter anwesenden. Studien über Interaktionssysteme.* [Communication among the present. Studies about interaction systems]. Suhrkamp.

Kreisky, E., & Spitaler, G. (2006). *Arena der Männlichkeit. Über das Verhältnis von Fußball und Geschlecht* [Arena of masculinity. About the relationship between football and gender]. Campus.

Lewis, C. J., Roberts, S. J., & Andrews, H. (2018). 'Why am I putting myself through this?' Women football coaches' experiences of the Football Association's coach education process. *Sport, Education and Society, 23,* 28–39.

Luhmann, N. (1988). Frauen, Männer und George Spencer Brown. [Women, men and George Spencer Brown]. *Zeitschrift für Soziologie, 1*(1), 47–71.

Luhmann, N. (2006). *Organisation und Entscheidung* [Organisation and Decision]. Westdeutscher Verlag.

Meuser, M. (2008). It's a men's world. Ernste Spiele männlicher Vergemeinschaftung. [It's a men's world. Serious games of male community]. In G. Klein & M. Meuser (Eds.), *Ernste Spiele: Zur politischen Soziologie des Fußballs* (pp. 113–134) [Serious games: On the political sociology of football]. Transcript.

Murray, P., Lord, R., & Lorimer, R. (2020). How the perceived effectiveness of a female coach is Influenced by their apparent masculinity/femininity. *The Sport Journal, 21.* http://thesportjournal.org/article/how-the-perceived-effectiveness-of-a-female-coach-is-influenced-by-their-apparent-masculinity-femininity/#more-6993

Nesseler, C., Gomez-Gonzalez, C., & Gasparetto, T. (2020, online first). Head coach tenure in college women's soccer. Do race, gender, and career background matter? *Sport in Society* https://doi.org/10.1080/17430437.2019.1710133.

Norman, L. (2010a). Feeling second best: Elite women coaches' experiences. *Society of Sport Journal*, 27, 89–104.

Norman, L. (2010b). Bearing the burden of doubt: Women coaches' experiences of gender relations. *Research Quarterly for Exercise and Sport*, 81, 506–517.

Norman, L. (2019). 'I don't really know what the magic wand is to get yourself in there': Women's sense of organizational fit as coach developers. *Women in Sport and Physical Activity Journal*, 28, 119–130.

Oakes, P. J., Haslam, S. A., & Turner, J. C. (1994). *Stereotyping and social reality*. Blackwell.

Pfister, G. (2004). *Mentoring im Sportverein oder Sportverband* [Mentoring in sports clubs and sports associations]. Bundesausschuss Frauen im Deutschen Turner-Bund.

Pfister, G. (2010). Women in sport: Gender relations and future perspectives. *Sport in Society*, 13, 234–248.

Pfister, G., & Fasting, K. (2003). Geschlechterkonstruktionen auf dem Fussballplatz [Constructions of gender on the football pitch]. In O. Arter (Ed.), *Sport und Recht* (pp. 137–152). Stämpfli.

Reid, K., & Dallaire, C. (2019). 'Because there are so few of us': The marginalization of female soccer referees in Ontario, Canada. *Women in Sport and Physical Activity Journal*, 27, 12–20.

Ridgeway, C. (2001). Interaction and the persistence of gender inequality in employment. *Kölner Zeitschrift für Soziologie und Sozialpsychologie*, 41, 250–275.

Rustemeyer, R., & Thrien, S. (1989). Die Managerin—der Manager. Wie weiblich dürfen sie sein, wie männlich müssen sie sein? [The manager. How female can they be, how male must they be?]. *Zeitschrift für Arbeits- und Organisationspsychologie*, 32(2), 108–116.

Schlesinger, T., & Weigelt-Schlesinger, Y. (2012). 'Poor thing' or 'Wow, she knows how to do it': Gender stereotypes as barriers to women's qualification in the education of soccer coaches. *Soccer & Society*, 13(1), 56–72.

Schlesinger, T., & Weigelt-Schlesinger, Y. (2013). 'Coaching soccer is a man's job!' The influence of gender stereotypes on structures for recruiting female coaches in soccer clubs. *European Journal of Sport and Society*, 10(3), 241–265.

Schneider, D. (2005). *The psychology of stereotyping*. Guilford Press.

Schreiner, R., & Thiel, A. (2011). Die Rekrutierung von Trainern im deutschen Spitzensport [The recruitment of coaches in German high-performance sports]. *Sport & Gesellschaft*, 1, 28–53.

Scraton, S., Fasting, K., Pfister, G., & Bunuel, A. (1999). It's still a man's game? The experiences of top-level European women footballers. *International Review for the Sociology of Sport*, 34, 99–111.

Shaw, S., & Slack, T. (2002). 'It's been like that for donkey's years': The construction of gender relations and the cultures of sport organizations. *Culture, Sport, Society*, 5, 86–106.

Sinning, S. (2006). *Trainerinnen im Frauenfußball eine qualitative Studie* [Female coaches in women soccer a qualitative study]. Hofmann.

Stichweh, R. (2005). *Inklusion und Exklusion. Studien zur Gesellschaftstheorie*. [Inclusion and exclusion. Studies in social theory]. Transcript.

Sülzle, A. (2011). *Fußball, Frauen, Männlichkeiten. Eine ethnographische Studie im Fanblock* [Football, women, masculinity. An ethnographic study in the fan corner]. Campus.

Taylor, S. E. (1981). A categorization approach to stereotyping. In D. L. Hamilton (Ed.), *Cognitive processes in stereotyping and intergroup behavior* (pp. 83–114). Erlbaum.

Theberge, N. (2000). Gender and sport. In J. Coakley & E. Dunning (Eds.), *Handbook of sports studies* (pp. 322–333). Sage.

Thiel, A., & Mayer, J. (2009). Characteristics of voluntary sports club's management: A sociological perspective. *European Sport Management Quarterly, 9*, 81–98.

Weigelt-Schlesinger, Y. (2008). *Geschlechterstereotype—Qualifikationsbarrieren von Frauen in der Fußballtrainerausbildung* [Gender stereotypes—Qualification barriers for women in football coach education]. Czwalina.

Weinbach, C. (2004). *Systemtheorie und Gender: Das Geschlecht im Netz der Systeme* [Gender and system theory: Gender in the net of systems]. Verlag für Sozialwissenschaften.

Weinbach, C., & Stichweh, R. (2001). Gender differences in functionally differentiated society. *Kölner Zeitschrift für Soziologie und Sozialpsychologie, 41*, 30–52.

West, C., & Fenstermaker, S. (1995). Doing difference. *Gender and Society, 9*, 8–37.

Wetterer, A. (2006). Von der Frauen- zur Geschlechterforschung? Kontinuitäten, Ausdifferenzierung und Perspektivenwechsel [From woman to gender research? Continuities, differentiation and change of perspectives]. In I. Hartmann-Tews & B. Rulofs (Eds.), *Handbuch Sport und Geschlecht* (pp. 14–25) [Handbook sport and gender]. Hofmann.

Part II
Strategies for Supporting a More Gender-Inclusive Sport Coaching Workforce

3 Transformational Change

Creating a New Culture of Sport Coaching

Guylaine Demers, Cari Din and Penny Werthner

> Coaching is a social process that is inherently laden with power.
> (LaVoi, 2016, p. 17)

Introduction

For more than 30 years, there have been many strong and creative women and organisations, working to improve sport for girls and women globally. The initiatives have been excellent, and the dialogue and critical reflection have been rich. We have seen great improvements in participation levels of girls and women in sport. However, this rate of improvement is not the same for women in leadership positions in sport, particularly in sport coaching. Globally, the number of women in leadership positions has, over the last 10–15 years, grown from 16% to 29% (Institute of Sport and Leisure Policy, 2004; Sport Canada, 2018), which is certainly an improvement. However, the number of women in coaching positions, particularly at a high-performance level, is stagnant at 11–16% (IOC, 2018). The purpose of this chapter is to argue for equality (50/50) for women coaches at all levels of sport participation and sport competition. The chapter will (1) detail the historical and current statistics on women and coaching, (2) illustrate a number of recent critical initiatives, (3) briefly highlight why the number of women coaches is still low and how LaVoi's Ecological Intersectional Model (2016) and various research studies help us understand the complexity of the issues, and finally (4) propose a clear path forward for equality for women coaches in the world of sport.

Historical and Current Statistics

In terms of women in leadership positions in sport, an internet-based measurement tool (the Sydney Scoreboard) found that only a few countries have achieved a critical mass of 30% representation that is suggested as the minimum number of women needed to have any impact. For example, in Norway, women make up 37.4% of the members of boards of sport organisations,

Sweden 32.1% (Adriaanse, 2016). The percentage in Canada increased to 35% in 2020 which is an improvement (Canadian Women & Sport, 2020). In 2019, the Council of Europe developed an online tool to measure both the number of women coaches as well as the number of women in leadership positions. Eighteen European countries participated in this data collection. For coaches, the findings indicated that only 22% of the employed elite-level coaches in the sport federations are women. The data revealed that women are under-represented among elite-level employed coaches in all countries. For women in leadership positions, the findings indicate that the percentage and distribution of women in National Olympic sport federations are as follows: 8% presidents, 18% vice-presidents, and 22% board members (Council of Europe, 2019). Around the world, women occupy 23% of the international executive positions in mainstream sports (Sport Canada, 2018).

In Canada's post-secondary educational institutions, the majority of Athletic Directors and their respective affiliate organisations are men, with only 21% of these positions occupied by women (CAAWS, 2016). Among the active Athletic Directors of all member colleges within the Canadian Collegiate Athletics Association (CCAA), 27% of these positions are held by women (CAAWS, 2016). While there is a stronger presence of women administrative leaders at both national sport organisations (NSOs) and multi-sport organisations (MSOs) (Sport Canada, 2018), it is troubling that the percentages are so low within universities and colleges given that they constitute influential components of the Canadian sport system and are leaders in achieving equity in many other areas.

In terms of sport coaching, it is much more discouraging. Data collected in Canada show that women coaches comprise no more than 25% of coaches at all levels of sport (Banwell et al., 2019). At the university-level sports in 2017, the 1,021 varsity sport teams were equally divided between men's and women's teams (511 women's teams and 510 men's teams). However, of these 1,021 teams, there were only 122 women head coaches (Norman et al., 2017). Researchers from the Centre for Sport Policy Studies revealed that the percentage of women coaches in university-level sports is decreasing, from 19% reported in 2011 to 17% in 2013 to 16% in 2015 and 2017 (Donnelly et al., 2013; Norman et al., 2017). At more competitive levels, these figures are equally concerning. According to data collected by Sport Canada, across 54 Canadian national teams, both men and women's teams, only 16% of all head coaches are women ($n = 9$) (Sport Canada, 2018). At the international level, only 11% of coaches representing Canada at the most recent 2018 Winter Olympic Games in PyeongChang, South Korea, were women, while 17% of coaches at the 2016 Summer Olympic Games in Rio, Brazil, were women (Canadian Olympic Committee, 2016). This is despite the fact that Canada's Olympic teams are relatively balanced in terms of the number of men and women athletes.

In 2017, the European Commission published *The Gender Equality in Sport Proposal for Strategic Actions 2014–2020*. That report presents a range of statistics that demonstrate the under-representation of women coaches across the European Union (EU). It is estimated, based on figures from seven EU member states, that between 20% and 30% of all sport coaches in Europe are women. For example, Finland reported 30% of coaches are women; Northern Ireland reported 20%; the Czech Republic reported 28% of female athletes were coached by a woman; and the UK reported 17% of qualified coaches were women. In looking at sport-specific statistics, Northern Ireland found approximately 40% of female coaches were in the sports of field hockey and athletics, whereas there were no female coaches in cricket, only 2% in rugby, and less than 10% in football. Denmark reported female coaches dominated in gymnastics (73%) but were largely underrepresented in handball (28%), tennis (20%), athletics (14%), and football (7%). In 2019, the number of elite-level women coaches working in Europe was 22%, and 31% of registered coaches in Europe were women (Council of Europe, 2019).

In terms of high-performance sport and Olympic-level sport, the research clearly shows the number of female coaches at the highest levels of competition is particularly low. For example, the numbers of accredited women coaches at recent Olympic Games are shown in Table 3.1 (IOC, 2018):

Critical Initiatives

Overall, the statistics highlighted clearly illustrate that there is still much work to be done, particularly in the profession of coaching. And yet, at the same time, we must acknowledge terrific initiatives, in education, mentorship, and policy development, which have been taking place over the last 30 years addressing gender equity in sport leadership. For example, the International Olympic Committee (IOC) has launched a Gender Equality Review Project that is a joint initiative of the IOC Women in Sport and Athletes' Commissions. The project presents 25 IOC Gender Equality Recommendations with one specific recommendation for women coaches: balanced gender representation for coaches selected to participate at the Olympic Games (recommendation #6).

Table 3.1 Numbers of accredited coaches at Olympic Games (including summer and winter)

Olympics Games	Women coaches (%)
Vancouver 2010	10
London 2012	11
Sochi 2014	9
Rio 2016	11

In the United States, the Tucker Centre conducts research and numerous knowledge dissemination activities focused on girls and women in sport (e.g., Kane & LaVoi, 2018). In Canada, a national women and sport conference, Conversations 2015, brought together women from across Canada to work together for three days on solving practical problems and dismantling barriers to women in sport. A second conversation is planned for 2021 (www.conversation2021.ca). As well, in Canada, there have been numerous other initiatives, such as a Federal Government Standing Committee Report (Fry, 2017) and a Women and Sport Working Group that each presented a list of recommendations to increase the number of women in leadership positions, including coaches. The International Working Group (IWG) in 2010 created a score board to increase women's representation on sport boards globally. This score board provided real-time data tracking of the gender of board members, chairpersons, and top managers in national and international sport organisations. The IWG also coordinates an international conference, every four years, which brings together women from across the globe to discuss women and sport issues and solutions. In addition, the European commission has mapped and analysed education for coaches from a gender perspective. In 2018, the Commonwealth Games Federation (CGF) launched their Gender Equality Strategy (GES) to ensure women are represented in all aspects of the Games, including: vice presidential positions, as technical officials, as women coaches, and as athletes. Finally, the International Council for Coaching Excellence (2018) has developed a Women and Coaching Strategy to improve opportunities for women coaches. Tables 3.2 and 3.3 (Fasting et al., 2018) illustrate the

Table 3.2 Types of action taken to increase the number of female coaches/instructors and game officials/judges/umpires

	Coaches/Instructors n*	(%)	Game officials/Judges/Umpires n*	(%)
Workshops, seminars, and so on for female coaches/instructors	86	(70)	56	(62)
Implemented an action plan/strategy	63	(52)	50	(55)
Mentoring programmes	60	(49)	38	(42)
Education/courses for girls and women only	59	(48)	45	(49)
Establishing networks	43	(35)	28	(31)
Recruitment campaigns targeting girls and women	41	(34)	31	(34)
Dedicated resources for female coaches/instructors	35	(29)	23	(25)
Other	11	(9)	11	(12)

Source: Fasting et al. (2018, p. 15)
* n is the number of sport organisations who have taken those types of action ($n = 122$).

Table 3.3 Actions taken to increase the number of women in decision-making positions (Fasting et al., 2018, p. 16)

	n*	(%)
Workshops, seminars, and so on for females in decision-making positions	92	(72)
Campaigns to encourage women to stand for decision-making positions	56	(44)
Network for females in decision-making positions	48	(38)
Education/courses for girls and women only	46	(36)
Mentoring programme for women in decision-making positions	43	(34)
Quotas in elections	42	(33)
Changes in statutes	40	(31)
Seats reserved for women	38	(30)
Specific arrangements to facilitate participation in meetings, i.e., childcare	18	(14)
Other	20	(16)

* n is the number of sport organisations who have taken those types of action ($n = 128$).

actions implemented globally to increase the number of women coaches, officials, and women in leadership positions. These actions were taken by women sport organisations, national federations/organisations, national Olympic committees, and international/continental federations between 2013 and 2017.

While these initiatives have been substantial and have anecdotally affected change at an individual level, we still have not seen significant change to the number of women in the profession of sport coaching (Culver et al., 2019; Kraft et al., 2020). So, the question remains—why is that?

Why Are the Number of Women Coaches Still Low?

One possible answer lies in the work of Nicole LaVoi. In the introduction to her book, *Women in Sports Coaching*, she writes, "Individuals who are seen and known in the world of sport, like coaches, communicate who and what is valued (and who is not)" (2016, p. 3). And, as we have already noted, the statistics and the research show us clearly that women are nearly absent from positions of power in sport coaching. For example, in Germany, 10% of high-performance coaches and 13% of professional coaches are women; in Australia, there are women as national managers only in gymnastics and netball; and in Finland, men occupy two-thirds of head coaching positions (Robertson, 2016). In fact, and as noted in this chapter, the number of women coaching at an elite level is declining (Demers et al., 2019).

In 2016, LaVoi published the Ecological Intersectional Model of women in coaching, making vivid links to the systemic forces influencing women's exclusion from coaching from an intersectional and life course perspective.

Specifically, LaVoi's model documents the individual, interpersonal, organisational, and sociocultural forces influencing women's experiences with sport coaching. This comprehensive model enhances our ability to understand, in depth, the barriers and sources of support women experience in sport coaching at multiple levels. It brings into focus the overlapping influences of age, parental status, sexual orientation, gender, class, (dis)ability, and race on women in coaching. The model also speaks to the need for a critical analysis of power and position in relation to women's complex identities. It surfaces the "forms of systemic injustice, oppression, and social inequality" women face in sport (LaVoi, 2016, p. 19). It moves beyond framing gender as the singular influence on women in coaching roles and helps us understand the dominant and essentialist narratives which sustain coaching discourses that ensure women are not coaching in the world of sport.

LaVoi (2016) also writes of the "blame-the-women" narrative that continues to marginalise, oppress, and deter women from becoming coaches (p. 20). LaVoi argues women are blamed for not possessing the skills or confidence required and thus, not fitting in to the sport system. Many initiatives and programmes focus on preparing women to be competent individually, and while this works to the degree that these programmes can certainly strengthen the skills of individual women coaches and leaders, these women go back to work in a sport system that has not changed. It is a system that often frames a woman's assertiveness as aggressive behaviour (Catalyst, 2007). What is described as assertiveness or confidence in a man is regularly depicted as arrogant or shrill in a woman (Ely et al., 2011). This dominant bias results in women in positions of authority being subjected to constant criticism or a double standard (LaVoi, 2016).

Another framework that helps us understand the barriers women coaches and leaders in sport face is role congruity theory (Eagly & Karau, 2002). This is a theory that proposes the perceived incongruity between the female gender role and a leadership position leads to two forms of prejudice: (1) perceiving women less favourably than men as potential occupants of leadership roles and (2) evaluating behaviour that fulfils the prescriptions of an effective leader less favourably when they are enacted by a woman. One obvious consequence of this is that attitudes are less positive towards female than male leaders. This makes it more difficult for women to become leaders and to achieve success in a leadership role. Certainly, the phenomenon of women gaining preliminary access to an organisation, as workers, voters, students, and athletes, yet making little headway when it comes to positions of leadership and coaching, is common and long-standing.

The notion of the leadership labyrinth, described by Eagly and Carli (2007), also details how individuals are resistant to women's leadership. Researchers have consistently shown that individuals associate men and women with different traits and that men are considered to demonstrate traits more broadly associated with leadership when compared to women (Eagly & Karau, 2002). Furthermore, women who demonstrate leadership traits face the double bind of acting outside of what is expected of women and not being liked for doing so (Eagly & Karau, 2002). This double bind in leadership results in women often developing a leadership style that includes characteristics women are expected to demonstrate (being communal) along with the characteristics expected to be a successful leader (being agentic). This is the unfortunate double bind that women in coaching experience (LaVoi & Dutove, 2012).

Ultimately, LaVoi's Ecological Intersectional Model clarifies why conditions have not improved for women in coaching over time. Systematic oppression, gender bias, damaging narratives, and double standards create untenable conditions for women in coaching. The model supports the demand for culture change and the systemic transformation we are advocating for in this chapter.

The Path Forward for Equality for Women Coaches

LaVoi's work (2016; LaVoi & Dutove, 2012) helps us to understand the complexity of the problem for women in sport, and how we must consider the impact of societal and organisational influences as well as the individual when imagining how to transform sport coaching. It also helps us understand why we still have the same low numbers of women coaches at all levels of sport. We have seen change for women in leadership positions, but we still need to develop specific strategies for women coaches. We need to set specific targets and regularly audit those targets for gender equality. The next section describes three strategies that will ensure we reach gender equality for women coaches: (1) advocate for more women coaches, (2) use political levers, and (3) establish quotas.

Strategy 1: Decision-Makers Must Advocate for Women Coaches

The first challenge we face in ensuring equality for women coaches is to be able to answer the simple question *why*? Why is it important or necessary to have women coaches? To understand why women are needed within the profession of coaching will improve our strategic approach towards recruiting more women. The literature on women as leaders provides scientific arguments to answer the *why*. These arguments are divided into three categories as follows: systemic discrimination, impact of diversity, and impact of role models.

Systemic Discrimination

Around the world, gender equality in sport is an issue of social justice. The current sport system cannot claim to properly represent all individuals, as women are significantly less present than their male colleagues, as noted earlier in this chapter. The most recent statistics in any country are clear.

(Note: you need to know the statistics of your own country and sport organisations.) While this situation is not necessarily voluntary discrimination, it is systemic discrimination. Navarro (2015) defines systemic discrimination as follows:

> Because of traditions and a history in which power has been exercised by men, the system in which we live has established itself in a particular way that gives them certain advantages (higher wages, greater power of decision, authority). Because of this system, women have been kept out of various aspects of social life. This does not mean that men want it or that women are happy with it. A system can change when we take steps to make it happen.
>
> (p. 19)

Thus, it is important to recognise that the current sport system places numerous obstacles before fully competent women. And yet, we can ask—why would we do this? The sport system is depriving itself of 50% of the available talent and, as the quote from Navarro (2015) indicates, perhaps there are many in the sport system who would be willing to embrace change—in this case, gender equality in coaching. So, with an understanding of systemic discrimination, establishment of a clear target (50%), and a great many conversations with both women and men, it is possible to achieve gender equality in coaching.

Impact of Diversity

Rachel Argaman, former TFE hotels CEO, said:

> Anyone who discriminates against a proportion of the population to get their talent is not getting the best. My belief is if you want the best of a population it's inevitable your ratios will fall out near the ratios of that population.
>
> (Fox, 2018, p. 124)

It is increasingly recognised that diversity brings many benefits to organisations (Adams & Ferreira, 2009; Bart & McQueen, 2013; Conference Board of Canada, 2014). Why would the sport world be different? Currently, the face of sport leadership globally is that of, more often than not, a middle-aged, Caucasian male. This is not about questioning their presence. However, it is about installing and supporting women in key positions which will transform and enrich the culture of sport.

The mixing of different people with unique backgrounds favours the development of creative and innovative ideas since each individual brings their way of thinking, life experience, and problem-solving approach. Diversity enables decisions that consider the varying needs of all members of an organisation. Diversity ensures different talents and skill sets hold seats around the table, allowing all members of an organisation to learn and grow. When diversity is embraced, the organisation becomes more effective.

To illustrate the impact of diversity, Ng and Muntaner (2018), two public health researchers, note that between 1976 and 2009, the percentage of women in provincial government in Canada increased sixfold, from 4.2% to 25.9%. Controlling for several confounding factors and looking at how expenditures in education and healthcare changed, their research indicates that the inclusion of six times more women resulted in significant drops in mortality rates within their provinces. Ng and Muntaner (2018) argue that increasing the number of women in positions of power not only promotes gender equity but also promotes greater health and well-being—an argument that bodes well for changing the culture of sport. Their explanation for this impact is that "women in government as collective political actors, are more committed to advancing women's interests, to achieving a more equal distribution of societal resources, and to triggering government spending in health-promoting ways" (p. 1).

In another study related to the positive impact of diversity, Brière (2019), examined ten traditionally male professions in Quebec, Canada (e.g., construction inspector, police officer, engineer, surgeon, etc.). The case of prison guards is particularly interesting. For that context, Brière documented the changes that occurred as women were introduced to the profession. Her findings demonstrate that, by creating a workplace that was much more equitable and diverse, the culture within the prison changed over the course of ten years—there was less physical violence and intimidation between prisoners and between the guards and the prisoners. This changed the climate for all involved—prisoners and prison guards. However, it was certainly not simply the introduction of women into the culture that created change. Rather the author argues that along with introducing diversity and more women into an environment, it was critical that the organisation committed itself to diversity and inclusion. Change does not happen unless the organisation is intentional about change. Brière identified multiple and specific strategies and actions that influenced the positive changes: adapting recruitment processes, reviewing work processes, establishing good working conditions, reconciling work and personal life, improving the work climate, creating a culture of equality and diversity, providing individual support, and adapting the processes linked to decision-making positions and specialisations. Certainly, this is sage advice for the sporting world.

Another recent example that demonstrates the benefits of diversity comes from the recent global COVID-19 pandemic. Since the beginning of the crisis, numerous articles report a relationship between the presence of women leaders at the head of certain countries and the effectiveness of their management of the crisis (e.g., Chamorro-Premuzic, 2020). The ranking of the World Economic Forum (WEF) Global Gender Gap Report 2020 notes that the countries which fought the pandemic most effectively, based on the criteria of number of individuals who became ill and number of deaths, were the countries that were seen to be most equitable (WEF, 2020). Diverse perspectives potentially lead to healthy confrontations of vision and pave the way for richer and more complete solutions. Therefore, the WEF report leads us to suggest that more egalitarian societies will be better managed. Sport is part of our greater society and therefore it seems that an equal number of women and men in coaching and leadership roles would have a positive impact on the way sport is managed.

Impact of Role Models

> You can't be what you can't see.
>
> Marian Wright Edelman

We do not have a great deal of research documenting the impact of women as role models in sport, likely because so few women hold positions of power in the system. Research with university-aged female athletes indicates a lack of interest in becoming a coach can be linked to a lack of women in coaching roles in performance sport (Imeson, 2017). The influence of same-sex role models in positively developing girls and women has been studied in numerous fields. In education, women in leadership positions help other women overcome misperceptions and stereotypes of women in power (Lockwood, 2006). Research in science, technology, engineering, and mathematics (STEM) shows women role models can increase the sense of belonging and performance for girls (Drury et al., 2011). One of the top six reasons girls in the US leave sport is a lack of positive women role models (Women's Sports Foundation, 2020). It is not difficult to imagine the positive influence women in numerous head coaching positions will have on the experiences of girls and women in sport in the future, if we get this right!

Strategy 2: Use Political Levers

There are three political levers that can be used to ensure sport organisations have a gender balance of individuals in coaching positions. These levers are powerful tools that can be implemented with low, and sometimes at no cost to an organisation. These three levers should be accessible in the majority of countries.

Inclusion in Strategic Plans

The integration of principles of equality (gender mainstreaming) in sport organisations' strategic plans is required to achieve equal gender representation of coaches in sport. The Federal-Provincial/Territorial Sport Committee (FPTSC) working group in Canada (FPTSC, 2018) has identified the necessity for the integration of equity and equality principles in sport organisation corporate planning. Brière (2019), in her study on women in traditional male professions, also concluded that leadership commitment to increasing the representation of women in organisations is essential to sustainable and meaningful change. One important commitment is the inclusion of gender equity measures in strategic plans, accompanied by action plans that are implemented and monitored. These plans can serve as a conceptual guide to ensure mechanisms and approaches are informed by gender and intersecting identity factors. To ensure success, sport organisations must commit to transparent reporting on the progress of action plan implementation.

Accountability Measures and Monitoring Progress

Accountability and monitoring go hand in hand. To create opportunities for women coaches that are equitable, funding agencies must implement compliance incentives and enforcements backed by policy. Drawing from research, the IOC (2018, p. 29) discovered a "consensus of opinion identifying a list of factors necessary for the values and practice of gender equality to take hold throughout an organisation". One of the identified factors relates to the accountability measures: monitor progress, measure and evaluate outcomes, and instil accountability. Agencies need to adjust funding frameworks for every sport organisation to build and ensure an intentional link between accountability and funding. Effective monitoring and evaluation of progress towards gender equity must be tied to funding and compliance.

Specifically, in relationship to monitoring, sport organisations must commit to the annual collection, collation, and sharing of gendered data. Indeed, one of the key factors for ensuring that gender equality is implemented and sustained is the need for consistent monitoring, measuring, and evaluation (FPTSC, 2018; IOC, 2018). It is important to track change over time. This can be done with a centralised reporting tool to assess and audit the state of equity among coaching positions.

Following are some examples of how to do it:

- Include a gender-based analysis in every funding framework
- Link funding of sport event hosting to a requirement for parity in coaching
- Integrate accountability and specific details into "report cards"
- Publicly report on the representation of women coaches

Careful monitoring and auditing of the policy level changes required to change sport and bring gender equality to decision-making positions are needed to ensure sustainable systemic change. The statistics, socio-cultural factors, and 30 years of work towards a more equitable sport system tell us for true change, political levers must be utilised, and accountability embedded in bylaws and electoral processes. Transparency is a key element in achieving gender equality and equity in coaching positions.

Strategy 3: Establish Quotas

In the latest WEF report, it is written that if the trend continues, it will be necessary to wait until the year 2234 so that the equality between men and women is reached in the world. Following the publication of this report, Rima Elkouri, a journalist in Montreal, Canada, shared her reaction in the *La Presse* edition on April 10, 2018:

> I'm kind of patient. But two centuries to achieve equality, I admit that I find it a bit long. That is why I am in favour of measures to support the parity accelerator. Too many headwinds tell us it will not happen by itself.

Indeed, 2234 is far too long into the future. This is why this chapter strongly argues for the implementation of corrective measures (quotas and targets). Only with such measures will equality between women and men coaches be realised long before the year 2234. When gender becomes balanced, sport culture will be transformed. For those who fear the idea of quotas, Pascale Navarro's 2015 essay *Femmes et pouvoir: les changements nécessaires* (Women and Power: The Changes Needed [free translation]) is particularly inspiring and debunks the myths surrounding the implementation of such measures. A review of the myths and the arguments associated with them are presented in the following sections.

Myth 1: Reserving Positions for Women Is Discrimination Against Men

According to Navarro (2015), "we do not impose gender quotas without reason. It is done to achieve parity in the name of the principle of equality" (p. 35). In 2021, we are far from achieving equality. In other words, quotas are not discrimination against men, but rather a way of eliminating systemic discrimination. It is therefore a question of temporarily favouring a historically discriminated group—women—to restore equal opportunities between the sexes.

> One of the questions we often face when there is talk about setting quotas or reserving certain positions for women is the following: Is reserving positions for women legally considered discrimination? In Canada, the Charter of Rights and Freedoms notes two important criteria: 1) Is this measure (e.g., quota) for an under-represented group? and 2) Is

this measure put in place by a non-profit organisation? In our case, in Canada, setting quotas for women coaches would not be discriminatory. (Note: this may be different in different countries.) Thus, installing measures to favour a group that is under-represented is justified, because these measures are necessary if one wishes to achieve equality between women and men. Moreover, the Charter is very explicit in that it does not prohibit "the establishment of laws, programs or activities intended to improve the situation of disadvantaged individuals or groups".

(Government of Canada, 1982, Article 15)

Myth 2: Quotas Undermine Quality and Competence When Hiring a Candidate

The idea of imposing gender quotas to achieve parity, regardless of what domain, has always displeased many people, including women. As Noemie Mercier explains, the reluctance for quotas sometimes goes as follows:

> Quotas would be an affront to the principles of meritocracy . . . Under a regime like this, second-rate candidates could take the place of men more qualified and the whole political class would be weakened. Elected officials must be chosen for their competence and not according to their gender.
>
> (2017, pp. 46–47)

Therese Mailloux and Pascale Navarro (2018) indicate that:

> the argument most commonly used to oppose parity is to assume the incompetence of women, and the fear that they do not deserve their place. Have we ever wondered about that of men? If we believe this logic, women by default are incompetent, and men, by default, competent.
>
> (p. 12)

In fact, when quotas have been put in place in several organisations, in different countries, there has not been a loss of competence or quality of work. On the contrary, studies show policies of parity increase organisational competence because the competent men keep their positions and the least competent are replaced by competent women. In their extensive analysis of gender quotas in the Swedish political system, Besley et al. (2017) state:

> Our main finding is that gender quotas increase the competence of the political class in general, and among men in particular. Moreover, quotas are indeed bad news for mediocre male leaders who tend to be forced out . . . Because new leaders—on average—are more competent,

> they feel less threatened by selecting more able candidates, which starts a virtuous circle of higher competence.
>
> (p. 2240)

Quotas can actually elevate the quality of individuals in an organisation as competence attracts competence. To be clear, it is not a question of hiring an incompetent woman in the place of a competent man, but rather of encouraging the hiring of a competent woman who has been unjustly dismissed. As Argaman said, "I believe there is no shortage of qualified women as candidates for roles, so a shortage, used as an excuse, doesn't cut it in my book" (Harrison, 2018, para. 20).

Conclusion

This chapter has strongly argued for a mandate of 50/50 gender equality for women coaches in the world of sport. We have noted historical and current statistics that clearly illustrate little has changed for women coaches over the last 30 years. We have also highlighted a number of excellent initiatives that have been implemented globally. However, we also note, for women coaches, the sport world has barely shifted. It is for this reason we have clearly outlined a number of specific solutions that will ensure we have women coaches in all areas of the sporting world. As authors, we argue the time has come, long overdue, to ensure we create transformational change in the world of sport coaching. LaVoi's model, briefly discussed here, but presented in greater depth in another chapter, helps us understand why we have not moved forward and what we must consider in order to transform sport.

We must deeply understand and address the systemic barriers that are embedded within the world of sport in order to transform it. There is still little research at the organisational level and LaVoi's model points to the critical relevance of the intersection of societal, organisational, and individual norms and beliefs, while considering the social identities of race, class, sexual identity, (dis)ability, age, and parental status. While still requiring more research, we must be willing to act, and that action must include a mandate of a 50/50 split of coaches of either gender, throughout the system. We need to create programmes, in every sport, in every country, that place women into coaching positions and provide ongoing support and learning opportunities for those women coaches. Women have the capability to be excellent coaches and leaders. We have seen the growth of women in the fields of education, law, and medicine and sport must now implement policy and practices to achieve gender equality.

Finally, let's not forget that women are not a minority. They make up 49.6% of the world population (Worldometers, 2020). They are present in all minority groups. It is inconceivable that they are not represented on equal terms with their male colleagues in the profession of sport coaching.

References

Adams, R. B., & Ferreira, D. (2009). Women in the boardroom and their impact on governance and performance. *Journal of Financial Economics, 94*(2), 291–309. https://doi.org/10.1007/s12197-017-9397-7

Adriaanse, J. (2016). Gender diversity in the governance of sport associations: The Sydney scoreboard global index of participation. *Journal of Business Ethics, 137*(1), 149–160. https://doi.org/10.1007/s10551-015-2550-3

Banwell, J., Stirling, A., & Kerr, G. (2019). Towards a process for advancing women in coaching through mentorship. *International Journal of Sports Science & Coaching, 14*(6), 703–713. https://doi.org/10.1177/1747954119883108

Bart, C., & McQueen, G. (2013). Why women make better directors. *International Journal of Business Governance and Ethics, 8*(1), 93–99. https://doi.org/10.1504/ijbge.2013.052743

Besley, T., Folke, O., Persson, T., & Rickne, J. (2017). Gender quotas and the crisis of the mediocre man: Theory and evidence from Sweden. *American Economic Review, 107*(8), 2204–2242. https://doi.org/10.1257/aer.20160080

Brière, S. (2019). *Les femmes dans les professions traditionnellement masculines* (Women in traditionally male occupations). Les Presses de l'Université Laval.

CAAWS. (2016). *Women in sport: Fuelling a lifetime of participation.* https://womenandsport.ca/resources/research-insights/fuelling-a-lifetime-of-participation/#:~:text=Canadian%20Women%20%26%20Sport%20understands%20the,of%20Participation%E2%80%9D%20in%20March%202016

Canadian Olympic Committee. (2016). *Rio 2016.* https://olympic.ca/games/2016-rio/

Canadian Women & Sport. (2020). *Women in sport leadership: 2020 snapshot.* https://womenandsport.ca/wp-content/uploads/2020/03/Women-in-Leadership-Snapshot_2019-2020_Canadian-Women-Sport.pdf

Catalyst. (2007). *The double-bind dilemma for women in leadership: Damned if you do, doomed if you don't.* www.catalyst.org/wp-content/uploads/2019/01/The_Double_Bind_Dilemma_for_Women_in_Leadership_Damned_if_You_Do_Doomed_if_You_Dont.pdf

Chamorro-Premuzic, T. (2020, April 10). Are women better at managing the COVID-19 pandemic? *Forbes.* www.forbes.com/sites/tomaspremuzic/2020/04/10/are-female-leaders-better-at-managing-the-covid19-pandemic/?sh=330f0edb28d4

Conference Board of Canada. (2014). *The business case for women on boards.* www.conferenceboard.ca/docs/default-source/public-pdfs/womenonboards_en54712006f28d67c19cc2ff0000c4b4d4.pdf?sfvrsn=4efc4713_2

Council of Europe. (2019). *All in! Towards gender balance in European sport: Analytical report of the data collection campaign.* https://rm.coe.int/analytical-report-of-the-data-collection-campaign-all-in-towards-gende/1680971a71

Culver, D., Kraft, E., Din, C., & Cayer, I. (2019). The Alberta women in sport leadership project: A social learning intervention for gender equity and leadership development. *Women in Sport and Physical Activity Journal, 27,* 110–117. https://doi.org/10.1123/wspaj.2018-0059

Demers, G., Thibault, L., Brière, S., & Culver, D. (2019). Women in leadership positions within Canadian sport. In N. Lough & A. Geurin (Eds.), *Routledge handbook of the business of women's sport* (pp. 106–123). Routledge.

Donnelly, P., Norman, M., & Kidd, B. (2013). *Gender equity in Canadian interuniversity sport: A biennial report (No. 2).* Centre for Sport Policy Studies. https://kpe.utoronto.ca/sites/default/files/cis-gender-equity-report-2013.pdf

Drury, B. J., Siy, J. O., & Cheryan, S. (2011). When do female role models benefit women? The importance of differentiation recruitment from retention in STEM. *Psychological Inquiry*, 22, 265–269. https://doi.org/10.1080/1047840X.2011.620935

Eagly, A., & Carli, L. L. (2007, September). Women and the labyrinth of leadership. *Harvard Business Review*. https://hbr.org/2007/09/women-and-the-labyrinth-of-leadership

Eagly, A., & Karau, S. J. (2002). Role congruity theory of prejudice toward female leaders. *Psychological Review*, 109(3), 573–598. https://doi.org/10.1037//0033-295X.109.3.573

Elkouri, R. (2018, April 10). La parité sans pitié. *La presse*. http://mi.lapresse.ca/screens/40505c24-a72a-49bd-b3af-47309b7e8380__7C___0.html

Ely, R. J., Ibarra, H., & Kolb, D. M. (2011). Taking gender into account: Theory and design for women's leadership development programs. *Academy of Management Learning & Education*, 10(3), 474–493. https://doi.org/10.5465/amle.2010.0046

Fasting, K., Pike, E., Matthews, J., & Svela Sand, T. (2018). *From Helsinki to Gaborone: IWG progress report 2013–2018*. https://iwgwomenandsport.org/wp-content/uploads/2020/01/6-2018-From-Helsinki-to-Gabarone-Progress-Report.pdf

Federal-Provincial/Territorial Sport Committee Work Group on Women and Girls in Sport. (2018). *Recommendation report*. https://sirc.ca/wp-content/uploads/2020/01/FPTSC-WG-WIS-Recommendation-Report-v14-Sept-27-2018-final.pdf

Fox, C. (2018, March). Taking care of business. *Virgin Australia Voyeur*, 123–126.

Fry, H. (2017). *Women and girls in sport. Report of the standing committee on Canadian heritage*.www.ourcommons.ca/Content/Committee/421/CHPC/Reports/RP9068268/chpcrp07/chpcrp07-e.pdf

Government of Canada. (1982). *Canadian charter of rights and freedoms*, article 15. https://laws-lois.justice.gc.ca/eng/const/page-15.html

Harrison, T. (2018, April 3). TFE Hotels CEO talks pay parity and empowering staff. *Travel Weekly*. www.travelweekly.com.au/article/tfe-hotels-ceo-talks-pay-parity-and-empowering-staff/

Imeson, T. D. (2017). *Understanding the absence of female coaches in sport and the value of same-sex role models for female athletes in their coaching pursuits* (Master's thesis). University of Windsor, Electronic Thesis Depository. https://scholar.uwindsor.ca/etd/5990

Institute of Sport and Leisure Policy. (2004, January). *Femmes et fonctions dirigeantes dans le mouvement olympique*. https://library.olympic.org/Default/doc/SYRACUSE/57403/women-leadership-and-the-olympic-movement-final-report-january-2004-research-undertaken-by-the-insti

International Council for Coaching Excellence. (2018). *Ideas for the IOC Working Group to include in the action plan to achieve recommendation 6 of the IOC gender equality review*. [Unpublished report].

International Olympic Committee. (2018). *Gender equality review project*. https://stillmed.olympic.org/media/Document%20Library/OlympicOrg/News/2018/03/IOC-Gender-Equality-Report-March-2018.pdf

Kane, M. J., & LaVoi, N. M. (2018). An examination of intercollegiate athletic directors' attributions regarding the underrepresentation of female coaches in women's sports. *Women in Sport and Physical Activity Journal*, 26(1), 3–11. https://doi.org/10.1123/wspaj.2016-0031

Kraft, E., Culver, D., & Din, C. (2020). Exploring a women-only training program for coach developers. *Women in Sport and Physical Activity Journal*, 1–7. https://doi.org/10.1123/wspaj.2019-0047

LaVoi, N. M. (2016). A framework to understand experiences of women coaches around the globe: The ecological-intersectional model. In N. M. LaVoi (Ed.), *Women in sports coaching* (pp. 13–34). Routledge.

LaVoi, N. M., & Dutove, J. K. (2012). Barriers and supports for female coaches: An ecological model. *Sports Coaching Review*, *1*(1), 17–37. https://doi.org/10.1080/21640629.2012.695891

Lockwood, P. (2006). Someone like me can be successful: Do college students need same-gender role models? *Psychology of Women Quarterly*, *30*(1), 36–46. doi:10.1111/j.1471-6402.2006.00260.x

Mailloux, T., & Navarro, P. (2018, April 14). *Pourquoi tant d'opposition à la parité?* https://quebec.huffingtonpost.ca/therese-mailloux/pourquoi-tant-d-opposition-a-la-parite_a_23410937

Mercier, N. (2017, May 3). *Moins compétentes, vraiment?* https://lactualite.com/societe/moins-competentes-vraiment

Navarro, P. (2015). *Femmes et pouvoir: les changements nécessaires—Plaidoyer pour la parité.* www.lemeac.com/catalogue/1531-femmes-et-pouvoir-les-changements-necessaires.html

Ng, E., & Muntaner, C. (2018). The effect of women in government on population health: An ecological analysis among Canadian provinces: 1976–2009. *Population Health*, *6*(141), 141–148. https://doi.org/10.1016/j.ssmph.2018.08.003

Norman, M., Donnelly, P., & Kidd, B. (2017). *Gender equity in Canadian interuniversity sport: A biennial report (No. 3).* Centre for Sport Policy Studies. https://kpe.utoronto.ca/sites/default/files/cis-gender-equity-report-2013.pdf

Robertson, S. (2016). Hear their voices: Suggestions for developing and supporting women coaches from around the world. In N. M. LaVoi (Ed.), *Women in sports coaching* (pp. 159–201). Routledge.

Sport Canada. (2018). *Gender equity in the Canadian sport system: Graphs and observations.* [Unpublished report].

Women's Sports Foundation. (2020). *Do you know the factors influencing girls' participation in sports?* www.womenssportsfoundation.org/do-you-know-the-factors-influencing-girls-participation-in-sports/

World Economic Forum. (2020). *Insight report: Global gender gap report 2020.* http://www3.weforum.org/docs/WEF_GGGR_2020.pdf

Worldometers. (2020). *World population.* www.worldometers.info/world-population/

4 Barriers and Supports in the Career Trajectories of Graduate-Level Female Sports Coaching Students

Stephen Harvey and Letitia Price

Introduction

Despite the dramatic increase in the number of women and girls participating in sport, the number of coaching positions and, the number of women to fill them being higher than ever, data indicate that the majority of sport leadership positions continue to be held by men, globally (e.g., Acosta & Carpenter, 2014; Lapchick, 2016; LaVoi, 2016; Young, 2020). Scholars have likened the process of securing high-level leadership positions as a *leadership labyrinth* for women because they are forced to navigate a complex variety of challenges that obstruct and reroute their path, such as discrimination in the workplace (Eagly & Carli, 2014). The leadership labyrinth suggests that many women have, and will, continue to navigate numerous and often predictable barriers to obtaining and maintaining a coaching role (e.g., navigate the power structures of a predictably male-dominated profession; Burton & LaVoi, 2016).

The conceptualisation and professionalisation of sports coaching has significantly evolved around the development of effective education for coaches to empirically legitimise the coaching profession (Duffy et al., 2011). While there continues to be a significant breadth of scholarly discourse on the various realms of coaching education (Duffy et al., 2011), little is known about the impacts of degree-level coaching education upon female coaches and their career trajectories. A graduate-level coaching education programme should be deemed and positioned as a valuable supporting entity for the female coaches within the programme. Advanced coaching education has a social responsibility in being a pivotal factor in alleviating the barriers that female coaches face within their future career trajectory. Additionally, graduate-level coaching education should be intended as an important entity of support for female coaches, bolstering their skills required to remain and progress along their coaching careers effectively. It is aspired that a graduate-level coaching education degree consists of critical pedagogies that will allow for female coaches to better understand the barriers they have faced and to provide them with the necessary skills to address them. It is well-intentioned effort for female coaches to ascertain an advanced-level degree to facilitate their coaching development and greater their career prospects. However, several interdependent forces work to suppress the development of women coaches, meaning that despite holding an advanced-level qualification such as a graduate degree, they will remain locked out of the coaching profession, facing systemic barriers. Therefore, it remains unknown across research and in practice, as to how an advanced-level coaching education degree can better support its female coaches in the context of gender inequities in coaching. What is required within the programme to ensure that females can remain and progress effectively with their careers? How can a graduate-level coaching programme better serve female coaches with identifying supports and deconstructing their career barriers?

In this chapter, we hope to illustrate some examples of the barriers and supports that female graduate-level sports coaching students face in pursuit of the sports coaching profession, to facilitate a greater understanding as to how a graduate-level coaching education programme can better serve its female coaches. Consequently, gleaning these lived experiences of their graduate-level education it is hoped that we can yield a greater understanding as to what types of "calls to action" are required for graduate-level coaching education programmes to provide better support to its female coaches. It is posited that graduate-level coaching education programmes can be a critical asset in deconstructing the gender inequities in sport coaching.

Ecological-Intersectional Approach

LaVoi and Dutove (2012) proposed an Ecological Systems Model that identifies factors that hinder women as well as factors that support women in pursuit of the sports coaching profession. These barriers and supports exist on four levels: (1) the individual level, (2) the interpersonal level, (3) the organisational level, and (4) the sociocultural level. According to the Ecological Intersectional Model (LaVoi, 2016), the barriers and supports experienced by women coaches at each level are influenced by *power structures*, such as *patriarchy* and *intersectionality*. Intersectionality refers to a person's multiple identities, such as age, race, gender, sexuality, class, ability, and ethnicity, and how these multiple identities influence the types of oppression that women coaches experience, such as ageism, sexism, and racism (LaVoi, 2016). This model underpinned this research by providing an analysis of how advanced-level coaching education can help deconstruct the barriers and augment support for female coaches.

Methods

Participants

Participants for this current investigation were nine students from one graduate coaching education programme within the US collegiate system who all identified as female. The demographics of the participants cited is highlighted in Table 4.1.

Design

Using a phenomenological design, the aim was to explore the research phenomenon of the barriers and supports female coaches experience and how these could inform graduate-level coaching education programmes to help better support female coaches (Van Manen, 2014). The narratives collected from the participants were used to construct the conscious awareness of female coaches, highlighting the significant, textual, and structural essences within their experiences (Creswell & Poth, 2018).

Data Generation

After obtaining Institutional Review Board approval from a large mid-Western university in the United States, data collection was conducted after gaining participant-informed consent. Two focus groups were conducted that followed a semi-structured interview format: one for those in a campus-based version of the programme and one for those students in the online programme. Interview questions were developed from a previous study (Harvey et al., 2018), and an overview of these questions can be found in Appendix A. Focus groups lasted 90 minutes and were recorded and transcribed. Before analysis, participants were asked to review the transcripts and agree that they were an accurate representation of the interviews that were conducted.

Data Analysis

To support a naturalistic mode of inquiry, an abductive content analysis was used to analyse the data (Partington et al., 2015) which was conducted in

Table 4.1 Study's participant demographics

Participants	Level of coaching	Years coaching	Sport(s)	Nationality	Race	(Dis)ability
Anne	Interscholastic	9	Tennis, softball, soccer	USA	White	N
Becky	Interscholastic	6	Multi-sport	USA	White	N
Courtney	Club	8	Gymnastics	USA	White	N
Dianne	Club	9	Soccer	Ghana	Black	N
Emily	Interscholastic	5	Softball	USA	White	N
Harriet	Interscholastic	10	Softball	USA	White	N
Jane	Intercollegiate	9	Strength and conditioning	USA	White	N
Joan	Interscholastic	20	Softball	USA	White	N
Miriam	Interscholastic	8	Soccer	USA	White	N

three phases. The first phase began with unitising the data, with the first and second authors independently conducting a line-by-line analysis of each of the three interviews. This unitising process led to initial data reduction by "separating [data] along their boundaries and identifying them for subsequent analysis" (Lincoln & Guba, 1985, p. 203). In Phase 2, we categorised the data by grouping related text segments into sub-categories. This process became more focused through repetitive and comparative text examination. The objective of these first two sub-processes was to organise and interpret the unstructured qualitative data generated (Glaser & Strauss, 1967) and resonate any conflicts in analysis between the two study authors. In Phase 3, the categories generated were assigned by the authors to LaVoi's (2016) Ecological Intersectional Model. Note that participant pseudonyms are utilised throughout the presentation of results.

Findings

We applied the principles of LaVoi's (2016) Ecological Intersectional Model of Barriers and Supports to our salient themes (Table 4.2) to guide our understanding as to how an advanced-level coaching education can better support female coaches.

Marginalising Effects of Gender Construction in Coaching

Emerging from our findings was the notion that gender can be constructed in sports coaching from various socio-cultural practices that compound gender roles and determined female involvement in sports coaching. From a sociocultural perspective, the construction of gender in coaching within this study pertained to, *Stereotypes, Gender Marking, Misinformed Gender Behaviours* and *Implicit Biases*. The stereotypes established in this research aligned with those highlighted by LaVoi (2016, p. 26), Burton (2015, p. 160), and Norman (2010), that noted how women are marginalised out of coaching/leadership roles due to the roles being erroneously characterised as requiring "masculine" attributes. Gender marking pertains to the notion of only specifying gender to women's sports, thus depicting men's sports as the ubiquitously "true" representation of a sport (e.g., Women's FIFA World Cup) (Bruce, 2016; Tanner et al., 2011). The participants emphasised that gender marking became an additional tacit method to marginalise them as coaches, as their women's teams were segregated from their organisation's main branch of sports. Misinformed gender behaviours in this study emerged as a novel theme, where the participants highlighted that throughout their experiences in the graduate-level coaching education course, the male coaches were often confused or unsure of what type of behaviour was expected or acceptable when working with other female coaches or athletes. Implicit biases in this research pertained to the social cognitive theory concept, that reflects an individual who makes decisions based on stereotypes that negatively impacts the respective identities to which the stereotypes have been cultivated from (Walker & Bopp, 2011). The participants in this study revealed that this graduate-level coaching education offered the opportunity for discussions with male coaches as to how implicit biases have negatively impacted their careers and personal trajectory, thus were in favour of education being an effective tool to educate male coaches into how to unpack their personal implicit biases.

It became evident that each of the female coaches possessed a significantly heightened consciousness surrounding the negative effects of how gender is constructed across the coaching landscape. It was highlighted that: "There is a gendering nature in coaching and so you will be exposed to it and you have to kind of be able to look inside and be like, okay—I need to be prepared" (Courtney, FG1). The gendering of coaching is a deeply embedded phenomenon, that has derived from the societal construction of gender ideologies. These gendered constructions assign specific behavioural traits to either male or female, therefore, consequently when an individual perturbates this well-established patriarchy, causes inquisition into their lack of conformity to gendering behaviours (Lorber & Farrell, 1994, p. 310). The reductive gendering ideologies have compounded women's coaching experiences by consequently creating gendered coaching pathways, which have limited their career prospects. As revealed in this research, the traits equated to being a successful coach were naturalised as being "male-specific traits", while other traits that were deemed more negatively as being more "female-specific traits". Additionally, the participants highlighted this gendering as being equally interwoven across race, sexuality, and age, thus creating a further deepening of intersectional gendering ideologies. The female coaches posited this as negatively impacting their ability to recruit females within their sport, due to the negative perception that females involved in certain sports are more likely to be associated with homosexuality: "Hey, you know, why don't you play rugby? No, I don't want people thinking I'm gay—that's why they don't play" (Miriam, FG1). Consequently, this negatively impacted their coaching experiences, as they perceived negative stereotypes to be associated with their gender identity and thus, created misguided consensus regarding their self-efficacy in sport coaching. Consequently, this has presented these coaches with challenges such as recruiting athletes, coaching athletes, and coaching opportunities in coaching, due to the gendered devaluation, ambivalence, and infantilisation of females in coaching. The gendering of sport coaching was also seen as convoluting women's understanding of their own identity, with negative labels such as "tomboy" compounding their interpersonal challenges: "It separated me . . . it made me somebody different to that, than just enjoying doing the same things that the guys enjoy doing" (Joan, FG1).

As these societal factors unfolded to reveal their influence in constructing gender in sport, an *anthropological identity* of these female coaches emerged as a theme in relation to the individual perspective of the

Ecological-Individual Model. Here, the term anthropological identity is used to refer to and encourage a deeper exploration into an individual's ever-evolving journey of identity, pertaining specifically to its impact on their intersectional characteristics, as opposed to simply the journey itself. The participants depicted how their personal identity developed throughout their career: "as I got older, I really like leaned into that tomboy kind of perception" (Anne, FG1). Their personal identity journeys provide us with further insight into the negative influences on female coaches throughout a period, thereby enabling incomparable understanding of how perceptions towards female coaches evolve. An anthropological identity becomes a pivotal notion to consider as the female coaches depicted a complex journey through their personal identities throughout their careers. This reveals the importance of understanding the chronic effects of sociocultural and individual barriers on the development of a woman's coaching career.

In graduate-level coaching education programmes, it becomes pertinent for the faculty/staff to understand their proactive role in deconstructing the gendering of coaching by educating their constituents on the sociological constructions that creates a labyrinth of barriers for its fellow female coaches.

Career Development in Coaching: Barriers and Strategies

The female coaches within this study postulated a conflicting and dyadic relationship pertaining to *gender resume[1] despotism* and *superfluous resume complex.* The gender resume despotism emerged from this study as a novel concept pertaining to the female coaches' experiences in applying for coaching roles and facing infantilisation of their skills and coaching experience. They noted that coaching administrations were essentially dismissing their extensive coaching resumes, due to being of a lesser significance and achievement to their male counterparts, as it is perceived that male coaches "are more likely" to have coached in "more competitive" environments, even if a woman is coaching at the same level, men's coaching is held at a much higher standard. The superfluous resume complex represents the reaction of female coaches to the systemic gender resume despotism, in that, they bolster their resumes with superfluous amounts of experiences, skills, and educational qualifications in order to be deemed as a highly credible coach on a level playing field with their male counterparts: "We're just going to have to add one more thing to my resume because we have to have more to get less on somewhat an equal footing" (Courtney, FG1). Pertaining to the organisational factors, coaches felt their athletic administrations marginalised female coaches within recruitment by exercising their power in an oppressive manner by dismissing a female coach's experience entirely "So, I have, thirteen years of head coaching experience, job comes open, the guy that has no experience and has never coached, got the job" (Joan, FG1). In graduate-level coaching education programmes, the understanding and knowledge of this dyadic relationship of gender resume despotism and superfluous resume for female coaches become a powerful tool to be used to educate the fellow coaches throughout the programme. The coaches within these programmes are either future coaches or current coaches in athletic administrations, where it is a significant opportunity for them to be made aware of such challenges.

Marginalisation within recruitment was also highlighted in the sociocultural factors, where the gender resume despotism becomes an effective tool to cultivate homologous reproduction of hiring male coaches, thereby dismissing female coach aptitude and not necessarily acting in the best interests of the athletes or sport programme:

> He's in the boy's club. And you know, our athletic director, our high school principal, they all have daughters in these programmes, they're not necessarily picking the best options for their kids, but they kept the boys club role in there, they're not going to break that up.
>
> (Joan, FG1)

Main themes	Sub-themes	Codes
Marginalising effects of gender construction in coaching	Stereotypes	Parental enforced stereotypes
		Negative stereotypes
		Stereotype denunciation
	Identity	Anthropological identity
		Parental influences
	Gender marking	Male sports defined as the norm
	Misinformed gender behaviours	Uncertainty of correct "gender behaviour"
	Implicit biases	Using education to help reveal biases
Career development in coaching: barriers and strategies	Equifinal career trajectories	Various career paths lead to coaching careers
	Gender resume despotism	Unjust coaching recruitment practices
		Infantilisation of coaching
		Avoiding tokenism of females
	Superfluous resume complex	Gaining more so to be on an equal footing with male coaches
	Coaching alacrity	Embracing inevitable challenges that exist in coaching
	Altruism in coaching	Selfless advice, teaching, and career guidance

Main themes	Sub-themes	Codes
Benefits of graduate-level coach education for women coaches	Coaching didactics	Coaching education leads to learning coaching
	Feminism embedded curricula	The need for feminism tenets embedded within coaching content
	Coaching degree empowerment	Success in coaching Greater employability Increased self-efficacy Remuneration benefits
Organisational discrimination and social responsibility	Organisational support for females	Lack of support for female coaches
	Organisational unfairness/inequity	Salary inequities Promotional inequalities Differential gender treatment with sports teams
	Gender bias training	Organisational employee training
Strategies in finding gumption within a marginalising coaching profession	Female coaching valour	Importance of remaining courageous Challenging the "boys club" Reaffirming self-efficacy Bringing your voice to the table
	Covert mentors	Inspirational individuals who are unaware of their mentorship
	Ancillary mentors	Indirectly involved in sport Lacking other support groups

Source: Adapted from BHS (2020a, 2020b) and IGEQ (2019)

Furthermore, the female coaches noted that they do not advocate for a sociocultural approach where "women get free handouts" (Harriet, FG1). They highlighted that it requires a societal approach which embodies a notion of gender equity:

> I want women to be equally looked at for a job position, that's why I almost just hate that on job applications they ask what your gender is. What does it matter? Here's my qualifications and here's why I deserve this job, if I'm not qualified enough, then that's great.
>
> (Harriet, FG1)

Despite the organisational and societal barriers that the female coaches were confronted with, they revealed an amalgamation of daedal solutions to surmount these challenges pertaining to *equifinal career trajectories, coaching alacrity,* and *altruism in coaching.* The equifinal career trajectories refer to the notion that there is more than one pathway that leads to careers in coaching. This novel concept emerged as a way for female coaches to overcome being closed out of the coaching profession, by establishing their own unique career pathways into coaching:

> I think younger people get really stressed out about focusing on other people in their careers and the path that they took, but you know I am currently the women's golf graduate assistant coach and I am a strength and conditioning coach.
>
> (Jane, FG2)

These coaching experiences parallel with Lorde's (1984) compelling feminist call to action "the master's tools will never dismantle the house" (p. 113). Lorde (1984) advocates that the marginalised are better served by reconstructing the sociological system with tactics that reflect the authenticity of marginalised identities, as opposed to merely sustaining patriarchy by using the oppressor's tools to attempt to deconstruct patriarchy. While female coaches continued to experience discrimination within recruitment for coaching positions, our participants revealed that they have become accomplished at establishing a pathway to their desired coaching role: "Sometimes paths look like that they're not going to take you where you want to go, but I feel like they give you well rounded experiences" (Jane, FG2). This proactive approach, however, results in female coaches cultivating a sense of coaching alacrity, which alludes to female coaches' readiness for establishing effective solutions to the inevitable challenges that exist for them in the coaching landscape: "There is always going to be adversity, which you know, you have to go through, if you want to achieve what you want to do in coaching" (Dianne, FG2). This coaching alacrity allowed for the female coaches to cultivate more positive coaching experiences and create an increased sense of agency over their coaching careers. The female coaches relied heavily upon the sociocultural factors that pertain to altruism in coaching. This notion posits that the female coaches relied on selfless support from other coaches within the domain to provide a significant degree of teaching and support: "I think it was people willing to teach me things, and also here where people and coaches are willing to take you in" (Becky, FG2). The female coaches revealed that they had established effective solutions to overcome the sociocultural and organisational barriers, thus providing an important insight for graduate-level coaching educators to consider including as part of their curriculum. These solutions can be discussed from an empirical perspective and thus provide significant support to female coaches by involving them in the dissemination of potential solutions.

Benefits of Graduate-Level Coaching Education for Women Coaches

The female coaches discussed the positive impact this advanced-level coaching education has upon a coach's career path from an organisational perspective. They noted the importance of empirical knowledge of coaching: "I believe education is a huge part, if you don't have the knowledge of what you are doing, then you are obviously going to fail" (Emily, FG2). The coaches placed greater emphasis on the more reflective aspects of the *coaching didactic* journey: "I guess, you don't have to be an exceptional in everything you do, it's a learning process and everything you do is a new learning experience, and you need to educate yourself in whatever sport you are in" (Becky, FG2). From a societal perspective, however, the coaches revealed that the coaching education domain has a powerful opportunity to significantly convalesce gender equity in coaching. They highlighted the potential benefits of embedding a more feminist lens into the curriculum as it can perpetuate the critical consciousness of all coaches within coaching education programmes, thus enhancing their understanding of the symbiotic relationship between sport and wider sociological marginalisation. Anne (FG1) highlighted a question that one of her male peers, a fellow graduate coach, asked her in response to a class reading that highlighted the significant marginalisation women face in sports coaching regarding maternity:

> So, he asked me "What are things that we can do to help mothers that have children keep coaching jobs above them?" . . . He then went on to say, "I did that research and I thought it was absolutely ridiculous that [in] this country there's no organisation that allows for official maternity or paternity leave."

Additionally, the female coaches revealed that male coaches who are coaching female athletes need to comprehend entirely the extensive challenges facing female athletes: "If they're going to be coaching girls' sports, they should have extensive mentor support from a female coach who is in the game" (Joan, FG1). The female coaches gleamed upon the positive empowerment of obtaining a graduate coaching degree: "I think the more that women are getting educated, the better off we're all going to be" (Harriet, FG1). Many of the coaches discussed how the graduate-level coaching education degree, elevated their personal self-efficacy in sports coaching, which subsequently perpetuates a more positive coaching career trajectory: "If you don't have a master's degree, you're not getting a phone call, so I needed to forward my career and then also just to learn, and I need to learn" (Courtney, FG1).

Organisational Discrimination and Social Responsibility

There was unanimous agreement across most of the coaches that there was an absence of support from their athletic administrations: "Support . . . there is no support?" (Harriet, FG1). All the coaches revealed a plethora of factors that supported the notion of *organisational unfairness* and *inequities*, they all related to, *salary inequities, promotional inequalities*, and *differential gender treatment* with sports. Further compounding these problems was the reality of the chronic paucity of hiring female coaches across their athletic programme:

> In the history of our girls' basketball programme, there has never been a female head coach . . . only at one point in time was there a female track coach that I'm aware of, and for softball, there's never been a female head coach.
>
> (Joan, FG1)

The coaches highlighted the oppressive impact that these chronic discriminatory practices had upon the organisational culture and climate of the athletic department:

> One of the coaches actually pushed me when I was trying to help this boy bench press, and this guy was just super sexist. So, he literally shoved me out of the way, saying "You don't know what you're doing" . . . Even though I knew what I was doing was right, I kinda felt intimidated and honestly, I didn't even know what to say.
>
> (Emily, FG2)

Despite the negative impacts that these marginalising practices had upon the female coaches, they highlighted several solutions with a significant sense of aplomb. The salient solution noted by the coaches was the importance of *gender bias training* as a tool for combatting the prevalent gender discriminatory attitudes across athletic departments: "Some solutions and one of the things that it suggested was like a gender bias training for University or a company" (Anne, FG1). They further noted, however, that a comprehensive and purposeful implementation of gender bias training would be required consistently to address the deeply entrenched oppressive culture and climate of many athletic departments. Graduate-level coaching education could serve as an important empirical asset in contributing to the content and implementation of gender bias training. If the programme has a robust critical theory curriculum alongside evidence-based solutions to address the barriers female coaches face, then these could be used as an educational tool to share with athletic administrations and bridge the gap between the empirical and practical aspects of coaching education, to serve as a proactive tactic in better supporting female coaches.

Strategies in Finding Gumption Within a Marginalising Coaching Profession

There was a notable consensus from the coaches' emphasising the importance of *female coaching valour*. The coaches exuberantly advocated for other female coaches to persist with challenging the oppressive status quo: "People have done it before us, so why can't we, there are so many questions that need to be asked" (Dianne, FG2). To change the scarcity of female coaches across the domain, the coaches asserted that the coaching landscape should relinquish "Blame the Women" narratives (LaVoi, 2016, p. 21), and offered an alternative narrative which was, to provide support for women to have a greater sense of gumption in applying for coaching roles: "In order to advance more women in coaching we have to go for those jobs, somebody has to do it why not you?" (Courtney, FG1). The coaches were not remiss in highlighting the additional barriers that female coaches face; however, the notion of purposeful reflection was an apparent influence for cultivating significant female coaching valour:

> There are going to be challenges, there is going to be adversity, there's going to be tears, everything—it is up to you to decide if you are going to stop or are you going to continue go through these things.
> (Dianne, FG2)

Notably, in engaging with purposeful reflection, the female coaches highlighted the impact it had upon their coaching experiences by surmounting sociological hurdles: "What are the intersectionalities? What do you think you can do, despite what people think . . . focus on yourself and not what people expect you to do?" (Emily, FG2). Furthermore, it became apparent that the female coaches were optimistic regarding forging male allies in the coaching domain and supported the importance of cultivating male advocacy in empowering female coaches: "some of those guys are really wanting to discuss this stuff, and they're really open to it" (Joan, FG1). Mentoring emerged as a salient theme for the female coaches, further highlighting the importance of mentorship within sports coaching. *Covert mentors* became an interesting strand of mentorship revealed by our coaches, with covert mentors referring to individuals who became role models for the coaches, despite not having direct relation to these individuals: "She gave me the motivation to be like her. What she is doing—I want to do the same. She was my mentor secretly, she might not know it, but she's taught me so much without knowing" (Dianne, FG2). These sociological facets become an important consideration for faculty/staff within graduate-level coaching education as it posits the question as to how coaching education can embody content that encourages coaching valour? Additionally, the concept of covert mentors becomes a pivotal asset for graduate-level coaching education, as its faculty/staff should embrace the opportunity to empower agency amongst its female coaches to establish their mentors.

The findings presented in this research highlighted several novel salient themes that were aligned to various levels of the Ecological Intersectional Model, portraying the deeply entrenched barriers that exist in the coaching profession. However, the coaches also highlighted effective opportunities that could positively influence female coaching career trajectories.

These findings have illuminated how a graduate-level coaching education programme has the potential to serve as a valuable multifunctional tool in providing support for female coaches. This multifunctional tool has to the potential to both deconstruct some of the barriers that female coaches face and augment the support for female coaches via purposeful and systemic actions. The following section discusses these "calls to action" for graduate-level coaching education programmes pertaining. The actions discussed are framed through the lens of providing better support for female coaches in coaching education programmes, by embracing their social responsibility towards improving gender equity in coaching.

Calls to Action

The dichotomy of females continuing to enrol into graduate-level coaching education degrees while simultaneously being locked out of the coaching profession situates coaching education as having a significant social responsibility in cultivating gender equity in coaching. Therefore, based on the findings from this research, the following calls to action are categorised by three major themes: pedagogies of opportunity, mentorship opportunity, and advocacy opportunity.

Pedagogies of Opportunity

Pedagogies of opportunity emerge as an adaptation from Freire's (1994) "Pedagogies of Possibility". Pedagogies of possibility has been a well-established concept used by feminist scholars to provide educational tactics that have "yet to be imagined, that which might become thinkable and actionable when prevailing relations of power are made visible when understandings shake loose from normative perspectives and generate new knowledge and possibilities for engagement" (Manicom & Walter, 2012, pp. 3–4).

The selection of opportunity as opposed to possibilities aligns with the emphasis upon advanced-level coaching education programmes as having significant opportunities within their educational pedagogies to better support female athletes. Therefore, the pedagogies of opportunity for these calls to action pertain to the teaching of gender equity in graduate-level coaching education degrees. To achieve this, advanced-level coaching education programmes need to *embed critical theory pedagogies* within the entire curriculum. In practice, this includes:

- *Ubiquitous equity, inclusion, and diversity* content across all topics as opposed to having a mere individual course/module that only addresses these topics.
- *Include critical thinking questions* that address gender equities in coaching, for example, how do gender inequities coaching negatively affect the entire coaching profession?

- *Beginning a programme with a critical theory module* to unpack gender and other interconnected marginalised inequities in coaching, allowing for student coaches to consider these notions as a priority before any other coaching education.
- *Rich diversity of faculty/staff* who have a heightened critical consciousness of gender inequities in coaching, thus able to formulate a more critical theory curriculum.
- *Varied pedagogical sources* that embody critical theory notions pertaining to gender, race, sexuality, and (dis) ability—for example, Bell Hooks, Audre Lorde, Paulo Freire, "A class divided".
- *Female scholarly citations* to be widely used across the coaching education courses avoiding a male hegemonic scholarly environment.
- *Diversity in sport examples* used within course content that avoids sport examples being dominated by professional male sport examples.

The aim of these calls to action are to ensure that graduate-level coaching education "avoids the dangers of a singular story" (Adichie, 2009) by adopting a critical feminist lens that provides a rich, robust, and inclusive pedagogical framework. As female coaches are continuously marginalised from the coaching profession, despite having a superfluous resume complex and enrolling in advanced-level coaching education, coaching education programmes are an opportunity to contribute to the deconstruction of this problem by educating current and future coaches and involving them as part of the solution to alleviate these challenges. By embedding a critical theory pedagogical approach within advanced-level coaching education, better supports its female coaches as it augments the understanding of how gender inequities negatively impact all aspects and coaches within the coaching profession (Clark, 2012).

Mentorship Opportunities

Mentorship opportunities emerge as a call to action to address the career development support that is required for female coaches within graduate-level coaching education programmes. As the duration of these programmes provides ample time for faculty/staff to provide mentorship guidance, this provides a significant opportunity for these programmes to better support female coaches. In practice, this includes:

- *Establishing different entry points* into the coaching profession with female coaches, which could include coaching educator positions, sport management roles, coaching committee positions, and coaching across a variety of sports/disciplines.
- *Creating a coaching network action plan* for female coaches to identify other coaches to with which to professionally connect.

- *Developing a mentorship programme* for female coaches within the programme by connecting them with similar successful female coaches.
- *Job application assistance* for female coaches, helping with devising an impactful job application and providing support with tactics to get organisations to recognise their skills.
- *Individual development* focusing on the female coach's personal identity and philosophies as a coach.

Consistent with previous research that has highlighted discriminatory hiring practices (LaVoi & Dutove, 2012), the female coaches in this study revealed the impacts this had upon their career development as it pertained to applying for jobs process. Therefore, providing effective mentor support for female coaches by identifying equifinal career trajectories and establishing viable entry points into the coaching landscape via the non-traditional pathways is a potential solution that addresses the labyrinth journey that female coaches too often endure (Burton & LaVoi, 2016). Additionally, this approach will also require for coaching education programmes to facilitate in supporting female coaches with establishing professional coaching networks. Consistent with recent research highlighting the importance of professional networks for female coaches (Katz et al., 2018), our coaches posited the importance of having a variety of mentors that positively influence their coaching careers, including covert mentors. Therefore, working with female coaches to identify the types of mentors they need while also empowering them to connect with these mentors serves as a powerful supporting tactic for female coaches. Furthermore, connecting female coaches with other successful female coaches bolsters this networking and mentoring empowerment.

Findings in this research revealed a conflicting dyadic relationship between gender resume despotism and the superfluous resume complex, aligning with previous research noting that female coaching experiences are often infantilised and deemed as incomparable to their male counterparts (Crolley & Teso, 2007). By mentoring female coaches through the job application process can augment the support for female coaches on these coaching education programmes, who may be feeling exacerbated at the fact that their advanced-level degrees are not propelling them through their coaching career trajectories as they expected.

Our findings highlighted the importance of understanding a female coach's anthropological identity throughout their coaching career, as barriers such as stereotypes, implicit biases, and gender marking negatively impacted their perspective of their personal identity. Therefore, as previous research highlighted the importance of alleviating the negative impacts of self-limiting behaviours (Norman, 2016; Burton, 2015), mentoring female coaches in the context of individual development can support female coaches establishing personal agency.

While faculty/staff are temporally constrained due to the nature of the profession, as our findings revealed, to better support female coaches, we need a greater sense of altruism and alacrity across the coaching profession. Advanced-level coaching education programmes are in an advantageous role to offer support in mentorship due to its scholarly practitioner nature.

Advocacy Opportunities

Advanced-level coaching education programmes should play a leading role in advocating for improved gender equity in coaching. As our findings revealed, there is a significant need for organisations to provide more holistic and focused support for female coaches as opposed to just lip service support, because they have a social responsibility to galvanise gender equity in coaching (Hartzell & Dixon, 2019). In practice, this includes:

- *Increasing visibility of female coaches* by lobbying for; greater media representation and for coaching textbooks to include examples/imagery of female coaches.
- *Partnering with female sport organisations/movements* such as WeCoach, Women Sports Foundation, or the International Working Group for Women in Sport (IWGWS; Young, 2020).
- *Collaborate with athletic administrations* to provide empirical coaching educational tools such as gender bias training or forming collaborative equity, inclusion, and diversity committees.

The advanced-level coaching education programme in this study is part of a well-established public higher education organisation that consists of an array of powerful entities that could serve as significant support in proactively advocating for gender equity in coaching. While gender bias training was posited as a potential solution for organisations to address organisational unfairness/inequities in this study, for this to be effective, the leaders of the organisation must possess a transformative desire to change. Therefore, advanced-level coaching education programmes that are apart of large public higher education organisations can better support their female coaches, by devising extensive strategies that consist of proactively advocating on their behalf, using the advantageous resources and social capital available within publicly powerful organisations.

This approach addresses the wider and more systemic gender-equity issues in sport coaching; therefore, while success of advocacy requires extensive commitment, the very notion of proactively advocating for female coaches provides better support for female coaches. Additionally, female coaches within the programmes could potentially benefit in the long-term if the programmes are able to prevail in cultivating their powerful resources to advocate for gender equity, thus providing support that transcends across all areas of their Ecological-Intersectional system.

Conclusion

The current study conveyed the complexity of the various barriers and supports that are interdependently woven across the Ecological Intersectional Model for female coaches in a graduate-level coaching education programme. While this study is limited in breadth, it nonetheless provides a fruitful "coup d'oeil" into how advanced-level coaching education programmes can better serve its female coaches by providing a pedagogical environment that provides scholarly and practical support for female coaches to help deconstruct gender inequities in coaching.

Note

1. We use the term resume in this chapter but recognise that some in the coaching profession may prefer to use the term "curriculum vitae".

References

Acosta, R. V., & Carpenter, L. J. (2014). *Women in intercollegiate sport. A longitudinal, national study, thirty-seven-year update. 1977–2014.* Retrieved April 22, 2020, from www.acostacarpenter.ORG

Adichie, C. (2009, October 07). *The danger of a single story: Chimamanda Ngozi Adichie.* Retrieved November 16, 2020, from https://youtu.be/D9Ihs241zcg

Bruce, T. (2016). New rules for new times: Sportswomen and media representation in the third wave. *Sex Roles, 74*(7–8), 361–376.

Burton, L. J. (2015). Underrepresentation of women in sport leadership: A review of research. *Sport Management Review, 18*(2), 155–165.

Burton, L. J., & LaVoi, N. M. (2016). An ecological/multisystem approach to understanding and examining women coaches. In N. LaVoi (Ed.), *Women in sports coaching* (pp. 49–62). Routledge.

Clark, H. (2012, April 11). *Helen Clark: Inclusion and equality: Why women's leadership matters.* Retrieved November 16, 2020, from www.undp.org/content/undp/en/home/presscenter/speeches/2012/04/10/helen-clark-inclusion-and-equality-why-women-s-leadership-matters.html

Creswell, J. W., & Poth, C. N. (2018). *Qualitative inquiry and research design: Choosing among five approaches* (4th ed.). Sage.

Crolley, L., & Teso, E. (2007). Gendered narratives in Spain: The representation of female athletes in Marca and El País. *International Review for the Sociology of Sport, 42*(2), 149–166.

Duffy, P., Hartley, H., Bales, J., Crespo, M., Dick, F., Vardhan, D., . . . Curado, J. (2011). Sport coaching as a 'profession': Challenges and future directions. *International Journal of Coaching Science, 5*(2), 93–123.

Eagly, A. H., & Carli, L. L. (2014). *Through the labyrinth: The truth about how women become leaders.* Harvard Business Press.

Freire, P. (1994). *Pedagogy of hope: Reliving pedagogy of the oppressed.* Continuum Press.

Glaser, B. G., & Strauss, A. L. (1967). *The discovery of grounded theory: Strategies for qualitative research* (1st ed.). Adline Transaction.

Hartzell, A. C., & Dixon, M. A. (2019). A holistic perspective on women's career pathways in athletics administration. *Journal of Sport Management, 33*(2), 79–92.

Harvey, S., Voelker, D. K., Cope, E., & Dieffenbach, K. (2018). Navigating the leadership labyrinth: Barriers and supports of a woman collegiate coach in a 20-year leadership role. *Sports Coaching Review, 7*(1), 45–62.

Katz, M., Walker, N. A., & Hindman, L. C. (2018). Gendered leadership networks in the NCAA: Analyzing affiliation networks of senior woman administrators and athletic directors. *Journal of Sport Management, 32*(2), 135–149.

Lapchick, R. (2016). *Gender report card: 2016 International sports report card on women in leadership roles*. The Institute for Diversity and Ethics in Sport. Retrieved April 22, 2020, from https://43530132-36e9-4f52-811a-182c7a91933b.filesusr.com/ugd/7d86e5_9ab8fc8f9e124398aaa29f66ef0873f3.pdf

LaVoi, N. M. (Ed.). (2016). *Women in sports coaching*. Routledge.

LaVoi, N. M., & Dutove, J. K. (2012). Barriers and supports for female coaches: An ecological model. *Sports Coaching Review, 1*(1), 17–37.

Lincoln, Y. G., & Guba, E. G. (1985). *Naturalistic inquiry*. Sage.

Lorber, J., & Farrell, S. A. (1994). *The social construction of gender* (1st ed.). Sage.

Lorde, A. (1984). The master's tools will never dismantle the master's house. In A. Lorde (Ed.), *Sister outsider: Essays and speeches* (1st ed., pp. 10–14). Ten Speed Press.

Manicom, L., & Walters, S. (2012). Introduction: Feminist popular education: Pedagogies, politics, and possibilities. In L. Manicom & S. Walters (Eds.), *Feminist popular education in transnational debates building pedagogies of possibility* (1st ed., pp. 3–12). Palgrave Macmillan.

Norman, L. (2010). Feeling second best: Elite women coaches' experiences. *Sociology of Sport Journal, 27*(1), 89–104.

Norman, L. (2016). Lesbian coaches and homophobia. In N. LaVoi (Ed.), *Women in sports coaching* (pp. 65–80). Routledge.

Partington, M., Cushion, C. J., Cope, E., & Harvey, S. (2015). The impact of video feedback on professional youth football coaches' reflection and practice behaviour: A longitudinal investigation of behaviour change. *Reflective Practice, 16*(5), 700–716.

Tanner, S., Green, K., & Burns, S. (2011). Media coverage of sport for athletes with intellectual disabilities: The 2010 Special Olympics national games examined. *Media International Australia, 140*(1), 107–116.

Van Manen, M. (2014). *Phenomenology of practice: Meaning-giving methods in phenomenological research and writing* (1st ed.). Routledge.

Walker, N. A., & Bopp, T. (2011). The underrepresentation of women in the male dominated sport workplace: Perspectives of female coaches. *Journal of Workplace Rights, 15*(1), 47–64.

Young, J. (2020, March 06). *Sydney score board*. Retrieved November 16, 2020, from www.sydneyscoreboard.com/

Appendix A
Overview of Questions

Part 1: Life History
- Experiences of physical education and sport.
- Lived experiences of coaching (challenges, constructive, and negative experiences).
- Role of mentors in coaching career.
- Supporting mechanisms throughout coaching career.

Part 2: Experiences of Graduate-Level Education
- Desire to go into graduate-level education.
- Experiences within graduate-level education (support, challenges, content, and areas for development).
- Professional development activities.
- Guidance for future female coaches on the graduate-level coaching education programme.

5 Can Sex-Integrated Sport Provide a Gender-Equitable Coaching Environment?

Donna de Haan and Lucy Dumbell

Introduction

The majority of Olympic sports remain sex-segregated, meaning men and women compete in separate competitions. In more recent years, there has been an increase in the number of mixed-sex team competitions, where there needs to be a representation from both sexes, such as table tennis and tennis at the Rio Olympics 2016. There is also one Olympic sport, which is sex-integrated meaning participation opportunities are open to men and women to directly compete against one another. This sport is equestrianism, which involves a horse and human as a competitive partnership.

The Olympic equestrian disciplines, Showjumping, Dressage, and Eventing, have evolved from a traditional masculine military foundation. Originally, the equestrian disciplines were only open to men competitors. Women were allowed to compete in Dressage in 1952, followed by Showjumping in 1956 and Eventing in 1964 (de Haan & Dumbell, 2016). Within the Olympic context, nations are free to choose the best riders, for individual and team selection, irrespective of their sex. Research shows, however, that the most successful equestrian nations demonstrate more equitable participation than other nations (Dumbell et al., 2018). At the 2016 Rio Olympics, women made up 45% of the 11,237 athletes who competed in the games and 47% of the events were open to women (either sex-segregated or mixed). This figure was closely mirrored in the 38% of women athletes competing in the Equestrian events (de Haan & Dumbell, 2019). Reflecting the wider representation of women in the Olympics, the number of women athletes competing in equestrian disciplines has increased over the years but has not yet reached 50%.

Despite improved opportunities for women to participate, they continue to encounter barriers to involvement in many aspects of sport. For example, during the last two consecutive Summer Olympic Games, only 11% of accredited coaches were women (Olympic.org, 2020). Whilst we are understanding more about the gendered nature of participating in sex-integrated sport, we know very little about those involved in coaching such sports. The purpose of this chapter therefore is to explore the extent to which a sex-integrated sport can provide a gender-equitable coaching environment and what can be learnt from this. Specifically, we use Bourdieu's concepts of field, habitus, and capital to review how the structure of equestrian sport, including coach education systems, may disrupt, challenge, or reinforce dominant ideologies of gender. We begin the chapter by outlining our theoretical position in the context of discussing the coaching landscape of equestrian sport. Throughout the chapter, we present quantitative data pertaining to participation rates of men and women, whilst also drawing on the narratives of two elite-level coaches. Finally, we draw conclusions from our study and present recommendations for future inquiries or directions for research and policymakers.

An Introduction to Equestrian Sport Using Bourdieu's Concept of Field

Bourdieu was one of the first social commentators to consider sport as a serious sociological issue. He acknowledged sport as a field of social significance and one that can be seen to epitomise issues of class, power, and the representation of body practices (Bourdieu, 1979). We acknowledge that Bourdieu's work has been criticised by some feminist scholars as being androcentric (Laberge, 1995; Thorpe, 2009), but we highlight the fact that sport as a field is patriarchal and Bourdieu's placement of social class over gender relations certainly resonates with the evolution of equestrian sport in the Olympic context. We also highlight that there are links between habitus, practice, and gender in some of Bourdieu's (1990) work and our purpose in this chapter is to identify similar associations and their implications for the coaching experience in a sex-integrated sport.

Bourdieu's concept of a field refers to the social system "within which struggles or manoeuvres take place over specific resources" or access to such resources (Jenkins, 2002, p. 84). In this case, Olympic sport constitutes a partially autonomous field within the broader field of high performance or elite sport. Each field has its own historical norms, which include the fields' explicit and formal rules and regulations, alongside informal, tacit and implicit customs, ceremonies, and etiquette that are collectively known as practice (Bourdieu, 1990). The Olympic Games are unquestionably entrenched in ritual and customs, from the symbolic rings on the flag, displays of nationalism and performance in the opening and closing ceremonies and medal table rankings. In the Olympic context, there are formal rules which may prohibit women from participating in certain events, but there are no equivalent rules that prevent women from coaching athletes, yet women coaches remain predominantly excluded from this field. Individual sports do however have formal rules which they use to regulate the practices of coaches. In equestrian sport, for example, one such organisation is the International Group for Equestrian Qualifications (IGEQ).

The IGEQ was formed in 1992 is an independent voluntary organisation with a mission "To improve horse welfare by developing, promoting and maintaining equestrian qualification standards" (IGEQ, 2019). As such, the IGEQ is responsible for explicitly formalising the rules and regulations associated with coaching qualifications for equestrian sport. It is open to membership from National Equestrian Federations, governing bodies and any organisation authorised by a government to deliver equestrian qualifications. Each member has a named representative as the IGEQ lead. As of February 2020, 39% of IGEQ named representatives were men and 61% were women.

The IGEQ system provides standardisation of qualifications that supports international comparability, sharing good practice and recognition of a coach's ability. By mapping their qualifications against three internationally agreed coaching minimum standards, members can be issued with an international coaching passport. The IGEQ therefore facilitates an arena of production, circulation, and appropriation and exchange of goods, services, coaching expertise, and practice (knowledge) or level of coaching qualification (status), and the competitive positions held by coaches (actors) in their struggle to accumulate, exchange, and monopolise different kinds of power resources (capitals). For Bourdieu, these are all key characteristics of a field.

The idea of standardising and recognising coaching qualifications across several countries is not unique. There are similar initiatives seen in other sports, for example, football. However, each sport provides a unique setting in which the actors (coaches) and their social positions are located. The Union of European Football Associations (UEFA), for example, has coaching levels (Pro, A, and B licences) that national coaching qualifications can be aligned with. UEFA made it mandatory in 1997 for those in key coaching positions to hold a UEFA licence. They introduced this to improve standards and to support free movement of coaching across Europe (UEFA, 2020). To some extent, this may be a way of creating equitable practices through the standardisation of qualifications. Norman and McGoldrick (2019), however, found inequitable recruitment practices of men and women coaches with the same coaching qualifications. Clubs placed a higher value on experience rather than qualifications and women coaches with the same qualifications as men were given less opportunity to acquire on-field experience. Furthermore, several studies highlight the women participants' experiences of the structural practices of the football coaching system left them feeling undervalued and marginalised (i.e., Norman, 2016; Lewis et al., 2015). Therefore, whilst the explicit and formal rules and regulations of the football coaching field appear gender-equitable, the informal tacit and implicit customs create a field in which the appropriation and exchange of knowledge or status, and the competitive positions held by actors in their struggle to accumulate, exchange, and monopolise different kinds of power resources (capital) is inequitable.

The Habitus of Coaching in Equestrian Sport

The UK was one of the original members of IGEQ and has a world-renowned equestrian education programme in the British Horse Society (BHS) Equine Excellence Pathway (BHS, 2020a), which includes a coaching pathway (see Table 5.1). The BHS maintain a register of accredited professional coaches (BHS, 2020b) that is publicly available on its website. The register contains member coaches who have current skills and knowledge and who complete a programme of continual professional development to remain so. Coaches with an international passport may become members and appear on the register.

In the United Kingdom, whilst 51% of the population are women, 67% of the 1.8 million regular riders (who ride at least once a month) are women (BETA, 2019). However, 91% of BHS accredited professional coaches are women and only 9% men (see Table 5.2). Interestingly, the odds ratio of a coach being male increases as the coaching level increases, from only 0.01 at BHS level 2, to 0.25 at BHS level 5 to 0.44 at accredited Fellow of the BHS to 0.89 of active Fellows. Having reviewed senior women coaches experience in the UK in cricket, hockey, football, and netball, Norman (2008, p. 455) describes the numeric distribution of women coaches at different levels as "comparable to a narrow 'bottle neck' occurrence whereby the higher the women climb, the more constricted the pathways and opportunities

Table 5.1 British Horse Society (BHS) qualifications

International level	BHS qualification	Coach ability level	Number of affiliated BHS coaches
None	Stage 2 Complete horsemanship 2	Communicate foundation skills under supervision	89
1	Stage 3 Coach	Teaching with limited responsibility usually under supervision of higher-level coach	952
2	Stage 4 Senior coach	Independent instructor with responsibility for all aspects of teaching	575
3	Stage 5 Performance coach	Independent master instructor	235
International expert	Fellow of the British Horse Society (FBHS)	Ambassador for the equestrian profession and thought leader for the sector. Expert in equitation and horsemanship	53

Source: Adapted from BHS (2020a, 2020b) and IGEQ (2019)

Table 5.2 The representation of the sexes in the British Horse Society (BHS) register of accredited professional coaches and active fellows (OR is odds ratio)

BHS level	Male Headcount	Percentage of males	Female Headcount	Percentage of females	Male:Female Percentage of coaches	Odds ratio
2	1	0.6	88	5.2	1:99	**0.01**
3	53	33.8	899	53.1	6:94	**0.06**
4	53	33.8	522	30.8	9:91	**0.10**
5	42	26.8	167	9.9	20:80	**0.25**
FBHS	8	5.1	18	1.1	31:69	**0.44**
Active FBHS	25	-	28	-	47:53	0.89
Total	**157**	**100**	**1694**	**100%**	**8:92**	**0.09**

Source: BHS (2020b)

become and so only a very few women manage to reach the top of their profession".

In the context of the Olympics, male coaches occupy the position of incumbents, meaning they are the dominant actors in the higher echelons of coaching. As such, male coaches will generally be invested in maintaining the field in its current form, as changes to the rules of competition risk destabilising their dominant position. The position of each particular actor in the field is a result of interaction between the specific rules of the field, actor's habitus, and actor's capital. Therefore, the gendered distribution of coaches at different levels in sport cannot solely be explained by the structure of coaching qualifications.

The "drop out" of women in numerous career paths is often discussed using the "leaking pipeline" metaphor (Aman et al., 2018). Hancock and Hums (2016) discuss that in the United States despite more women working in intercollegiate athletics than ever before, the number of women assistant and associate athletic directors is declining. As such, fewer women are in the "pipeline" to achieve the position of Athletic Director. They identified perceptions of gender and professional value incongruence (habitus) as factors which affected women's career choices and opportunities for advancement. In equestrian sport, at the highest levels of UK coaching, whilst more than two-thirds of coaches are women a large number of these coaches are not currently active and the proportion of active BHS coaches at the highest level is approximately equal between men and women. This could be regarded as a highly desirable balance and is certainly unusual compared to other sports. What makes the UK figures potentially concerning, however, is the much smaller overall number of men coaches and raises questions of how and why they seem to progress to the highest levels and remain active there in much greater proportions than women. This requires further investigation to gain more detailed insights into this phenomenon.

The collective entity by which and into which dominant social and cultural conditions are established and reproduced is referred to by Bourdieu as habitus. Specifically, Bourdieu (1994, p. 170) defines habitus as a property of social agents, individuals, groups, or institutions (athletes, coaches, and sport federation) that comprises a "structured and structuring structure". Scholars have previously applied the concept of habitus to specific sports, for example, rowing (de Haan & Norman, 2019), professional football (Cushion & Jones, 2014; Blackett et al., 2015), snowboarding (Thorpe, 2005), and rock climbing (Beames & Telford, 2013). Whilst the three Olympic equestrian disciplines share historical norms and collective practices, there are distinct discipline-specific nuances.

The habitus of coaching equestrian sport is different to coaching leisure riding and those learning to horse ride. One female international coach described how leisure riders will often use qualifications and accessibility to choose a coach, and then if they find they can build "a rewarding relationship with that coach, they will return to them". She described competitive riders as "very different, frequently using competitive background above or combined with qualifications" to choose to engage with a coach. This was reinforced by the male coach as well. The capital that is accrued for coaching leisure riding and competitive equestrian sports therefore differs. Perhaps because horse riding can be experienced with no reference to competitive requirements and has a large number of competitive discipline-specific nuances, it is unsurprising that competitive background and experience is used to differentiate coaches of competitive equestrian sports.

This is quite different to other sports, for example, football. Even when played as a leisure pursuit, football is usually experienced in a competitive setting, with a game taking place following the rules of the sport and a winner being declared. Equestrianism is not like this and participants usually learn to horse ride with no reference to competition rules, expectations, or arguably, skills. In equestrian sport, some coaches may specialise and build a reputation in one specific discipline, whilst others may be more generalists. Riders can access coaching in group or individual settings, they may have a coaching session that works on improving them and the horse in combination or they may pay for a coach to ride their horse, thereby the focus is on training the horse not the horse/rider combination. Equestrian sport therefore creates numerous different types of coaching habitus.

Furthermore, Taylor and Garratt (2010, p. 126) highlight that coaching habitus will vary depending on the "system of acquired dispositions or categories of perception and assessment held by the coach at the level of practice". For example, a coach cannot create effective training programmes if they have no experience of the sport. So only once a coach has internalised the "rules and requirements" of the sport (in the sense of the structured structure), can they adapt and communicate an effective training programme to their athlete (in the sense of a structuring structure). A habitus is "structured" by one's past and present circumstances. As most coaches first experience a sport as an athlete, their experience of being coached will inevitably influence their own coaching experience (Cushion et al., 2003). It is "structuring" in that one's habitus helps to shape one's present and future practices. Thus, coaches may be reproducing the discourses about gender and other social power relations into which they were disciplined during their athletic careers.

The Valourisation of the Gendered Body in Coach Education

A dominant social and cultural discourse describes elite sport as a heterosexual male domain and/or as a place where practices associated with desirable heterosexual masculinities are celebrated (Theberge, 1993). The discourses about desirable (masculine) bodies in sport not only pertain to performing bodies but also regulate which bodies become and are seen as leaders in sport such as coaches (Connell & Messerschmidt, 2005). Kane (1995) and McKay et al. (2000) point to the social construction of differences between women and men athletes as one of the most powerful techniques employed to support male hegemony in sport. Indeed, Hargreaves (2002) suggests the historical justification for segregating sport was built around the ideas of sexual difference and the belief in the unsuitability of sport and physical activity for women. Equestrian sport challenges this notion of desired physicality in sport as it is not the human athlete's body that is judged. In equestrian sport, however, there is no sex-based biological advantage for either men or women, as Dashper (2012, p. 215) explains, "masculine sporting abilities such as speed and strength are less significant . . . strength of a rider plays a role, but this is limited as within the equestrian partnership the horse will always be the stronger partner".

For Bourdieu, the habitus instils a world view in its subjects by conferring (cultural) value upon things, be they material or immaterial. Put simply, within the habitus, some things are valourised and some are not. Even at the seemingly intimate level of the body, the habitus posits and bestows specific properties. Some of these are constructed as "good", while others are "bad" and stigmatised (such as physical strength and athleticism). Coach education material is an indicative guide to the valourisation of the athletic body. Coaching texts tend to emphasise physical differences between men and women (Yoshiga & Higuchi, 2003). In general, coach education materials tend to be based on a biomedical framework (Denison et al., 2017) that views gender as a physical binary (LaVoi et al., 2007).

Fielding-Lloyd and Mean (2016), and Lewis et al. (2015), explored the gendering of coach education. They found that instructors and male students were complicit in constructing male coaches and athletes as the norm for the development of coaching methods that emphasised practices associated with desirable athletic masculinity. In our review of UK equestrian coach education material, we found a distinct lack of gender pronouns or gendered language. For example, in the BHS coaching syllabi, we found 220 references to "riders", 13 references to "learners", and then use of "coaches" or "horse trainers" or "clients". But there was no reference to "males" and "females" or "men" or "women". When we reviewed the key BHS coaching text (Print, 2011), we noted consistent use of the word "rider" and "instructor" but again no use of gendered pronouns. We found content referring to the rider's body shape, having three main somatotypes but these were not ascribed or discussed with regards to a specific sex. The only sex-related discussion pertained to the difference in anatomy of the pelvis and acknowledgement that male riders may make different mistakes than female riders as a result of their "conformation". In her study of the lived experience of equestrian sport in the Olympic context, de Haan (2015) also noted the absence of gender pronouns in the stakeholder narratives of those involved in supporting athletes, including coaches.

How Equestrian Coaches Accumulate Power and Recognition: Bourdieu's Concept of Capital

For Bourdieu (1977), valorised properties within the habitus come to constitute cultural capital, the possession of which affects how social and cultural relations are made and remade, and importantly by whom and for whom. The concept of capital sits at the centre of Bourdieu's (1985) construction of social space: "The structure of the social world is defined at every moment by the structure and distribution of the capital and profits characteristic of the different particular fields" (p. 734). In short, capital refers to the different forms of power held by different social agents. Bourdieu (1986) identifies various forms of capital including economic, social, cultural, symbolic, linguistic, academic, and corporeal. The ability of an actor, an athlete, or coach to accumulate capital is proportionate to their position in the social space. In the same way that the habitus of equestrian coaches differs both when coaching leisure riding or competitive equestrian sport, and between competitive sporting disciplines, the forms of capital available to them also differs.

Bourdieu (1988) understood society to be structured along differences in the distribution of capital with individuals striving to maximise their own personal capital. The amount of capital that can be accumulated by an individual makes a significant contribution to determining the range of available choices open to that individual (Bourdieu, 1989). Purdy et al. (2009) explain that in this context capital becomes the capacity to exercise power over ones' own future and the future of others. However, the ability of an individual to accumulate various forms of capital is proportionate to their position in the social space. In equestrian sport, horses are an essential asset which at the elite level requires significant economic capital. Horse owners therefore have considerable capital as they make the decisions as to which rider have access to their horse. In order to truly exercise power over their own future, riders would ideally also be the owner of their horses. At the

Rio Olympic Games in 2016, only three Team GB riders were part owners of their horse, and these were all men (Dumbell et al., 2018). This reinforces Bourdieu's belief that women are not typically capital-accumulating objects; rather they are capital-bearing objects, whose value accrues to the primary groups in which they belong (Lovell, 2000).

In equestrian sport, capital/power may come from being an owner/rider but there is another dual role many hold within the equestrian sport and that is rider/coach. As a sex-integrated sport men and women can accumulate capital as riders; however, this may be easier if they are an owner/rider which at an elite level appears to be a male-dominated domain. In equestrian sport, capital/power may come from being an owner/rider but there is another dual role many hold within the equestrian sport and that is rider/coach. Carl Hester for example has ridden for Team GB at five Olympic Games and went to the Rio Olympics in 2016 as a team rider and coach for the Dressage team. When describing his career, he refers to himself as a rider and a coach, and a horse trainer. For the purpose of this chapter, we are utilising the term horse trainer as a person who trains horses directly, meaning they are likely to ride the horse themselves. The coach focuses on the combination of rider and horse. In fact, three of the four Team GB horses at the Rio Olympics had been trained by Carl himself (Braddick, 2017), meaning he had ridden the horses to develop their athletic potential.

The concept of rider and coach, and horse trainer, is not unusual, although the scale of Hester's success is. What is unusual in equestrian sport is for coaches not to have ridden, in fact most still ride, albeit to varying levels. When equestrian coaches adapt a coaching plan, they do so in response to not only the riders behaviour but also the horses responses to the rider (Hall, 2017). In fact, it is considered good practice in BHS examinations to be able to ride the horse to experience what the rider experiences. Perhaps it is this multiple role paradigm (coach, rider, horse trainer, and horse owner) that makes equestrian coaching unusual.

Our female coach said "unless at elite level, I will be expected to offer insights into what the rider will feel, how they can improve and also how to improve the horse". Additionally, Lewis (2013) found that high-level competitive riders would frequently engage several coaches who they perceived offered different advantages. For example, one might act as a mentor and provide performance feedback, behaving as a "sounding board" for ideas, another might be very good at training horses and offer insights in that capacity, another might be very good at "the art of competition" and offer insights into how to maximise marking rewards in a discipline. These roles, where the rider is the one who decides on tactics and selectively engages different coaches for different roles, are quite unusual in the sporting world, where in many sports typically it is the coach who would decide tactics. At this point, we do not know if these different coaching roles are more likely to be taken by a coach who is a man or a woman, and we do not know if riders prefer working with men or women coaches. Clearly, the gender distribution would be linked to opportunities to accrue capital in these areas; therefore, this is an area of research that should be investigated further.

Our male international coach also believed he accrued considerable capital from his multiple, simultaneous roles within, and wider association with, the sport, "people know I am an international showjumping course builder. They come to me for insights into courses and how they can be ridden". Due to the longevity of equestrian athletes and the unique nature of equestrian sport, the simultaneous nature of these multiple roles is not unusual but is different from many other sports. For example, it would be hard to imagine an international football manager refereeing a first division game. It would be interesting to understand the gender and make up of these associated positions in equestrian sport; however, these data are not available at this time. What we do know is that showjumpers are more likely to be male and the majority of advanced showjumping course builders are also male (22 out of 30 Level 5) (British Showjumping, 2020).

In sport, in general, we know very little about coaches' acquisition of capital beyond association with winning athletes and position-taking (coaching position, such as head coach). Denison et al. (2017) argue that those who coach the elite are the coaches that are most respected and to whom others listen. This suggests that coaches in high-performance and international sport may exert a great deal of power on other coaches as well as athletes. We know that the more capital an actor has the more power that individual or group has to influence what is considered to be of value. In equestrian sport, it would seem that some methods of accumulating this capital may be through male-dominated activities (such as horse ownership and associated positions in equestrian sport).

Disrupting, Challenging, or Reinforcing a Gendered Coaching Environment

The field of sport is one in which the male heterosexual non-disabled body is seen as the ideal. It is built on a network of historical relations of power between positions held by individuals, social groups, or institutions all of which celebrate hegemonic masculinity. Men are the incumbents in sport and sport coaching. In the Olympic context, thanks to formal imposed rule changes, women athletes have been able to slowly intrude into this space. Unfortunately, the same cannot be said for coaching. During the last two consecutive Summer Olympic Games, only 11% of accredited coaches were women (Olympic.org, 2020). The traditional gender binary of sex-segregated sport reinforces hegemonic masculinity and reinforces the gendered constructs and discourses that position women as other. In this study, we have tried to establish if sex-integrated sport disrupts, challenges, or reinforces this.

What we have found is that within the context of UK equestrian sport women coaches are arguably the incumbents. Of the BHS-accredited professional coaches, 91% are women. In other coach-related leadership roles, women are also well represented; for example, of IGEQ-named representatives, 61% are women. Team GB equestrian staff consist of 46 people, 25 females, and 21 males, and those that are directly related to coaching are five females and three males (TeamGBR Equestrian, 2020). Position-taking such as this is one way for coaches to accumulate capital. In the context of reviewing, the coaching environment using a Bourdieu framework, power is intrinsically linked to capital. We therefore suggest that this contrasts with many other sports, where the coaching and support staff are predominantly male. It is interesting to note however that the odds ratio of a coach being a man increases as the coaching level increases, from only 0.01 at BHS level 2, to 0.89 of active Fellows. We conclude therefore that the coaching pipeline in equestrian sport in the UK is probably not equitable, and we call for additional research to investigate the transition of men and women coaches throughout the system.

Within equestrian sport, we have noted unique position-taking opportunities and we have seen that some groups may be able to create capital through a unique combination of multiple roles. Such position-taking corresponds to agency, actions, and practices in the field which affords the actor with more symbolic capital than that of those with only singular status. Our preliminary review suggests that within the elite echelons of the sport these combined positions are often taken by men, although we stress the need for further research across all levels, and disciplines, of the sport to validate this. At this point, we do not have enough data to draw conclusions as to whether men or women are more likely to take these positions. We do however highlight the complexity of the intersectionality of capital acquisition within equestrian coaching.

In this chapter, we have also discussed how coach education material across sport is often gendered and how this can perpetuate discourses which frame men and male athletes as the desirable norm, problematising women athletes' bodies and their behaviours (Connell & Messerschmidt, 2005). We have noted that women are largely absent from coach education material. Having interviewed women senior national coaches of major team sports (football/soccer, field hockey, rugby league, rugby union, cricket, netball, basketball, and volleyball) Norman (2010) reported that these coaches felt undervalued and underrated. These feelings were the result of not overt discrimination but more subtle, insidious ideologically based oppression that contributes to women's continued under-representation (Halford & Leonard, 2001). Norman (2008) argued that ineffectual coach education contributes to women's lack of power within coaching.

Our research shows a lack of gendered discourse in the UK coaching material associated with equestrian sport. Equestrian coaches interviewed confirmed that they had been encouraged to refer to athletes as riders (through training and reinforced by educational materials) and as equestrian is a sex-integrated sport, even at the highest levels, that removes the implication of gender. This approach has been evident for at least the last 40 years in the UK and may have supported a large number of women becoming equestrian coaches. Whilst this does "level the field" in so far as promoting an assumption of participants being male or female, it may also not acknowledge the differences between female and male participants that may be important for effective coaching to occur. At this point, our perception is that coach education material in equestrian sport is not necessarily an example of a gender-equitable coaching environment but rather an example of one that is gender-blind. We believe therefore that equestrian sport is creating a different gendered coaching environment as far as coach education is concerned. At this point, it is unclear whether this is an intentional approach or simply an effectual outcome of the field. In order to truly disrupt gendered ideologies in coach education, materials need to challenge perceptions associated with the ideal body in sport. Therefore, being gender blind in sport cannot be considered a neutral position due to the overwhelming discourse of masculine hegemony. Men and women's bodies are different. Men and women athletes are different. Coaching material needs to acknowledge these differences to truly contribute to an equitable coaching environment. We believe there is potential for this type of coach education material to disrupt the dominant gendered discourses in coaching. However, further research is needed to fully understand the affect this has on the coaching environment.

Whilst our review has been limited in scope, we believe it provides a useful insight into this unique coaching environment. We argue that equestrian sport challenges dominant gender discourses in coaching but suggest additional research is required to ascertain if this equates to an equitable coaching environment. We began the chapter questioning if the sex-integrated competition structure would disrupt, challenge, or reinforce a gendered coaching environment. We end by suggesting that it is perhaps the paradigm of multiple roles within the coaching field that offers greater opportunity to acquire capital which in turn challenges traditional gender discourses of power within the coaching field. We appreciate these constructs are not directly transferable to other sports. We know additional research is required to fully understand the construct and context of capital in equestrian sport, and we call for other sports to do the same. We suggest that an equitable coaching environment will only be achieved if men and women coaches have equal opportunity to acquire capital. It is therefore critical that sporting lead bodies consciously work to understand what that capital is and create habitus in which all coaches have the opportunity to acquire it.

References

Aman, M. P., Yusof, A. B., Ismail, M., & Razali, A. (2018). Pipeline problem: Factors influencing the underrepresentation of women in the top leadership positions of sport organisations. *Malaysian Journal of Movement, Health & Exercise, 7*(2), 151–166.

Beames, S., & Telford, J. (2013). Pierre Bourdieu: Habitus, field and capital in rock climbing. In E. Pike & S. Beames (Eds.), *Outdoor adventure and social theory* (pp. 78–84). Routledge.

BETA. (2019). *The national equestrian survey 2019: Overview report*. BETA.

BHS. (2020a). *BHS career pathways*. Retrieved February 4, 2020, from https://pathways.bhs.org.uk/career-pathways/

BHS. (2020b). *Find an accredited professional coach*. Retrieved February 4, 2020, from www.bhs.org.uk/enjoy-riding/find-an-accredited-professional-coach

Blackett, A. D., Evans, A., & Piggott, D. (2015). Why 'the best way of learning to coach the game is playing the game': Conceptualising 'fast-tracked' high-performance coaching pathways. *Sport, Education and Society, 22*(6), 744–758. https://doi.org/10.1080/13573322.2015.1075494

Bourdieu, P. (1977). *Outline of theory and practice*. Cambridge University Press.

Bourdieu, P. (1979). *Distinction. A social critique of the judgement of taste*. Routledge.

Bourdieu, P. (1985). The social space and the genesis of the groups. *Theory and Society, 14*, 723–744.

Bourdieu, P. (1986/2004). The forms of capital. In S. Ball (Ed.), *The Routledge falmer reader in the sociology of education*. Cambridge University Press.

Bourdieu, P. (1988). *Homo academicus*. Polity Press.

Bourdieu, P. (1989). Social space and symbolic power. *Sociology Theory, 7*, 14–25.

Bourdieu, P. (1990). Structures, habitus, practices. In P. Bourdieu (Ed.), *The logic of practice* (pp. 52–65). Stanford University Press.

Bourdieu, P. (1994). *In other words: Essays towards a reflexive sociology*. Polity Press.

Braddick, T. (2017). Carl Hester – coach of entire British Olympic dressage team, Rider, 3 horses through his program—does he muck stalls, Too? *Dressage-News*. Retrieved March 3, 2020, from https://dressage-news.com/2016/07/11/carl-hester-coach-of-entire-british-olympic-dressage-team-rider-3-horses-through-his-program-does-he-muck-stalls-too/

British Showjumping. (2020). *Officials contacts*. Retrieved October 13, 2020, from www.britishshowjumping.co.uk/officials-contacts.cfm?region=&area=&type=CD&level=CDADV&name=

Connell, R. W., & Messerschmidt, J. W. (2005). Hegemonic masculinity: Rethinking the concept. *Gender & Society*. https://doi.org/10.1177/0891243205278639

Cushion, C. J., Armour, K. M., & Jones, R. L. (2003). Coach education and continuing professional development: Experience and learning to coach. *Quest, 55*(3), 215–230.

Cushion, C. J., & Jones, R. L. (2014). A Bourdieusian analysis of cultural reproduction: Socialisation and the 'hidden curriculum' in professional football. *Sport Education and Society, 19*(3), 276–298.

Dashper, K. (2012). Together, yet still not equal? Sex integration in equestrian sport. In M. Adelman & J. Knijnik (Eds.), *Gender and equestrian sport* (1st ed., pp. 37–53). Springer.

de Haan, D. (2015). *Evaluating the experience of the Olympic and Paralympic Games in the career histories of elite equestrian athletes* (PhD thesis). Loughborough University. https://repository.lboro.ac.uk/articles/Evaluating_the_experience_of_the_Olympic_and_Paralympic_Games_in_the_career_histories_of_elite_equestrian_athletes_/9604532

de Haan, D., & Dumbell, L. (2016). Equestrian sport at the Olympic games from 1900 to 1948. *The International Journal of the History of Sport, 33*(6–7), 648–665. https://doi.org/10.1080/09523367.2016.1195373

de Haan, D., & Dumbell, L. (2019). 10. From the battle field to the board room: The place of gender in sex-integrated sport. In N. Lough & A. N. Guerin (Eds.), *Routledge handbook of the business of women's sport* (1st ed.). Routledge.

de Haan, D., & Norman, L. (2019). Mind the gap: The presence of capital and power in female athlete—male coach relationship within elite rowing. *Sports Coaching Review*. https://doi.org/10.1080/21640629.2019.1567160

Denison, J., Mills, J. P., & Konoval, T. (2017). Sports' disciplinary legacy and the challenge of 'coaching differently'. *Sport, Education and Society, 22*(6), 772–783.

Dumbell, L. C., Rowe, L., & Douglas, J. L. (2018). Demographic profiling of British Olympic equestrian athletes in the twenty-first century. *Sport in Society, 21*(9), 1337–1350. https://doi.org/10.1080/17430437.2017.1388786.

Fielding-Lloyd, B., & Mean, L. (2016). Women training to coach a men's sport: Managing gendered identities and masculinist discourses. *Communication and Sport, 4*(4), 401–423.

Hall, C. (2017). *Teaching equitation science as a collaborative, communicative and ever-changing partnership of coach, student and horse*. ISES 2017–13th International Conference Proceedings. https://equitationscience.com/previous-conferences/2017-13th-international-conference

Halford, S., & Leonard, P. (2001). *Gender, power and organisations: An introduction*. Palgrave Macmillan.

Hancock, M. G., & Hums, M. A. (2016). A "leaky pipeline"? Factors affecting the career development of senior-level female administrators in NCAA division I athletic departments. *Sport Management Review, 19*(2), 198–210.

Hargreaves, J. (2002). *Sporting females: Critical issues in the history and sociology of women's sport*. Taylor & Francis.

IGEQ. (2019). *The international group for equestrian qualifications*. Retrieved February 4, 2020, from https://igeq.org/

Jenkins, R. (2002). *Pierre Bourdieu* (Revised ed.). Routledge.

Kane, M. J. (1995). Resistance/transformation of the oppositional binary: Exposing sport as a continuum. *Journal of Sport and Social Issues, 19*, 191–218.

Laberge, S. (1995). Toward and integration of gender into Bourdieu's concept of cultural capital. *Sociology of Sport Journal, 12*(2), 132–146.

LaVoi, N. M., Becker, M., & Maxwell, H. D. (2007). "Coaching girls": A content analysis of best-selling popular press coaching books. *Women in Sport and Physical Activity Journal, 15*(4), 7–20.

Lewis, C. J., Roberts, S. J., & Andrews, H. (2015). 'Why am I putting myself through this?' Women football coaches' experiences of the football association's coach education process. *Sport, Education and Society*. https://doi.org/10.1080/13573322.2015.1118030

Lewis, V. (2013). *Coaching the 'self-coached rider': What is the role of the coach in elite equestrian sport* (MSc thesis). Hartpury College. student.hartpury.ac.uk/Learning%20

Resources%20Centre/Dissertations/Postgraduate%202013/Victoria%20Lewis,%20Coaching%20the%20Self%20Coached%20Rider%20What%20is%20the%20Role%20of%20the%20Coach%20in%20Elite%20Equestrian%20Sport.pdf

Lovell, T. (2000). Thinking feminism with and against Bourdieu. *Feminist Theory*, *1*(1), 11–32. https://doi.org/10.1177/14647000022229047

McKay, J., Messner, M. A., & Sabo, D. (2000). *Masculinities, gender relations, and sport* (Vol. 11). Sage.

Norman, L. (2008). The UK coaching system is failing women coaches. *International Journal of Sports Science & Coaching*, *3*(4), 447–464.

Norman, L. (2010). Feeling second best: Elite women coaches' experiences. *Sociology of Sport Journal*, *27*(1), 89–104.

Norman, L. (2016). The impact of an 'equal opportunities' ideological framework on coaches' knowledge and practice. *International Review for the Sociology of Sport*, *51*(8), 975–1004.

Norman, L., & McGoldrick, M. (2019). *Understanding the impact of club cultural climates in the context of recruiting women coaches in the women's super league: Phase 2 final report for the English football association*. Carnegie School of Sport, Leeds Beckett University.

Olympic.org. (2020). *Statistics*. Retrieved February 4, 2020, from www.olympic.org/women-in-sport/background/statistics

Print, P. (2011). *The BHS complete manual of equitation*. Kenilworth Press.

Purdy, L., Jones, R., & Cassidy, T. (2009). Negotiation and capital; athletes' use of power in an elite men's rowing program. *Sport, Education & Society*, *14*(3), 321–338.

Taylor, B., & Garratt, D. (2010). The professionalisation of sports coaching: Relations of power, resistance and compliance. *Sport, Education & Society*, *15*(1), 121–139.

TeamGBR Equestrian. (2020). *Team staff*. Retrieve March 12, 2020, from www.equestrianteamgbr.co.uk/team/team-staff/

Theberge, N. (1993). The construction of gender in sport: Women, coaching, and the naturalization of difference. *Social Problems*, *40*(3), 301–313.

Thorpe, H. (2005). Jibbing the gender order: Females in the snowboarding culture. *Sport in Society*, *8*(1), 76–100. https://doi.org/10.1080/1743043052000316632

Thorpe, H. (2009). Bourdieu, feminism and female physical culture: Gender reflexivity and the habitus-field complex. *Sociology of Sport Journal*, *26*(4), 491–516.

UEFA. (2020). *Coach education*. Retrieved February 22, 2020, from www.uefa.com/insideuefa/football-development/technical/coach-education/index.html

Yoshiga, C. C., & Higuchi, M. (2003). Rowing performance of female and male rowers. *Scandinavian Journal of Medicine & Science in Sports*, *13*(5), 317–321.

6 It's on Boys! University Coach Educators and the Production, Maintenance, and Disruption of Gender Structures

Natalie Barker-Ruchti, Laura Purdy and Lolita Dudeniene

A Vignette About a Lecture in a University Sports Coach Education Programme

It's Tuesday morning and Tanja[1] is sitting in the fourth lecture of the exercise science course she is taking as part of the university sports coaching education programme she is reading as a year 2 student. The lecturer, Thomas, is talking about the identification and development of talented young athletes. Tanja is interested in this topic as she coaches girls and boys of this age. The topic has relevance because her athletes can be selected for regional teams and national championships. Thomas is a confident speaker, and his PowerPoint slides present the different measurements that can be taken to identify talent. Tanja listens carefully to Thomas, who is describing the findings of three different studies.

Who are these studies on? Tanja wonders. She quickly scans the slides for more information.

On one of the slides, she can read information about the sample.

Ah, now I can see it. It's on BOYS! Of course. Oh, wait, in one of the three studies they've included a female tennis player . . . that's typical. But at least there's one female athlete—that's more than zero.

Now, Thomas is talking about biological age. He confidently links early talent identification with early drop-out.

But what about girls? Tanja is sceptical. *How are girls being identified and developed? Do they even measure girls? How's this done? He's generalising, but he's excluding 50% of the population! Where are the girl research participants? Why aren't they part of this sample? I have to ask him. Oh gosh, but my questioning's probably going to come across as aggressive.*

Tanja carefully considers how she can ask Thomas about the lack of girls in the research sample. She does not want to come across as aggressive or challenging. She is a bit nervous now, which annoys her, but puts up her hand.

"I've noticed that the research you present is based on boys. What about girls? What would the results say if the research participants were female?"

The lecturer appears a little taken aback. Perhaps he is not used to being questioned. But Thomas agrees that the results are based on boy participants and that the results would differ if girls had been included. He also agrees that it would be interesting to know about girls.

"Ok, thank you, but why isn't this researched?", Tanja asks.

Tobias, who is sitting near them, rolls his eyes. "*Here we go*", he mutters.

"*Well, identifying talent and researching girls of this age is complicated; at that age, they've most likely started pubertal development, which makes it difficult to use standardised tests*".

The lecturer's answer disappoints Tanja. Suz, who sits next to her, sighs rather loudly. They exchange meaningful looks.

In the break, Tanja talks to some of her female student peers. John and Tobias are also listening. They speak in hushed voices about Thomas, his lecture, and the way he generalises. Anna is quite frustrated and says perhaps a little too loudly:

"*I can't believe we're presented with such lopsided material. I mean it's 2020. We're only learning about the identification and development of talented BOYS. Even the images on the slides are on boys. Gosh, for researchers to think it is okay to ONLY focus on boys, it's such an easy way out. And I don't like the way he talks. It's so certain! Even for boys, I know that talent identification and development is really complex*".

SUZ NODS AND RESPONDS: "*I agree, but you should be used to this from football education! That's how it is there. It's guys teaching about guys' football. Everything's based on men's football. Remember?*"

MATILDA THINKS ALOUD: "*But the courses are made up of men who're coaching men, so I guess this is why they're always the focus?*"

SUZ INTERJECTS: "*But the football federation has changed this. At least they use examples from women's football and the pictures aren't always of male players. I took some of their courses after the last Women's World Cup. They provided women's data on physical load, number of passes and so on. I was really happy about this, but some of the guys in the class were so pissed off that they had to learn about women's football!*"

Anna sighs. "*Yeah, one wonders why they can't do it here. I mean, Thomas isn't the only one who does what he does. We've even had female lecturers using mainly male examples*".

MATILDA: "*I haven't paid attention to that before, especially the pictures. I'm going to keep an eye on them now. I wonder if lecturers think about this when they prepare their material?*"

Tobias joins in the conversation: "*You're thinking too much about this and making it bigger than it is. A photo's just a photo. And, you heard what Thomas said, there isn't much research on girls so you really can't blame him for content that is one-sided. He just presents what he can cover in the time that he has. Besides, in that study there was a female tennis player*".

Thomas is calling to continue the class and the students return to the lecture room. Tanja is still thinking about the situation.

I must continue to question Thomas. My student peers won't say anything, they're too young or too scared. I don't want simple answers; I want to learn and discuss and understand the nuances of the subject, that's why I'm here! We have elite sport for women, so we should be taught about this as much as what's relevant for men.

After the session, John approaches Tanja.

"You know Tanja, I haven't really thought about what you asked and said earlier. But you're right. It's so male-dominated, and everything's about winning. You know, when I was doing circus education, it was different. They spoke about the human side, and how to influence individuals beyond performance. It was a bit more like the women coach educators in our programme. They make connections, relate it to the bigger picture, and they're much more open to discuss something. I like that!"

"Yeah, it's like that, isn't it? The women in the social sciences, the men in the lab". Tanja appears a bit lost. *"You know, I would love to choose a lab science research topic for my Bachelor thesis. Just to make a point. Women CAN do lab research! But I wouldn't know what to do. It just feels so natural for me to do a social science project. Something that's more real-life".* Tanja looks through the window, contemplating. *"Right, there's no time for more discussion. I've got a coaching session to plan!"*

As Tanja rushes out of the university building, she continues to reflect. *Lecturers have a responsibility to present results on men AND women. They have so much power to teach us knowledge and to affect us and our coaching practice. Why don't they tell us the herstories?*

Introduction and Background

Globally, except for a few women-dominated sports (e.g., synchronised swimming and netball), most coaches are men. This critique is also relevant in coach education (CE), in which the educator and participant populations are predominantly male. While research has looked at women's experiences in CE, how coach educators do and undo, gender has escaped attention. The purpose of this chapter is, thus, to (1) consider how university CE and coach educators produce, maintain, and disrupt gender inequalities and (2) present actionable recommendations to support universities and other institutions providing CE, in developing gender-equitable education. To do this, we use the aforementioned vignette that we had produced from in-class discussions with year 1, 2, and 3 university CE students in Lithuania, Sweden, and the UK on how they perceive and experience male and female coach educators and CE content. In what follows, we outline existing literature on CE and the role of coach educators and then present the three university CE contexts represented by the authors of the chapter. We then describe how we created and analysed the vignette and sketch Risman's (2009) "gender structure theory". After presenting the effects gender structures have on CE and CE programmes, curriculum content and delivery, and how these may be disrupted, we conclude the chapter with actionable recommendations to develop gender-equitable education.

Coach Education, the Role of Coach Educators, and Gender

CE has been identified as key to improved coaching and the appreciation of coaching as a profession (Armour, 2011; Woodman, 1993). Within CE, coach educators, and their positions, dispositions and actions are argued to play an important role in facilitating the learning of CE students (Cushion et al., 2019). Coach educators, however, do not simply and unproblematically deliver CE content. Their teaching does not occur in isolation of social ideals and norms and institutional boundaries. Rather, educators are engaged in a dynamic struggle over the representation and definitions of knowledge, a struggle that is constituted by social ideals and norms, and with relevance to sports coaching, socialisation in sport, previous CE and other forms of education, experiences coaching, and possibly sports science research (Cushion et al., 2019). This socialisation, and the expertise that it generates, has been argued to be synonymous with men and masculinity (Fielding-Lloyd & Meân, 2008).

Much literature has over the years discussed the gendered nature of CE and how those who are not White, middle-class, non-disabled, and male are "othered" (Graham et al., 2013; Lewis et al., 2018; Norman, 2008, 2018; Schlesinger & Weigelt-Schlesinger, 2012). Indeed, research on female participants has shown that CE contexts can be intimidating, and for curriculum content to be patronising and even irrelevant (e.g., Barker-Ruchti et al., 2015; Clarkson et al., 2019). Efforts and measures to amend this inequality have not provided satisfactory results (Banwell et al., 2019; Norman et al., 2018). Towards this end, Fielding-Lloyd and Meân (2008) argue that CE, in its various forms, represents a dominant mechanism that positions coaching knowledge as male/masculine and women coaches and women's coaching practices as "other" and thus inferior. Research examining these mechanisms to understand the influence gender ideals have on CE, coach educators, and curriculum content and delivery, has, however, received minimal scientific scholarship.

An area that researchers have shown to be impacted by gender is the educational materials that are being used in CE (Alsarve, 2018; Fielding-Lloyd & Meân, 2008; Grahn, 2014). This research demonstrates that the male-centred hegemony that infiltrates sport also affects educational texts, which in turn, (re)produce the male/masculine and female/feminine binary, and through this, normative hegemonic knowledge and practices. With relevance to CE, Grahn (2014; see also Alsarve, 2018; Svender et al., 2011) has shown how Swedish federation-legitimised CE textbooks reinforce gender ideals through the texts' essentialist descriptions of girls' and boys' bodies and bodily development during puberty. The authors write that a functional discourse assumes that boys are naturally suited to sport because of biological characteristics such as durability and muscle mass, whereas girls' bodies and their development are assumed problematic and non-performing.

In addition to educational materials, another important area discussed in relation to CE is learner compliance. Learner compliance as a form of gatekeeping to maintain the "status quo" of coaching knowledge and the coach educator has been identified as particularly concerning (Piggott, 2012). Thus, although scholars have not adopted a gender perspective to examine how CE and coach educators (re)produce, maintain, and disrupt gender inequalities, it is clear from the existing literature that coach educators have a central role in legitimising and recreating coaches' practice and acting as "linch-pins in educational reforms" (Cushion et al., 2019, p. 533; see also Blackett et al., 2015). In our view, it is thus possible to assume that the present mechanisms that gender CE (Fielding-Lloyd & Meân, 2008), the coach population (Norman, 2008, 2018; Purdy & Potrac, 2016), and CE texts (Grahn, 2014; Svender et al., 2011), significantly shape (i.e., gender) CE programmes, coach educators, curriculum content and delivery, and educator–student interactions. The vignette presented at the outset of this chapter highlights how this knowledge and practice is "lived" in a classroom setting and often "taken for granted".

Coach Education in Lithuania, Sweden, and the UK

CE in the three nations represented in this chapter—Lithuania, Sweden, and the United Kingdom—offers unique contexts as they have contrasting sport systems and structures that impact how coaching is perceived and understood and, consequently, how CE is positioned and delivered (González-Serrano et al., 2017; Hall et al., 2019; Hedberg, 2015; Piggott, 2012).

In Lithuania, only the Lithuanian Sports University offers CE: a four-year Bachelor of Sports that emphasises the biosciences (e.g., functional anatomy; biochemistry; sports and exercise physiology; motor control, neuromechanics, and learning; sports medicine; and nutrition). The dominant form of delivery is didactic, although applied coaching knowledge is also taught. The scientific content is delivered by an equal number of male and female staff; however, the pedagogical content is largely delivered by women. The student population is approximately 60% male and 40% female, who pay tuition to study at the university. As coaches are required to complete training in a higher education institution in the field of sport to gain employment, many of the coaching workforce in Lithuania have graduated from the programme offered by the Sports University, formerly the Lithuanian Academy of Physical Education.

In Sweden, CE is provided at universities and by the Swedish Sports Confederation and national sports federations (Hedberg, 2015). All major universities in the country offer sport science education, with several of them also providing sports coaching profiles. At the University of Gothenburg, where the chapter's first author was employed from 2011 to early 2019, a three-year bachelor programme in sports coaching is offered. The programme is broad, entailing courses in the common sport science areas (e.g., sport pedagogy; sport sociology; biomechanics and exercise science; and sport psychology). The programme's student population consists predominantly of male students with backgrounds in team sports (e.g., football, handball, and ice hockey). On average, 10% of students are female. In terms of teaching staff, the courses relating to the natural sciences were delivered by men and the social science courses by women. The dominant teaching approach was didactic; however, there was a push towards problem- and case-based pedagogy. To gain coaching employment in Sweden, students also complete the CE offered by national sports federations.

In the United Kingdom, over 245 undergraduate degree courses, offered by 95 providers, relate to sports coaching (UCAS, 2020; Hall et al., 2019). These programmes vary from single honours to joint programmes (e.g., Sports Coaching and Physical Education, and Sports Coaching and Management) and are 3–4 years long. The programmes range in emphasis with content aligned with sport and exercise sciences, and physical education or management. A search of university webpages identified that many of the sports coaching programmes have a higher percentage of male staff than female, a ratio that also extends to their students. Students pay to study and, in a majority of cases, they also must complete the CE of their national sports federations in order to gain employment.

Creating and Analysing the Vignette

Based on our reflections and discussions with students in Lithuania, Sweden, and the UK on their perceptions and experiences of male and female coach educators and CE content, the description of how Thomas gave a lecture on talent identification and development basing his comments on boy research samples was identified as a suitable plot for the vignette. Using this plot, the drafting of the vignette focused on the one hand on bringing together the students' attitudes, beliefs, and perceptions (Hings et al., 2018; Paquette et al., 2019; Schinke et al., 2016; Fancher & O'Connell-Whittet, 2018; Schinke et al., 2016), but on the other, to demonstrate how these commonalities could be disrupted (i.e., Tanja's questions in class). As much as possible, direct quotes from the discussion sessions were included. In a second step and in an attempt to ensure that the vignette represented our interpretations of students' experiences, we sent the draft vignette to the students who most directly featured in it. Their input further developed the vignette and provided us with the assurance that we could share the text with others.

To consider the vignette on how university CE and coach educators produce, maintain, and disrupt gender inequalities, we adopted Risman's (2009,

2018) "gender structure theory". Gender structure theory focuses on explaining how gender structures constitute inequalities through processes at the individual, interactional, and institutional levels. At the individual level, gender structures are understood to socialise individuals and to develop identities and selves (Risman, 2011); while at the interactional level, they normalise how individuals are expected to behave. These structures are organised and represented by formal institutions and, at the social and institutional level, create rules and categories that regulate (groups of) individuals. Importantly, Risman (2004) integrates the three levels of influence in a "web of interconnection between gendered selves, the cultural expectations that help explain interactional patterns, and institutional regulations" (p. 431). In focusing on these three levels of influence, we return to the vignette to outline how gender affects CE, coach educators and students, and their interactions.

Gendered Institutions: University Coach Education Programmes

At an institutional level, Risman (2018) theorises that gender structures are formalised into institutional laws, rules, and organisational norms, which in turn determine practice, and create gendered material goods and influence the distribution of resources. In our first step to analyse the vignette, it is thus important to understand the structures that frame and shape (and gender) the university CE degree programmes the vignette represents.

In the past two decades, university degrees in sports coaching have increased around the world (Hall et al., 2019). Such development has been welcomed by those in the field as it has been argued that offering a degree in sports coaching strengthens perceptions that it is an intellectual endeavour and a legitimate vocation (Bales, 2006; Jones, 2006; Hall et al., 2019). Adding to this are trends in higher education in which scientism has been used to gain and maintain legitimacy (Langbert, 2018). However, the rationalisation and domination of scientific knowledge have resulted in the promotion of a masculine culture (Bryant & Pini, 2006; Rhoten & Pfirman, 2007; Simon et al., 2017), which has led to exclusive educational contexts that are being defined as "chilly" for "others" (i.e. women, individuals with minority ethnic backgrounds and/or with disabilities and/or identify as LGBTQ+) (Allan & Madden, 2006; Simon et al., 2017). For instance, STEM subjects, which have similar characteristics to the field of sports coaching, have been criticised for being professions that are steeped in raced, classed, and gendered notions that have historically privileged White, middle-class men (Witz, 1990; Powell & Sang, 2015; Sattari & Sandefur, 2019). Consequently, they maintain occupational segregation through the construction of women (and other minorities) as different (Bolton & Muzio, 2007), and, by extension, inferior. The danger here is that gender structures, as Tobias, one of the students in the vignette, exemplifies through his impatience and eye-rolling, can lead to some perceiving this under-representation and treatment of those that are othered as "natural" and "their fault" (Francis et al., 2017; Fielding-Lloyd & Meân, 2011), rather than an issue that institutions produce because they are gendered. Thus, as Fielding-Lloyd and Meân (2011) argue, women (and other minority) coaches are expected to change or adapt, thereby reproducing the discursive practices that oppress them, as opposed to making changes at the institutional level in the way sport is constructed, maintained, and organised.

In relation to CE, degree programmes have traditionally been structured around the scientific elements of coaching with the socio-pedagogical receiving less attention (Cassidy et al., 2015). Typically, CE is compartmentalised and the scientific content is viewed as most important for/to coaches, with courses that are based on such sciences (e.g., biomechanics; exercise physiology; motor learning and sports nutrition; and match analysis) taking up a significant component of a degree programme. Furthermore, sports coaching is a field that has tended to attract White men (lecturers and students), a majority who are non-disabled and from middle-class backgrounds (Graham et al., 2013; Lewis et al., 2018; Norman, 2008, 2018; Schlesinger & Weigelt-Schlesinger, 2012). Therefore, in keeping with earlier arguments, the emphasis on science and a lack of diversity in the field has contributed to the socialisation of coaches who view coaching and scientific coaching knowledge as male/masculine. Here, the low representation of women, as individuals from minority backgrounds can, in part, be attributed to institutional characteristics that make the field of sports coaching unfriendly and exclusive (i.e., "chilly"). In CE, this side-lining or exclusion helps explain why female participants have found CE to often be patronising, irrelevant, and a negative experience (Barker-Ruchti et al., 2015; Norman, 2008; Purdy & Potrac, 2016; Schlesinger & Weigelt-Schlesinger, 2012).

Based on the preceding argument, at an institutional level, the education of sports coaches is rooted in a system of gendered, classed, ableist, and raced structures (Powell & Sang, 2015). There is often an unawareness of this as, through their routineness, the "isms" have been rendered invisible to most of those within the system (Powell & Sang, 2015; Webb, 2002). Despite recent efforts to include "other" voices, women are still made to feel that the "real" curriculum is a male-centred one (Rich, 1979). In the vignette, Tanja and Suz's frustrations with the one-sided representation of talent identification and development, as well as their experiences of male students' reactions to the presentation of data on women footballers in a football CE course are representative of this male-centring and the othering effects it has on female students.

Individual Gendering: Coach Educators' and Students' Socialisation

Risman (2004) theorises the socialisation of individuals as gendered and to entail an internalisation process that constitutes identities and constructs selves. This socialisation intersects with other social structures (e.g., class, ethnicity, ability, and age) and is shaped by historical and contextual specificity. This gendered socialisation has endurance; however, Risman (2004) acknowledges that individuals have, at least in today's Western contexts, possibilities to effectively reject dominant gender ideals, norms, and routines and through this, generate more gender-equitable outcomes.

Based on Risman's socialisation understanding, Thomas and the CE students' prior socialisation constitute gendered identities, selves, and actions. For Thomas, as is common for coach educators, his sport, sport science, and possibly sports coaching experiences would have played a key role in socialising him into the confident expert he represents in the classroom. The experiences would also have influenced his didactic teaching approach and the strategies he employed to give weight to his expert position, such as he adopted through confident demeanour, deterministic linking of causes and effects, and leaving out information that could be critiqued. His expression of surprise at Tanja's question about the sample, and his unwillingness to engage in a critical discussion on the lack of research on girl athletes, are also techniques that coach educators have been found to employ to deify certain "knowledge, rendering unassailable the ideas and practices they were presenting" (Piggott, 2012, p. 549).

For the students represented in the vignette, prior education experiences would also have been influential in socialising them to accept the passive learner role. Furthermore, and with relevance to CE, Piggott (2012) writes that students may be socialised to not challenge course content because questioning a teacher may be perceived to cause negative impressions and lower grades. Tanja's nervousness and efforts to prepare her questions, as other students not asking questions, is illustrative. In turn, students' infrequent questioning and apparent acceptance of curriculum content reinforce the authority of (male) teachers and the knowledge they (re)present. Focusing on female students in male-dominated university education, research has pointed to how the empowerment of teachers and particular knowledges marginalises, and importantly, creates a "chilly classroom climate" that discourages those that are "othered" to speak up (Allan & Madden, 2006). The "feminist fatigue" or "a collective eye roll" reactions that Tobias adopts when Tanja questions Thomas' presentation of the research he uses to deliver curriculum content is indicative of the chilly classroom climates this can create (Cruger, 2018, p. 87). Unfortunately, this chilliness is difficult to recognise as passive/quiet (male and female) student behaviour fits the dominant expectation.

Yet, interruptions are possible and Tanja's speaking up represents one such example. Despite concerns over how she is perceived by Thomas and her classmates, she is unwilling to accept the dominant-subordinate power relations that he is cultivating and the simplified knowledge that he presents. However, caution about the effectiveness of Tanja's challenge is warranted. Research on female students in male-dominated university education has demonstrated that women who ask questions may be perceived in a negative light because they are breaking traditional expectations (Allan & Madden, 2006; Banchefsky & Park, 2018). Certainly, Tanja is aware of this risk and Tobias' eye rolling may be a sign of her being labelled as a feminist troublemaker.

Gendered Interactions: Encounters in Coach Education

Risman (2004) theorises that gender structures create gendered interactional expectations that prescribe how individuals should act in social encounters. These expectations are shaped by individual socialisation and intersect with other social inequalities. They may also be constituted by laws and/or institutional regulations. As mentioned earlier, the gendered expectations are not set in concrete; changes in individual identities and moral accountability, as well as institutional laws, rules, and organisational norms, have and may change interactional expectations at any point in time.

Risman's lens points to the gendered interactions represented in the vignette: Tanja's exchange with Thomas is perhaps most typical of a male educator-female learner encounter (Allan & Madden, 2006). However, it is important to acknowledge that the institutionalised education expectations (i.e., learner compliance) also influence the way the encounter occurred. The interaction between Tobias and the female students discussing Thomas' teaching is such an example. Here, Tobias is embodying the non-challenging (male) student that Piggott (2012) has identified as common in CE, while the female students (i.e., Tanja) are adopting the "responsible student" role that is interpreted as feminist trouble making (Cruger, 2018).

Another interaction in the vignette that demonstrates gendered expectations is the role modelling between coach educators and female CE students. In the vignette, Thomas models the practices of sport science laboratories, an area that Tanja, and as research has shown female students, struggle to identify with, while the female coach educators, signify a social science approach that female students have been shown to prefer (Rhoten & Pfirman, 2007). According to Cushion and colleagues (2019), coach educators are indeed able to steer CE students' interests and learning. Fostering female students to engage with disciplines and research areas perceived distant to their gender, such as through mentoring programmes or efforts to represent a diverse population within professional fields (e.g., on university websites and advertising for education programmes), has shown to positively affect study and career goals (Cheryan et al., 2015; Reid et al., 2017). In Tanja's case, her interest in a lab-based Bachelor thesis project could possibly have been realised had strategic mentoring, advertising, and/or recruitment been implemented.

In summary of our three-level analysis using Risman's (2009, 2018) theorising, gender structures constitute CE, socialise coach educators and CE students, and normalise the interactions between and among them. As a result, gender structures are being (re)produced and maintained. The structures are not permanent though, and Tanja's questioning represents one example of how they may be interrupted. However, further interruptions are necessary to prevent CE from (re)producing gender inequalities. In the following, we present actionable recommendations that can support universities and other institutions providing CE programmes, in developing gender-equitable education.

Actionable Recommendations

In continuing with Risman's gender structure theory, particularly her suggestion that social change can begin by disrupting gender expectations, the actionable recommendations we present in the following first focus on minimal easy-to-implement actions that individual coach educators and students can adopt to create (more) gender-equitable CE. In a second step, we also outline recommendations that universities and other CE institutions can adopt.

At the *individual level*, a first action that coach educators can adopt is to include curriculum content and illustrations that feature girl/women athletes, as equally as possible to that of boys/men. Where this may be limited or not available, the educators should acknowledge the lack of data on girls/women and discuss with students how knowledge based on more diverse samples would differ between genders. Such presentation and discussions would better enable students to understand the nuances of the subject as they attempt to apply their knowledge to practice. Moreover, students would be socialised to view diversity of the population, as well as engage in discussions and debates about the material presented to them, as the norm. In turn, this should lessen the male/masculine and female/feminine knowledge binary and reduce prejudice towards (female) student questioning (e.g., in the vignette: eye rolling; "here we go again" comment) and frustrations about coach educators and educational content (e.g., in the vignette: Tanja feeling let down about the presented research being on boys; men being frustrated with content being on female footballers). Lastly, acknowledging the nuances of the subject (and its application) and discussing limitations has the potential to balance out the hierarchical educator–student relationship (Naskali & Keskitalo-Foley, 2019; Ylöstalo & Brunila, 2018).

A second action we wish to recommend at the individual level is for coach educators to move away from the traditional didactic approach to teaching, which research has argued to be synonymous with men and masculinity and to "other" those who are not White, middle-class, non-disabled, and male (Graham et al., 2013; Lewis et al., 2018; Norman, 2008, 2018; Schlesinger & Weigelt-Schlesinger, 2012). CE literature offers various non-traditional and innovative pedagogical strategies of delivery that have demonstrated to positively affect student engagement, classroom climates, and learning

(Driska & Gould, 2014; Jones et al., 2012; Roberts & Ryrie, 2014; Stoszkowski et al., 2017), and arguably, such pedagogical strategies would also contribute to being more (gender) inclusive (Naskali & Keskitalo-Foley, 2019; Ylöstalo & Brunila, 2018).

Lastly, we would like to direct an individual-level actionable recommendation at students. As Tanja did, we recommend students to (continue to) ask questions about curriculum content and if need be, highlight (gender) inequalities and gaps through asking questions in class, and through noting critique in course/modules and programme evaluations. We further recommend that students bring their perspectives and experiences of education into CE programme boards and student unions. If managed effectively, such involvement can facilitate students' understanding of educational challenges and provide solutions that suit both students and educators (Bilodeau et al., 2019).

At the *institutional level*, a first actionable recommendation we propose is for higher education authorities and international/national CE bodies that provide sports coaching programmes to check if and how their CE fulfils the (gender equality) requirements outlined in national Higher Education Acts. In the Swedish Higher Education Act (Swedish Higher Education Act, Initial provisions; Section 5), it is stated that "Equality between women and men shall always be taken into account and promoted in the operations of higher education institutions". In Lithuania and the UK, gender equality is not built into their Higher Education Acts (see Lithuania's Law on Equal Treatment, 2003, and UK's Equality Act, 2010[2]).

A second institutional recommendation is that those responsible for the coordination of CE programmes guide and follow up the implementation of gender equality in CE in general and curriculum content in particular. Possible ways ensure quality is through evaluation processes and/or educators' professional development. In terms of the former, questions regarding gender equality and gender-balanced curriculum content should be included, and its evaluations taken up to address possible shortcomings. In terms of the latter, research on professional development has shown that male university staff had the greatest increase in awareness of gendered structures and the inequalities these generate (Bird, 2011). We thus recommend professional development activities for coach educators and for such activities to focus on how curriculum content and delivery, and educator–student relationships and interactions can contribute to "chilly" classroom climates that disadvantage students, and how in turn, gender-balanced content, alternative delivery methods, and role modelling, can be less "chilly" and more inclusive.

A final institutional actionable recommendation is for universities, and sport science departments particularly, to create gender-balanced teaching teams. Sport science and sports coaching research indicate a gendered distribution of male and female scholars in the natural and social sciences (in the vignette: men in natural sciences and women in social sciences) and across all levels of the degree (women teaching at the introductory levels of CE). To change this gendered distribution, recruitment of staff to create gender-balanced educator teams, in combination with the actionable recommendations outlined previously, would most certainly facilitate inclusive education (Banchefsky & Park, 2018). Gender-balanced teams are further likely to result in research that is conducted with more heterogeneous research populations, which would result in literature that outlines the diverse nature of sport, coaching, and performance.

We believe that the actionable recommendations we have outlined earlier have the potential to disrupt the gender structures that Risman (2009) theorises to gender institutions, individuals, and interactions. Such disruptions are important for CE as they will contribute to creating gender-balanced CE curriculum, inclusive classrooms, engaged students, and ultimately, the knowledge that students have a right to acquire.

Conclusion

This chapter aimed to consider how university CE and coach educators produce, maintain, and disrupt gender inequalities and present actionable recommendations to support universities, and other institutions providing CE, in developing gender-equitable education. Through the vignette presented at the chapter's beginning and drawing on Risman's (2004, 2009, 2011, 2018) "gender structure theory", we demonstrated how CE programmes, coach educators, curriculum content and delivery, and educator–student interactions are gendered and gender, and in so doing, (re)produce gender inequalities. Particularly, the vignette reveals the "taken for granted" gender structures of which the lecturer and several of the students appeared to be unaware of, and consequently, reinforced by their (in)action. If the literature has identified that CE is limited in affecting student and coaching practice, then not addressing gender structures increases the risk of reproducing the status quo. Therefore, if CE is meant to have an impact, coach educators (e.g., lecturers) should have the professional responsibility to acknowledge and disrupt the gender structures which are reinforced in and through their practice. While additional research is necessary to further our knowledge of these areas, our actionable recommendations are hopefully a starting point to disrupt the existing gender structures in CE.

Notes

1. All names included in the vignette are pseudonyms.
2. Lithuanian www.lygybe.lt/data/public/uploads/2016/10/law-on-equal-treatment_no.-ix-1826.pdf / Swedish Higher Education Act: www.uhr.se/en/start/laws-and-regulations/Laws-and-regula-tions/The-Swedish-Higher-Education-Act/#chapter1 / UK Equality Act: www.legislation. gov.uk/ukpga/2010/ 15/contents

References

Allan, E. J., & Madden, M. (2006). Chilly classrooms for female undergraduate students: A question of method. *The Journal of Higher Education*, 77(4), 684–711.

Alsarve, D. (2018). Addressing gender equality: Enactments of gender and hegemony in the educational textbooks used in Swedish sports coaching and educational programmes. *Sport, Education & Society*, 23(9), 840–852.

Armour, K. (2011). Effective career-long professional development for teachers and coaches. In K. Armour (Ed.), *Sport pedagogy: An introduction for teaching and coaching* (pp. 229–243). Prentice Hall.

Bales, J. (2006). Introduction: Coach education. *The Sport Psychologist*, 20(2), 126–127.

Banchefsky, S., & Park, B. (2018). Negative gender ideologies and gender-science stereotypes are more pervasive in male-dominated academic disciplines. *Social Sciences*, 7(2), 27.

Banwell, J., Stirling, A., & Kerr, G. (2019). Towards a process for advancing women in coaching through mentorship. *International Journal of sports Science and Coaching*, 14(6), 703–713.

Barker-Ruchti, N., Lindgren, E. C., Hofmann, A., Sinning, S., & Shelton, C. (2015). Tracing the career paths of top-level women football coaches: Turning points to understand and develop sport coaching careers. *Sports Coaching Review*, 3(2), 117–131.

Bilodeau, P. A., Liu, X. M., & Cummings, B. A. (2019). Partnered educational governance: Rethinking student agency in undergraduate medical education. *Academic Medicine*, 94(10), 1443–1447.

Bird, S. R. (2011). Unsettling universities' incongruous, gendered bureaucratic structures: A case-study approach. *Gender, Work & Organization*, 18(2), 202–230.

Blackett, A. D., Evans, A., & Piggott, D. (2015). Why 'the best way of learning to coach the game is playing the game': Conceptualising 'fast-tracked' high-performance coaching pathways. *Sport, Education and Society*, 22(6), 744–758.

Bolton, S. C., & Muzio, D. (2007). Can't live with 'em: Can't live without 'em: Gendered segmentation in the legal profession. *Sociology*, 41(1), 47–64.

Bryant, L., & Pini, B. (2006). Towards an understanding of gender and capital in constituting biotechnologies in agriculture. *Sociologia Ruralis*, 46(4), 261–279.

Cassidy, T., Jones, R. L., & Potrac, P. (2015). *Understanding sport coaching: The pedagogical, social and cultural foundations of coaching practice*. Routledge.

Cheryan, S., Master, A., & Meltzoff, A. N. (2015, February 11). Cultural stereotypes as gatekeepers: Increasing girls' interest in computer science and engineering by diversifying stereotypes [hypothesis and theory]. *Frontiers in Psychology*, 6(49). https://doi.org/10.3389/fpsyg.2015.00049

Clarkson, B. G., Cox, E., & Thelwell, R. C. (2019). Negotiating gender in the English football workplace: Composite vignettes of women head coaches' experiences. *Women in Sport and Physical Activity Journal*, 27, 73–84.

Cruger, K. M. (2018). Applying challenge-based learning in the (feminist) communication classroom: Positioning students as knowledgeable change agents. *Communication Teacher*, 32(2), 87–101.

Cushion, C. J., Griffiths, M., & Armour, K. (2019). Professional coach educators in-situ: A social analysis of practice. *Sport, Education and Society*, 24(5), 533–546.

Driska, A. P., & Gould, D. R. (2014). Evaluating a problem-based group learning strategy for online, graduate-level coach education. *Kinesiology Review*, *3*(4), 227–234.

Fancher, P., & O'Connell-Whittet, E. (2018). Misogyny in the classroom: Two women lecturer's experiences. *Composition Studies*, *46*(2), 192–194.

Fielding-Lloyd, B., & Meân, L. J. (2008). Standards and separatism: The discursive construction of gender in English soccer coach education. *Sex Roles*, *58*(1–2), 24–39.

Fielding-Lloyd, B., & Meân, L. J. (2011). "I don't think I can catch it": Women, confidence and responsibility in football coach education. *Soccer & Society*, *12*(3), 345–364.

Francis, B., Archer, L., Moote, J., DeWitt, J., MacLeod, E., & Yeomans, L. (2017). The construction of physics as a quintessentially male subject: Young people's perceptions of gender issues in access to physics. *Sex Roles*, *76*, 156–174.

González-Serrano, M. H., Crespo Hervás, J., Pérez-Campos, C., & Calabuig-Moreno, F. (2017). The importance of developing the entrepreneurial capacities in sport sciences university students. *International Journal of Sport Policy and Politics*, *9*(4), 625–640.

Graham, L., McKenna, M., & Fleming, S. (2013). "What d'you know, you're a girl!" Gendered experiences of sport coach education. *Journal of Hospitality, Leisure, Sport & Tourism Education*, *13*, 70–77.

Grahn, K. (2014). Alternative discourses in the coaching of high performance youth sport: Exploring the language of sustainability. *Reflective Practice*, *15*(1), 40–52.

Hall, E. T., Cowan, D. T., & Vickery, W. (2019). 'You don't need a degree to get a coaching job': Investigating the employability of sports coaching degree students. *Sport, Education and Society*, *24*(8), 883–903.

Hedberg, M. (2015). Coaching and coach education in Sweden. *International Sport Coaching Journal*, *2*(2), 187–191.

Hings, R. F., Wagstaff, C. R. D., Anderson, V., Gilmore, S., & Thelwell, R. C. (2018). Professional challenges in elite sports medicine and science: Composite vignettes of practitioner emotional labor. *Psychology of Sport & Exercise*, *35*, 66–73. https://doi.org/10.1016/j.psychsport.2017.11.007

Jones, R. L. (2006). How can educational concepts inform sports coaching? In R. L. Jones (Ed.), *The sports coach as educator: Re-conceptualising sports coaching* (pp. 3–13). Routledge.

Jones, R. L., Morgan, K., & Harris, K. (2012). Developing coaching pedagogy: Seeking a better integration of theory and practice. *Sport, Education & Society*, *17*(3), 313–329.

Langbert, M. B. (2018). University scientism and American economic interests. *Industry and Higher Education*, *32*(3), 143–151.

Lewis, C. J., Roberts, S. J., & Andrews, H. (2018). 'Why am I putting myself through this?' Women football coaches' experiences of the football association's coach education process. *Sport, Education & Society*, *23*(1), 28–39.

Naskali, P., & Keskitalo-Foley, S. (2019). Mainstream university pedagogy in feminist perspective. *Gender & Education*, *31*(1), 100–116.

Norman, L. (2008). The UK coaching system is failing women coaches. *International Journal of Sports Science & Coaching*, *3*(4), 447–476.

Norman, L. (2018). "It's sport, why does it matter?" Professional coaches' perceptions of equity training. *Sports Coaching Review*, *7*(2), 190–211.

Norman, L., Rankin-Wright, A. J., & Allison, W. (2018). 'It's a concrete ceiling; it's not even glass': Understanding tenets of organizational culture that supports the progression of women as coaches and coach developers. *Journal of Sport and Social Issues*, *42*(5), 393–414.

Paquette, K., Trudel, P., Duarte, T., & Cundari, G. (2019). Participating in a learner-centered coach education program: Composite vignettes of coaches' and coach educators' experiences. *International Sport Coaching Journal*, *6*(3), 274–284.

Piggott, D. (2012). Coaches' experiences of formal coach education: A critical sociological investigation. *Sport, Education & Society*, *17*(4), 535–554.

Powell, A., & Sang, K. J. C. (2015). Everyday experiences of sexism in male-dominated professions: A Bourdieusian perspective. *Sociology*, *49*(5), 919–936.

Purdy, L., & Potrac, P. (2016). Am I just not good enough? The creation, development and questioning of a coaching identity. *Sport, Education & Society*, *21*, 778–795.

Reid, J., Smith, E., Iamsuk, N., & Miller, J. (2017). Balancing the equation: Mentoring first-year female STEM students at a regional university. *International Journal of Innovation in Science and Mathematics Education*, *24*(4), 18–30.

Rhoten, D., & Pfirman, S. (2007). Women in interdisciplinary science: Exploring preferences and consequences. *Research Policy*, *36*(1), 56–75.

Rich, A. (1979). *On lies, secrets, and silence: Selected prose*. Norton and Co.

Risman, B. J. (2004). Gender as social structure theory: Wrestling with activism. *Gender & Society*, *18*(4), 429–450.

Risman, B. J. (2009). From doing and undoing: Gender as we know it. *Gender & Society*, *23*(1), 81–84.

Risman, B. J. (2011). Gender as structure or trump card? *Journal of Family Theory & Review*, *3*(1), 18–22.

Risman, B. J. (2018). Gender as a social structure. In B. J. Risman, C. M. Froyum, & W. J. Scarborough (Eds.), *Handbook of the sociology of gender* (pp. 19–43). Springer.

Roberts, S. J., & Ryrie, A. (2014). Socratic case-method teaching in sports coach education: Reflections of students and tutors. *Sport, Education & Society*, *19*(1), 63–79.

Sattari, N., & Sandefur, R. L. (2019). Gender in academic STEM: A focus on men faculty. *Gender, Work & Organization*, *26*(2), 158–179.

Schinke, R. J., Blodgett, A. T., McGannon, K. R., & Ge, Y. (2016). Finding one's footing on foreign soil: A composite vignette of elite athlete acculturation. *Psychology of Sport and Exercise*, *25*, 36–43.

Schlesinger, T., & Weigelt-Schlesinger, Y. (2012). 'Poor thing' or 'Wow, she knows how to do it'—gender stereotypes as barriers to women's qualification in the education of soccer coaches. *Soccer & Society*, *13*(1), 56–72.

Simon, R. M., Wagner, A., & Killion, B. (2017). Gender and choosing a STEM major in college: Femininity, masculinity, chilly climate, and occupational values. *Journal of Research in Science Teaching*, *54*(3), 299–323.

Stoszkowski, J., Collins, D., & Olsson, C. (2017). Using shared online blogs to structure and support informal coach learning. Part 2: The participants' view and implications for coach education. *Sport, Education & Society*, *22*(3), 407–425.

Svender, J., Larsson, H., & Redelius, K. (2011). Promoting girls' participation in sports: Discursive constructions of girls in a sports initiative. *Sport, Education and Society*, *17*(4), 463–478. https://doi.org/10.1080/13573322.2011.608947

UCAS. (2020). *Universities and Colleges admission services*. Retrieved November 3, 2020, from www.ucas.com/

Webb, J., Schirato, T., & Danaher, G. (2002). *Understanding Bourdieu*. Allen and Unwin.

Witz, A. (1990). Professions and patriarchy: Gender and the politics of occupational closure. *Sociology, 24*(4), 675–690.

Woodman, L. (1993). Coaching: A science, an art, an emerging profession. *Sport Science Review, 2*(2), 1–13.

Ylöstalo, H., & Brunila, K. (2018). Exploring the possibilities of gender equality pedagogy in an era of marketization. *Gender and Education, 30*(7), 917–933.

7 Gender-Equity Policies in Sport in Practice

From Words to Action

Susanna Soler, Ingrid Hinojosa-Alcalde, Pedrona Serra and Ana Andrés

Contextual Issues

In recent decades, state, regional, and local governments in Spain have developed several policies to promote women's participation in sports at different levels and in different roles. An analysis of these policies confirms how, over the years, public policies have gone from equal opportunities promoted at the start of democracy to effective equality and equity in the early 21st century (Martin et al., 2017).

This shift has been particularly fostered by the Constitutional Law on Effective Equality between Men and Women 3/2007 dated March 22, 2007 (the 2007 Equality Act). Article 29 of the 2007 Equality Law gave a strong boost to the promotion of women in sport:

> All public sports development programmes will incorporate the principle of real and effective equality between women and men in their design and execution. The government will promote women's sports and encourage the effective opening of sports disciplines to women through the development of specific programmes at all stages of life and at all levels, including those of responsibility and decision-making.
> (Art. 29)

Under this principle of equity, public administrations are required to promote a dual strategy that simultaneously focuses on gender mainstreaming and positive actions to address gender inequalities in sport. Together with specific bodies dedicated to equality issues—such as the Women and Sports Programme of the Superior Sports Council—administrative departments must also be involved and incorporate the gender perspective in all areas and phases of sports policy development. This new paradigm is intended to ensure that all internal management processes carried out by administrations and sports entities are viewed from a gender perspective: from planning, design, and execution to evaluation of the gender impact of interventions.

For elite sports, in 2019, the Spanish government launched the Woman's Universe Programme, considered an Event of Exceptional Public Interest (AEIP), which provides significant tax breaks to organisations that collaborate in disseminating female sports events or make donations to this programme.

Within this framework, much progress has been made in recent years in the normative and public recognition of women's rights and the incorporation of a gender and diversity perspective in public sports policies. However, much remains to be done to turn intentions into actions. The implementation of gender policies is neither automatic nor free from challenges (Soler et al., 2017). In many cases, there is the so-called "mirage of equality" (Valcárcel, 2008), which leads to the belief that gender policies are no longer necessary. Likewise, Pfister (2010) warns of various withdrawal symptoms, the result of a set of ideological and political practices and movements, close to neoliberalism, that limit or reject demands for equality and ignore the gender variable or that even show outright disapproval and contempt for the term "feminism".

Shattering the Mirage of Equality: Research into Suggested Changes

Research on the gender perspective in sport in Spain shows how effective the equality between women and men is not yet a reality. Despite the legal, social, cultural, and sports changes of the last 40 years, women remain under-represented in sport management, as coaches and among Physical Activity and Sport Science (PASS) degree holders (Hinojosa-Alcalde et al., 2018; Serra et al., 2019; Viñas & Pérez, 2014). Furthermore, from a qualitative point of view, the research also confirms the persistence of resistance to change in sports organisations (Soler et al., 2017).

Decrease of the Presence of Women in PASS and Related Academic Studies

Women hold a disproportionately low share of PASS degrees and vocational training qualifications in physical activity and sports (Serra et al., 2019). Statistics show that the percentage of women enrolled in these studies has been decreasing in the last 20 years. In relative terms, women aspiring to take PASS degrees have gone from representing 39.4% in 1989 to 21% in 2018. A longitudinal analysis of female presence in PASS studies does not show any improvement: data collected in the last 25 years shows a progressive masculinisation of physical activity and sports in higher education.

Similar to what has happened with PASS degrees, the percentage of women with vocational training qualifications related to physical activity and sports has decreased from approximately 32% in 2000–2001 to 20%

Table 7.1 Coach certification courses according to gender in Catalonia 2010–2017

	Men (%)	Women (%)	Total (N)
Level 1	84.2	15.8	13,607
Level 2	89.2	10.8	7,013
Level 3	92.3	7.7	1,357
Total	86.3	13.7	21,977

Source: Hinojosa-Alcalde and Soler (2018)

in 2017–2018, a drop of 12 points in over the first two decades of the 21st century.

This low representation of women is mirrored in coach training courses in Catalonia, where women represent just 13.7% (Table 7.1). If we take a closer look, we can also see that the number of women decreased significantly at higher levels of coach training, showing a consistent downward trend in the last seven years (Hinojosa-Alcalde & Soler, 2018).

The changes in the educational, sports, and university system that have occurred in the last third of the 20th century in Spain and the early 21st century—including consolidation of mixed physical education, increased female participation in sports, increased female presence of women in university studies, and gender policies—have not led to a greater female presence in PASS degrees, quite the opposite. The situation has worsened, therefore, rather than improved.

According to the data for Catalonia, of the total number of graduates who are physical activity and sports professionals, 67% are men (Pérez-Villalba et al., 2018). Considering the negative evolution of PASS degree female uptake, the percentage of women in the sports workforce will be even smaller in the future.

Where Are the Women Coaches?

The low participation of women in positions of responsibility in Spanish sports organisations, including technical management and leadership positions, continues to evolve very slowly (Alfaro et al., 2018; Azurmendi, 2016; Hinojosa-Alcalde & Soler, 2018). Within the Catalan sports-related labour market, sports training is the main field of work for 28.6% of PASS graduates. It is in this important field of work where the gender gap is greatest, as men account for 84.1% of employment (Viñas & Pérez, 2014). Women with PASS degrees are less likely than their male counterparts to work as coaches. Catalan sports federations confirmed that women accounted for just 12% of all coaches in 2015 (Hinojosa-Alcalde et al., 2018). This strong under-representation of women points to a significant horizontal segregation in the coaching profession, reflecting in turn employment segregation.

Gender inequality in leadership positions in the sports field is especially evident in high-performance sports training. In the 2016 Rio de Janeiro Olympic Games, only ten of the 79 accredited coaches in the Spanish delegation were women (12.7%) and in the Paralympic Games, only two of the 26 accredited coaches were women (8.7%) (Hinojosa-Alcalde & Soler, 2018). A study of the profiles of both male and female coaches in Catalonia (from recreational to international level) found female under-representation and unequal distribution when assessing 27 sports at different competitive levels (Hinojosa-Alcalde et al., 2018). This study revealed that women accounted for 17.7% of coaches and were also significantly younger than men. There was also a significant difference between weekly hours of coaching: more men worked in full-time coaching positions, while 20.7% of women worked under five hours per week. In terms of competitive level, women mostly occupied coaching positions at the participatory/recreational level (Hinojosa-Alcalde, 2019).

Although men and women coaches work within the same profession, their sociodemographic characteristics are significantly different (Hinojosa-Alcalde et al., 2018). Knoppers' (1992) theory of the sexual division of labour as applied to the coaching sector can be used to interpret the shortage of women and sociodemographic differences between men and women through three key aspects: opportunity, power, and proportion.

In terms of opportunity, although women may have a more advanced competitive experience, this does not benefit their professional development as coaches (Hinojosa-Alcalde et al., 2018). Another issue is the significant differences in family structure, since most women are not married or cohabiting and, a high percentage of the women did not have children (84.0%), in contrast to the male coaches (61.8%). Another aspect to highlight is that women mostly train women, as confirmed in sociocultural studies of coaching contexts (LaVoi et al., 2019; Reade et al., 2009; Walker, 2016), and most women train grassroots teams (boys and girls). Men, in contrast, train at all levels, and typically occupy the main role at the head of senior teams (both male and female) that yield greater social recognition.

In terms of power, male coaches have more years of experience in the profession (see Table 7.2) and occupy key decision-making positions within sports organisations. Their time dedication to coaching is also higher (greater weekly workload) and the competitive levels at which they work also tend to be higher (see Table 7.3). Women coaches, in contrast, systematically occupy positions of less power within sports organisations.

In terms of proportions, that of men is significantly higher, with the data from the study by Hinojosa-Alcalde et al. (2018) confirming that the under-representation of women coaches in Catalonia follows patterns similar to those described in countries such as the United States, the UK, Norway, New Zealand, Germany, Canada, and the Czech Republic (Acosta & Carpenter, 2014; Allen & Shaw, 2013; Fasting et al., 2013; Pfister & Sisjord, 2013; Reade et al., 2009).

Table 7.2 Years experience as sport coaches according to gender

Years as coach	Men		Women	
<3 years	166	(12.0%)	79	(26.4%)
3–5 years	344	(24.8%)	91	(30.4%)
6–9 years	285	(20.6%)	54	(18.1%)
10–14 years	218	(15.7%)	37	(12.4%)
15–19 years	134	(9.7%)	17	(5.7%)
20 years or more	239	(17.2%)	21	(7.0%)

Source: Hinojosa-Alcalde (2019)

Table 7.3 Current position in coaching according to gender

Current role	Men		Women	
Technical management	178	(12.8%)	32	(10.7%)
Head coach	1,028	(74.2%)	204	(68.2%)
Assistant coach	146	(10.5%)	62	(20.7%)
Athletic trainer	34	(2.5%)	1	(0.3%)

Source: Hinojosa-Alcalde (2019)

The profession of physical activity and sports coach is clearly masculinised and marked by a sexual division of labour, such that opportunity, power, and proportion in benefit of women are significantly less than those of their male counterparts.

Resistance to Change

To change these numbers and the labour segregation by sex, in accordance with the gender policies promoted in Spain, sports clubs, sport federations, and educational physical activity and sport institutions need to implement actions aimed at changing the structural and organisational factors that limit women opportunities to coach. Nevertheless, the research also confirms the persistence of resistance to a cultural change in higher education institutions and sports organisations (LaVoi et al., 2019; Soler et al., 2017).

The traditional organisational culture of sports clubs, sport federations, and physical activity and sports higher education institutions in Spain is mostly androcentric and sexist (Azurmendi, 2016; Puig, 2007; Soler et al., 2018). Organisational culture refers to a wide spectrum of organisational practices, including values, unwritten norms, myths, ideas, aspects assumed as normal in organisational routines, objects and symbols, decoration and space environment, rituals and ceremonies, and social processes that include informal ways of interacting and working (Ely & Meyerson, 2000). These are often intangible issues key to understanding gender relations in an organisation. Analysing daily interactions and informal aspects of an organisation is a way of understanding the meanings that people give to their life in the organisation, their decisions, and their way of being, as well as the imperceptible mechanisms that generate exclusion (Shaw, 2006). One Catalan study (Observatori Català de l'Esport, 2016) has criticised sports clubs, for instance, for continuing to fail to reflect the routines and practices of women.

The development and implementation of gender-equity policies in sport organisations—such as affirmative action in recruiting, retaining, and promoting women coaches—are neither easy nor automatic (Hall, 1996; LaVoi et al., 2019; Soler et al., 2017). The implementation of new gender-equity policies therefore requires not only a move towards more transformative practices (Scraton, 2013), but also a shift from words to specific actions, engaging people to implement affirmative actions taking into consideration their own attitudes and experiences (Soler et al., 2017). During this process and due to its complexity and the different agents involved, resistance to change may arise from people (both men and women) inside an organisation at different levels, from leaders to staff members. It must also be taken into consideration that gender policies are sometimes implemented as a result of political pressure (Hovden, 2012; Shaw & Penney, 2003), which may also lead to resistance to change. Previous research has already accounted for different forms of resistance that need to be both acknowledged and explored in terms of underpinning factors (LaVoi et al., 2019; Slack & Parent, 2006) as part of the process leading to change.

Resistance to change is often the result of strongly internalised beliefs that may lead to behaviours that prevent individuals from engaging in actions for change. These beliefs are often based on the idea of individual responsibility or personal choice, it being argued that men and women make decisions under the same conditions and that, therefore, individual circumstances are the result of choice (LaVoi et al., 2019; Soler et al., 2017). Accordingly, the under-representation of women in coaching, sports organisations, and sport studies is seen as a consequence of personal choice. However, this point of view does not consider that, beyond individual choice, power relations and social, cultural, and structural factors are powerful elements that directly influence individual behaviours and choices.

A further argument against affirmative action, from a very different point, is the conviction that organisations cannot solve a problem of such magnitude, and so all efforts will be in vain, that is, "We are powerless to change the general tendency". Although this belief can come from people aware of gender inequalities, to believe that it is impossible to change inequalities is another source of resistance that must also be considered. The view that inequality in sport is the result of cultural determinism by which gendered models are reproduced is a demoralising argument. This belief has a direct impact on individual behaviours, as it will prevent people from engaging in actions to bring about change that may be perceived as a waste of time and may lead to apathetic responses (Soler et al., 2017).

Finally, the belief that gender-equity policies are not needed is another source of resistance. The reasons behind this belief are varied. The fear of feminism referred to by Weiner (2000) and the developing discourse that gender equity has been largely achieved challenge the need for gender policies (Scraton, 2013) and pose a barrier to their implementation. The viewpoints that an organisation does not need to change or that gender-equity policies may even be unfair to men are ideas related to this source of resistance.

Alongside the aforementioned beliefs, other barriers may arise focused not just on beliefs but more on behaviours. The implementation of gender-equity policies themselves require specific actions that have to be put into practice by multiple agents. In this regard and as Slack and Parent (2006) highlight, moving towards action can be seen by some professionals as costly, requiring an additional investment in work, resources, and time, as well as a specific effort to achieve meaningful change in raining female participation in sport organisations. This barrier is often underpinned by the idea that changing the situation is the responsibility of organisations themselves (Soler et al., 2017), but ignores the need for all individuals to be involved, as gender equity ultimately benefits both everyone.

The implementation success of gender-equity policies requires the engagement and involvement of individuals at all levels within sport organisations, from policymakers to professionals. Within this process, the knowledge of resistances that may arise can be helpful in order to tackle them during the process (Heffernan, 2018; LaVoi et al., 2019; Slack & Parent, 2006; Soler et al., 2017).

Actions for Change

The low presence of female coaches, the falling numbers of women in PASS studies, and the resistance to change that persists in the sports system reflect a situation that could be seen as discouraging. However, being aware of the current situation enables a better understanding of the causes of the problem as a first step to addressing all the issues that limit and condition the presence of female coaches.

Puig (2007) has proposed an extensive list of actions at the individual, organisational, and structural level to transform organisations committed to change. A good example of these new ways of promoting gender policies is the Spanish *Guide for the Incorporation of a Gender Perspective into Local Sports Management* (Consejo Superior de Deportes & Federación Española de Municipios y Provincias, 2011). The intervention strategies proposed are as follows: diagnosis and planning in the local sports field; gender budgets; normative development; affirmative actions; citizen participation channels; and awareness and training.

In Spain, there is currently no systematic intervention at all levels to transform the multicausal situations limiting the access, progression, and retention of female coaches. However, many organisations and institutions have taken action to try to reverse the situation. Together with various proposals already existing internationally as described earlier, in this chapter, we propose concrete actions focused on improving women's visibility and tackling the bias that limits individuals and organisations from considering women as potentially good as men at coaching.

We try to go forward to improving ratios from a quantitative point of view to focus on qualitative aspects that promote a more inclusive organisational culture. Quota policies, whereby institutions are obliged to increase the number of women in positions such as coaches, need to continue until gender parity is reached. However, this policy itself does not transform patriarchal sport into equal and equitable sport. Research has described multiple forms of gender bias and resistance to gender policies based on ideas such as: "If they want to, they can"; "It's not necessary"; "It's not possible to resolve this issue"; "There's no time or money"; "It's not fair to men" (Soler et al., 2017).

Research has found that it is not just a matter of numbers or of investing money, but of also working on the beliefs and relationships in organisations (Elling et al., 2019; LaVoi et al., 2019; Soler et al., 2017) and also those that permeate Spanish society, even despite the changes of recent decades (Soler & Martin, 2020).

For this reason, actions have been selected that seek to transform mechanisms that more or less unconsciously prevent more gender diverse configurations of organisations, especially in the coaching area. It is not a matter of tackling the issue as a "women's problem" or developing strategies "to fix things for women", but about changing the focus and directing it to the organisation itself. Along these lines, Shaw and Frisby (2006), drawing on the work of Ely and Meyerson (2000), propose going beyond existing conceptual frameworks based on liberal feminist theory to develop a new framework based on post-structural feminist theory as a means to analyse gender equity. This new perspective is focused on reflexivity and requires critique, experimentation, and narrative reviews of social practices inside organisations (Meyerson & Kolb, 2000).

Considering this new perspective, and also bearing in mind that in Spain (as in many other countries) most women coaches are lost through the pipeline (Azurmendi, 2016; Hinojosa-Alcalde & Soler, 2018), we propose four actions focused on reviewing usual social practices in career pathways for a coaching career. The actions are centred on engaging, recruiting, and retaining women, as follows: (1) seeding an interest in coaching in girls, (2) co-headcoaching, (3) incorporating gendered-lens training, and (4) women coaches talking to pupils, increasing the social visibility of women coaches as a way to show examples of women's leadership to boys and girls.

Developing a Taste for Coaching: Seeding Interest in Girls

To engage young women in coaching, it is necessary to use new and creative strategies, different from those traditionally used in sports clubs, which may be successful for men, but less so for most women.

Many sport clubs in Spain that have reaffirmed the commitment to actively advocate equality between men and women have developed campaigns to specifically recruit coach candidates from among women athletes in their club, for instance, combining the role of athlete and coach and encouraging retiring athletes to consider coaching (Julià, 2017; Mahmoud, 2017). Technical directors of these clubs discuss the issue with women who show special interest in the sport and may offer financial assistance to participate in training courses. Nevertheless, even when affirmative actions are designed, often no candidates come forward. Such situations are often blamed on women as being a matter of their choice in failing to apply (LaVoi et al., 2019; Soler et al., 2017): "Even with specific campaigns we cannot get women to enrol. They don't want to do it" (Prat et al., 2012). As research has revealed, the argument often used by sports managers to justify the lack of women coaches is women's lack of interest (Julià, 2017; Soler et al., 2017). Blaming women conveniently allows technical directors to leave the androcentric status quo intact (LaVoi et al., 2019).

Nevertheless, to achieve different results, different actions are required. Before asking to be a coach, it may be useful for girls not only to see women coaches, but also to have a taste for what it means to be a coach in a secure and encouraging context. According to that principle, one sports club has designed a campaign to seed an interest in coaching in girls. Girls in pairs from grassroots teams, for one day a month, perform assistant coach tasks for another team, during a match and/or during a training session. In this way, they can see what the profession consists of and assess whether they have suitable skills; thus, when they decide whether or not to become coaches, they can make that decision based on their experience, rather than on a stereotype.

Co-Headcoaching

Co-headcoaching, a practice in which two coaches come together to jointly coach a team as equals, has been revealed as an innovative organisational structure that helps women to continue the coaching career, while retaining female talent in sport clubs. Co-headcoaching is not the classical hierarchical model of a head coach and a second coach, but it is a way of mentoring and developing coaching skills. Often an experienced female coach and a novice female coach work together. As LaVoi et al. (2019) state, same-sex social support and role models matter. In co-headcoaching, the two coaches equally share the head coach responsibilities in a symbiotic manner, as has been described by Rytivaara et al. (2019) for their co-teaching practices. This symbiosis in the work relationship allows female coaches to avoid some of the barriers that LaVoi and Dutove (2012) describe at the organisational, interpersonal, and individual levels. For example, it is a way to elude the tokenism (Knoppers, 1992) and the old-boys club culture commonly found in sports clubs, incrementing the sense of community. Furthermore, working as a unit can reduce the great time commitment typical of coaching jobs and consequently favours a healthier work-life balance. As

Hinojosa-Alcalde (2018) argued, work–family conflict in Spain is a major barrier to retaining coaches, especially women coaches. Co-headcoaching is therefore especially useful to balance the complex intersection among coaching, family, and personal life.

Finally, co-headcoaching as a collaborative partnership is a tool for professional learning that can help bring down individual barriers. Moreover, co-teaching can encourage an effective learning environment within the context of a sports education season (Calderón et al., 2015).

Gender Lens Training

To improve occupational experiences for women coaches, to promote them within clubs, and to implement gender policies in organisations, decision-makers need to be aware of how gender bias and sexism are embedded in sports organisational culture and the larger sociocultural context (LaVoi et al., 2019; Soler et al., 2017). In 2015, only 2% of sports clubs in Catalonia, for example, considered gender as a challenge for the club (half a point less than in 2009) (Observatori Català de l'Esport, 2016). Providing gender lens training and raising awareness is an essential task in initial and ongoing training for coaches, sport leaders, and policymakers (Heffernan, 2018; Soler et al., 2017). Awareness, according to Heffernan (2018), is defined as men's and women's understanding of women's low representation in leadership positions and their power to influence the hiring of women. This awareness is necessary to develop allies and to find key people as referents and role models who underpin proposals with conviction. Furthermore, sport organisations need to incorporate a gender perspective not as a top-down imposition, but involving all staff through reflective processes, so that a gender perspective can be incorporated as an integral part of the organisation, as described in various works (Elling et al., 2019; Heffernan, 2018; Pfister & Sisjord, 2013; Shaw, 2006; Soler et al., 2017).

As Norman et al. (2018) argued, the under-representation of women coaches must be reframed as "a symptom, or an outcome of a deeper issue, rather than the problem in itself" (p. 395). Furthermore, as Clarkson et al. (2019) have stated, women coaches might be uncomfortable with affirmative discriminatory efforts, and so will men in positions of power. Hence, the need for training that raises awareness of the deeper issues that prevent equality between men and women.

We propose breaking with preconceived and internalised ideas, or to use Brown's words (2005, p. 20): "challenging the boundaries of what people perceive as gender inconceivable, improbable and acceptable in PE [physical education] and school sport until the inconceivable becomes the acceptable". Some examples of proposals to encourage this reflection and to detect the embedded sexism in organisations are to be found in the "Gender in the eyes" material developed by Rey-Cao and González-Palomares (2017), which aims to reveal the gender stereotypes present in photographs

Figure 7.1 Physical education textbook photographs reflecting leadership roles
Source: Rey-Cao and González-Palomares (2017, p. 10)

related to the body and movement, specifically in Spanish physical education textbooks. Examples are shown in Figure 7.1; students are invited to analyse and reflect on who is represented in a leadership role in the sport context and to then create a different image by changing the roles.

Another example of gender perspective training and promotion of critical reflection is that proposed by Monforte and Úbeda-Colomer (2019); using the video "Like a girl", with over 65 million views on YouTube, gender inequalities are made visible and challenged through provocation and debate. The video and subsequent debate are intended to stimulate the ability to perceive daily discrimination and gender violence practices that operate under the radar of sport and physical education, as proposed in critical pedagogy (Sánchez-Hernández et al., 2018).

In Spain, several guides have been developed to promote change directed at the decision-makers in education and PASS degrees (Serra et al., 2018; Soler et al., 2018). Using these guides, centres and teachers can carry out self-diagnoses regarding incorporation of a gender perspective in their daily lives in aspects such as curricular design, visual language of teaching materials, verbal and written language, the inclusion of women referents in all sports fields, work methods and group dynamics, criticism and prevention of objectification of the body, evaluation rubrics, dissertation and practicum design, and in research and involvement in overall institutional transformation. One known positive impact of this action is that following this guide, the teaching team of a PASS degree attended a specific course on gender in university teaching; as a result of this training, most of the 35 participants indicated their intention to change or include some aspects related to gender in their teaching programme, for example, check the number of women and men authors include in syllabus reference lists, increase the number of women, among other issues. Furthermore, the Catalan Basketball Federation has also included a gender-reflexive perspective in its coach training programme.

Women Coaches Talking to Pupils

Schools are considered a key setting to promote gender equality and critical competition in gender roles. The existing curricular opportunities in physical education make schools an ideal setting in which to deliver programmes designed to transform traditional gender relations and stereotypes.

The Catalan Soccer Federation, for example, in addition to providing financial assistance to girls wanting to take their coaching courses, has developed a more ambitious and long-term programme. Within the framework of its #Orgullosa programme, with a powerful communication campaign to promote women's football at all levels, it has also promoted #Orgullosa soccer for equality, aimed at secondary schools (Soler et al., 2020). The programme is structured into three blocks of work that allow football and indoor football to be approached from a social, cultural, educational, and sports perspective. *Block 1, Critical Reflection: Rethinking Sport* aims to promote awareness of gender stereotypes and gender discrimination, from physical education in schools to elite sports. *Block 2, The Playful Aspect: Let's Play Soccer* has ten motor activities that aim to foster cooperation and respect between boys and girls in the practice of more stereotyped sports. Finally, *Block 3, Our Environment: Approaching Clubs* has five activities that lead boys and girls to discover key women football players and coaches, including in clubs from their cities. As a whole, the proposal aims to empower girls and boys to take actions for change.

One of the activities implemented within the #Orgullosa programme is visits by women players and women and men coaches to educational centres, as ambassadors. To take full advantage of the visit, students are recommended to previously research the ambassador players and coaches and, in small groups, to prepare some questions for the ambassadors in advance. This action aims to increase the social visibility of women coaches as a way to promote women coaches as role models to boys and girls and challenge the male domination in sports coaching.

Future Directions for Researchers and Policymakers

While public administrations and sports institutions have attached great importance to the presence and role of women in decision-making positions, the presence of women in sports professions and coaching has received much less attention. In various measures to promote equality carried out in recent years by public administrations, fewest actions have been taken in relation to women coaches. For example, when gender indicators have been assessed for subsidies to sports organisations, the presence of women on the board and the number of female athletes have been taken into account, but not the number of female coaches.

The findings of this chapter also provide evidence of the need to encourage and support women as sports coaches in PASS degrees and of the need to transform sports organisational and PASS higher education culture. As Reifsteck (2014) points out, simply incorporating more women into a male-dominated institution without challenging underlying gender relations merely reinforces the lower status of women or reproduces the heteronormative femininity that perpetuates gender stereotypes. Although more women may be incorporated in sports clubs as coaches, if the "gender of the organisation" (Hall, 1996) does not change, the outcome is likely to be a glass ceiling or horizontal segregation (women coaching grassroots teams and women teams). It is necessary to change the day-to-day culture and pre-established ideas of organisations and their staff. It is for this reason that gender lens training and gender inequality awareness are essential.

Advancing gender policies in sport, therefore, requires not only economic, material, and organisational efforts, but also individual efforts. To a greater or lesser degree, we need to reflect on our own beliefs and ways of doing things. Our vision of sports and of gender models and relationships has historically been constructed within an androcentric and patriarchal context. We need, however, to learn to recognise and detect the different mechanisms that prevent equality between men and women and to consider what needs to be maintained, what needs to be changed and, if necessary, what needs to be unlearned. We also need to ensure that a gender perspective is present and mainstreamed in all aspects of politics and daily sports management.

The implementation of successful gender-equity policies is the result of a complex process that requires the participation and engagement of multiple agents at different levels. For policymakers down to sports organisation staff responsible for taking specific action, gender equity is a promising yet challenging goal.

References

Acosta, R. V., & Carpenter, L. J. (2014). *Women in intercollegiate sport: A longitudinal study: Thirty seven year update 1977–2014* (Unpublished Document). www.acosta-carpenter.org/

Alfaro, E., Mayoral, Á., & Vázquez, B. (2018). *Factores que condicionan el acceso de las mujeres a los puestos de responsabilidad en el deporte*. Subdirección General de Mujer y Deporte. Consejo Superior de Deportes.

Allen, J. B., & Shaw, S. (2013). An interdisciplinary approach to examining the working conditions of women coaches. *International Journal of Sports Science & Coaching, 8*(1), 1–17. https://doi.org/10.1260/1747-9541.8.1.1

Azurmendi, A. (2016). *Obstáculos psicosociales para la participación de las mujeres en el deporte como entrenadoras y árbitras* (Doctoral thesis). Universidad del País Vasco. https://addi.ehu.es/handle/10810/26195?show=full

Brown, D. (2005). An economy of gendered practices? Learning to teach physical education from the perspective of Pierre Bourdieu's embodied sociology. *Sport, Education and Society, 10*(1), 3–23.

Calderón, A., de Ojeda, D. M., Valverde, J. J., & Méndez-Giménez, A. (2015). "Ahora nos ayudamos más": Docencia compartida y clima social de aula. Experiencia con el modelo de Educación. Deportiva. *RICYDE. Revista Internacional de Ciencias del Deporte, 12*(44), 121–136. https://doi.org//10.5232/ricyde

Clarkson, B. G., Cox, E., & Thelwell, R. C. (2019). Negotiating gender in the English football workplace: Composite vignettes of women head coaches' experiences. *Women in Sport and Physical Activity Journal, 27*, 73–84.

Consejo Superior de Deportes & Federación Española de Municipios y Provincias. (2011). *Guía para la incorporación de la perspectiva de género a la XXXnterpr deportiva local*. CSD-FEMP.

Constitutional Law 3/2007 dated 22 March, Effective Equality between Men and Women (Equality Act). Spain.

Elling, A., Hovden, J., & Knoppers, A. (Eds.). (2019). *Gender diversity in European sport governance*. Routledge.

Ely, R. J., & Meyerson, D. E. (2000). Theories of gender in organizations: A new approach to organizational analysis and change. *Research in Organizational Behavior, 22*, 103–151.

Fasting, K., Sand, T. S., & Knorre, N. (2013). European female sport students as future coaches? *European Journal for Sport and Society, 10*(4), 307–323.

Hall, A. (1996). *Feminism and sporting bodies: Essays on theory and practice*. Human Kinetics.

Heffernan, C. D. (2018). *Gender allyship: Considering the role of men in addressing the gender-leadership gap in sport organizations* (Unpublished doctoral dissertation). University of Minnesota. https://conservancy.umn.edu/bitstream/handle/11299/201034/Heffernan_umn_0130E_19541.pdf?sequence=1&isAllowed=y

Hinojosa-Alcalde, I. (2019). *La professió d'entrenador/a des de la perspectiva de gènere I benestar laboral* (Doctoral thesis). Universitat de Barcelona. http://hdl.handle.net/10803/669649

Hinojosa-Alcalde, I., Andrés, A., Serra, P., Vilanova, A., Soler, S., & Norman, L. (2018). Understanding the gendered coaching workforce in Spanish sport. *International Journal of Sports Science & Coaching, 13*(4), 485–495. https://doi.org/10.1177/1747954117747744

Hinojosa-Alcalde, I., & Soler, S. (2018). On son les dones entrenadores? La desigualtat a la banqueta. *11è Quadern Dones i Esport, 11*, 64–74.

Hovden, J. (2012). Discourses and strategies for the inclusion of women in sport—the case of Norway. *Sport in Society, 15*(3), 287–301. https://doi.org/10.1080/17430437.2012.653201

Julià, H. (2017). *La transició de jugadora a entrenadora de bàsquet des d'una perspectiva de gènere. El cas de L'esquitx* (Master thesis). Universitat de Barcelona.

Knoppers, A. (1992). Explaining male dominance and sex segregation in coaching: Three approaches. *Quest, 44*(2), 210–227. https://doi.org/10.1080/00336297.1992.10484051.

LaVoi, N. M., & Dutove, J. K. (2012). Barriers and supports for female coaches: An ecological model. *Sports Coaching Review, 1*(1), 17–37. https://doi.org/10.1080/21640629.2012.695891

LaVoi, N. M., McGarry, J. E, & Fisher, L. A. (2019). Final thought on Women in sport coaching: Fighting the war. *Women in Sport and Physical Activity Journal, 27*, 136–140.

Mahmoud, M. (2017). *El futbol femenino en los clubes deportivos de la ciudad de Barcelona: un análisis de suXXXnterprn* (Doctoral thesis). Universitat de Barcelona. www.tdx.cat/handle/10803/405706

Martin, M., Soler, S., & Vilanova, A. (2017). Género y deporte. In M. García-Ferrando, N. Puig, F. Lagardera, R. Llopis-Goig, & A. Vilanova (Eds.), *Sociología del deporte* (4ª ed., pp. 97–124). Alianza editorial.

Meyerson, D. E., & Kolb, D. M. (2000). Moving out of the 'armchair': Developing a framework to bridge the gap between feminist theory and practice. *Organization, 7*(4), 553–571. https://doi.org/10.1177/135050840074002

Monforte, J., & Úbeda-Colomer, J. (2019). 'Like a girl': A provocative study on gender stereotypes in Physical Education. *Retos: nuevas tendencias en educación física, deporte y recreación, 36,* 74–79.

Norman, L., Rankin-Wright, A. J., & Allison, W. (2018). "It's a concrete ceiling; It's not even glass": Understanding tenets of organizational culture that supports the progression of women as coaches and coach developers. *Journal of Sport and Social Issues, 42*(5), 393–414. https://doi.org/10.1177/0193723518790086

Observatori Català de l'Esport. (2016). *Evolució dels clubs esportius a Catalunya de 2009 a 2015.* INDE Editorial.

Pérez-Villalba, M., Vilanova, A., & Soler, S. (2018). Mercado de trabajo en el deporte y género: un estudio comparativo entre las condiciones de trabajo de las tituladas y los titulados en Ciencias de la Actividad Física y el Deporte por las universidades catalanas. *Revista de Humanidades, 34,* 195–216. https://doi.org/10.5944/rdh.34.2018.19731

Pfister, G. (2010). Women in sport—gender relations and future perspectives. *Sport in Society, 13*(2), 234–248. https://doi.org/ 10.1080/17430430903522954

Pfister, G., & Sisjord, M. K. (2013). *Gender and sport: Changes and challenges.* Waxmann.

Prat, M., Soler, S., & Carbonero, L. (2012). De las palabras a los hechos: un proyecto para promover la participación femenina en el deporte universitario. El caso de la Universitat Autònoma de Barcelona. *Agora para la educación física y el deporte, 3,* 283–302.

Puig, N. (2007). Mujeres, puestos de decisión y organizaciones deportivas: Barreras y propuestas. In Diputación General de Aragón (Ed.), *Actas de las Jornadas sobre mujer y deporte* (pp. 120–131). Diputación General de Aragón.

Reade, I., Rodgers, W., & Norman, L. (2009). The under-representation of women in coaching: A comparison of male and female Canadian coaches at low and high levels of coaching. *International Journal of Sports Science and Coaching, 4*(4), 505–520. https://doi.org/10.1260/174795409790291439

Reifsteck, E. J. (2014). Feminist scholarship: Cross-disciplinary connections for cultivating a critical perspective in Kinesiology. *Quest*, *66*(1), 1–13. https://doi.org/10.1080/00336297.2013.824903

Rey-Cao, A., & González-Palomares, A. (2017). *El género en los ojos. Estrategias para educar con (y pese) las fotografías de los materiales curriculares.* Universidad de Vigo. http://xeneronosollos.webs.uvigo.gal/El_genero_en_los_ojos.pdf

Rytivaara, A., Pulkkinen, J., & de Bruin, C. L. (2019). Committing, engaging and negotiating: Teachers' stories about creating shared spaces for co-teaching. *Teaching and Teacher Education*, *83*, 225–235.

Sánchez-Hernández, N., Martos-García, D., Soler, S., & Flintoff, A. (2018). Challenging gender relations in PE through cooperative learning and critical reflection. *Sport, Education and Society*, *23*(8), 812–823. https://doi.org/10.1080/13573322.2018.1487836

Scraton, S. (2013). Feminism and physical education: Does gender still matter? In G. Pfister y M. K. Sisjord (Eds.), *Gender and sport. Changes and challenges* (pp. 199–216). Waxmann.

Serra, P., Soler, S., & Vilanova, A. (2018). *Jo SÍ incorporo la perspectiva de gènere a les Ciències de l'Activitat Física i l'Esport. Decàleg per a professorat universitari i personal investigador de Ciències de l'Activitat Física i l'Esport (CAFiE).* COPLEFC. www.coplefc.cat/fitxers/DEC%C3%80LEG%20PERSPECTIVA%20GENERE%20CAFIE.pdf

Serra, P., Soler, S., Vilanova, A., & Hinojosa-Alcalde, I. (2019). Masculinización en estudios de las ciencias de la actividad física y el deporte. *Apunts Educación Física y Deportes*, *135*, 9–25. https://doi.org/10.5672/apunts.2014-0983.es.(2019/1).135.01

Shaw, S. (2006). Scratching the Back of "Mr X": Analyzing Gendered Social Processes in Sport Organizations. *Journal of Sport Management*, *20*, 510–534.

Shaw, S., & Frisby, W. (2006). Can gender equity be more equitable? Promoting an alternative frame for sport management research, education and practice. *Journal of Sport Management*, *20*(4), 483–509.

Shaw, S., & Penney, D. (2003). Gender equity policies in national governing bodies: An oxymoron or a vehicle for change? *European Sport Management Quarterly*, *3*(2), 78–102. https://doi.org/10.1080/16184740308721942

Slack, T., & Parent, M. M. (2006). *Understanding sport organizations: The application of organization theory* (2nd ed.). Human Kinetics.

Soler, S., Hinojosa-Alcalde, I., Lecumberri, C., Sánchez-Hernández, N., Serra, P.,& Vilanova, A. (2020). *Futbol per a la igualtat.* Federació Catalana de Futbol-INEFC.

Soler, S., & Martin, M. (2020). La perspectiva de género en el deporte en las dos primeras décadas del siglo XXI. In N. Puig & A. Camps (Eds.), *Diálogos sobre el deporte (1975–2020)* (pp. 222–234). INDE.

Soler, S., Prat, M., Puig, N., & Flintoff, A. (2017). Implementing gender equity policies in a university sport organization: Competing discourses from enthusiasm to resistance. *Quest*, *69*(2), 276–289. https://doi.org/10.1080/00336297.2016.1226186

Soler, S., Serra, P., & Vilanova, A. (2018). *La igualtat en joc. Guia de bones pràctiques de gènere en els estudis de la família de les Ciències de l'Activitat Física i de l'Esport IE).* Institut Nacional d'Educació Física de Catalunya—INDE.

Valcárcel, A. (2008). *Feminismo en el mundo global.* Ediciones Cátedra.

Viñas, J., & Pérez, M. (2014). *El mercat de treball de l'esport a Catalunya. Especial incidència a la província de Barcelona.* INDE.

Walker, N. (2016). Cross-gender coaching. In N. M. LaVoi (Ed.), *Women in sports coaching* (pp. 111–125). Routledge.

Weiner, G. (2000). A critical review of gender and teacher education in Europe. *Pedagogy, Culture & Society, 8*(2), 233–247. https://doi.org/10.1080/14681360000200091

8 Organisation-Level Practices to Support Women in Coaching

Laura Burton and Ajhanai Newton

Introduction

In 2020, Katie Sowers became the first woman to coach in the US National Football League Super Bowl. Lisa Fallon became the first female coach of Cork City Football Club in Ireland and the National Basketball Association (U.S.) Boston Celtics hired Kara Lawson as an assistant coach in 2019. As we celebrate women coaching men's professional sport in the United States and internationally, we also see continued challenges and lack of equal opportunities for women to coach at the professional, intercollegiate, and international level of sport (Diversity Research, 2018; Lapchick, 2019).

Many scholars have considered why women continue to have fewer opportunities to coach sport (see LaVoi, 2016). We know the "pipeline" argument is inadequate as there are more girls and women playing sport in the United States and internationally than at any point in history. Furthermore, the number of women coaching at the assistant level of women's intercollegiate sport while significant is not leading to sustained number of women head coaches (Diversity Research, 2018). If there is an available population of potential women coaches why is there a lack of parity in coaching roles in both men's and women's sports? To help address the lack of parity, we first must situate sport as a gendered institution (i.e., a significant organisation in society) which has served as space to construct and reproduce traditional ideas of masculinity (Anderson, 2009). Therefore, women are often situated as "other" or not belonging, and their presence as athletes, coaches, managers, or leaders, is under constant scrutiny (Fink, 2016; Kane, 1995). Any discussion of women in coaching must include an understanding of gender as fundamental to both organisational and social processes in the sport sector (Pape, 2020). Gender has an influence on organisational and managerial practices, such that images, cultures, interactions, and gender-appropriate behaviours within organisational operations are linked to socially constructed ideals of masculinity and femininity. Understanding sport as a gendered institution helps us examine how and why gender is such a powerful factor in organisational processes and how gender bias and gender stereotypes influence the recruitment, hiring, retention, and advancement of women at all levels of sport coaching.

In this chapter, we advance strategies to make meaningful changes within sport organisations in support of women in sport coaching and highlight that any meaningful changes must first account for gender (intersectional) biases and the impact of these biases on women's experiences in coaching. We begin this chapter with a brief overview of biases that impact women in coaching and then provide a more detailed discussion regarding how biases impact women (intersectional identities) in coaching. We then consider how organisations can begin to address gender bias at the individual level and some of the challenges inherent in those practices. Finally, we will discuss organisational practices that can have an impact on mitigating bias and supporting the advancement of women in coaching.

Understanding Biases

Biases, both implicit and explicit, are prevalent and impact women in sport organisations in a myriad of ways (see Fink, 2016 for a discussion of sexism in sport). We provide a brief overview of how biases impact individuals by exploring stereotypes, prejudice, and discrimination (Cunningham, 2019).

Stereotypes have been defined as "the unconscious or conscious application of (accurate or inaccurate) knowledge of a group in judging a member of the group" (Banaji & Greenwald, 1994, p. 58). Stereotypes based on gender are derived from shared understanding of what are considered expected and appropriate attributes and behaviours for men and women (Wood & Eagly, 2012). These gender-based stereotypes have implications for women in sport leadership, in general (Cunningham & Ahn, 2019), but specifically, negatively impact the experiences of women in coaching (see Schull & Kihl, 2019; Walker & Bopp, 2010).

Prejudice operates at the affective level and is influenced by stereotypes individuals hold. Prejudice is a negative (pre)judgement of an individual who is different from oneself (Allport, 1954). However, prejudice involves both evaluations of individuals different from and similar to oneself, and that evaluations are more favourable towards similar individuals when compared to dissimilar individuals (Brown & Zagefka, 2005). Prejudice operates both explicitly and implicitly. Consider the continued explicit forms of sexism in sport (Fink, 2016). Implicit prejudice operates below a conscious level, even at times when individuals do not believe the attitude is accurate (Cunningham, 2019). Discrimination is a behavioural response directed towards individuals as a result of stereotypes or prejudice held by those perpetuating the behaviour (Cunningham, 2019).

To this point, we have discussed one category of social identity, gender. However, all individuals hold multiple social identities (e.g., race, ethnicity, sexual orientation, and physical ability). We, therefore, adopt an intersectional frame throughout this chapter to call attention to how the influence of sexism and racism cannot be parcelled out as discrete experiences for individuals (Collins, 1991; Crenshaw, 1989). Intersectionality provides a "critical insight" (p. 2) noting that race, gender, ethnicity, and other identities "operate not as unitary, mutually exclusive entities, but as reciprocally constructing phenomena that in turn shape complex social inequalities" (Collins, 2015, p. 2). Importantly, intersectionality is a theoretical lens linked to Black feminism and Black women's experiences (Crenshaw, 1989; Simien & Clawson, 2004). However, we are drawing upon critical aspects of intersectionality, like power and an individual's multiple identities, and how this informs their social and professional career navigation. In this chapter, we focused on the impacts of racism, sexism, and homophobia on women in coaching and applied an intersectional framing as we described organisational-level practices that can reduce biases.

Considering How Organisations Are Gendered and Racialised

Fink (2016) posed a significant question, "So how do we combat sexism in sport" (p. 4)? We propose sport leaders recognise biases based on gender, race, and sexuality. The experiences of women coaches must be situated in broader macro-level phenomena (Cunningham et al., 2019), as organisations are gendered (Acker, 1990) and racialised (Ray, 2019). Wells and Kerwin (2017) and McDowell et al. (2009) highlighted the realities of occupational segregation—organisational responsibilities being *segregated* by gender and race. Sport organisations must be "conducive" for women and racial minorities, in order for these historically marginalised communities to be successful (Wells & Kerwin, 2017). Furthermore, when women are token members of teams or when women on majority female teams do not perform to their fullest capabilities, gendered stereotypes informed their self-efficacy perceptions (Chen & Houser, 2019). "Single-gendered workplaces are not a solution, as women, in particular, continue to suffer from [gendered stereotypes] even in the absence of men" (Chen & Houser, 2019, p. 11). When sport leaders do not acknowledge and recognise that sport organisations are gendered and racialised (Acker, 1990; Burton, 2015; Ray, 2019), women coaches perceive gender and racial bias as something they have to address on their own.

Impacts of Biases on Women Coaches

In this section, we delve more deeply into how biases (stereotypes, prejudice, and discrimination) impact women in coaching. As described in the introduction of this chapter, sport is a gendered institution and as such, gender is a powerful factor in organisational processes; therefore, gender bias and gender stereotypes impact women's experiences in coaching. In the sections to follow, we detail how stereotypes of women impact women as coaches and how these stereotypes influence women's access to coaching

Stereotypes of and Impact on Women Coaches

Women in leadership positions and those aspiring to leadership are perceived differently than men due to the prevalence of gender stereotypes (Okimoto & Brescoll, 2010). In general, when we think about *how* women behave (descriptive stereotypes) and *how we want* women to behave (prescriptive stereotypes), we expect more nurturing, supportive, and "other-oriented" behaviours. Conversely, when we think about how men behave and are expected to behave they are to be assertive, independent, and dominant (Prentice & Carranza, 2002). An additional layer of gender stereotypes exists—proscriptive stereotypes that describe negative behaviours we want each gender *to avoid*. For men, that includes avoiding weakness (i.e., being insecure or emotional), and for women avoiding dominance (i.e., being aggressive or intimidating). When women are dominant or men are weak, both face "backlash" for violating proscriptive gender stereotypes (Williams & Tiedens, 2016). Although men face backlash for violations of gender stereotypes (Moss-Rascusin et al., 2010), women who act in dominant and more masculine ways generate a wider variety and stronger feelings of contempt, disgust, revulsion, and disdain from others who witness these dominant behaviours (Brescoll et al., 2018). This "dominance penalty" is likely based on the perceived threat to the gender status quo that women must holder lower status when compared to men (Rudman et al., 2012).

Gender and leadership stereotypes force women into a "double bind" when women seek out or act in the role of leader (Eagly & Karau, 2002). Gendered leadership stereotypes can be applied to coaches, as the coaching role is typically perceived as a more typical male pursuit (Koenig et al., 2011). In general, coaches are expected to be self-confident, demanding, and assertive. Furthermore, coaches are expected to hold leadership and more task-oriented qualities, and those are qualities more stereotypically ascribed to male coaches (Burton & LaVoi, 2016; Demers, 2004; Schlesinger & Weigelt-Schlesinger, 2012, 2013). Women seeking head coaching roles are expected to act "like a coach", meaning "act like a man" which violate traditional female gender stereotypes. When women coaches violate gender stereotypes, they are subject to backlash (Rudman et al., 2012). Women face this double bind when considered for leadership positions in college athletics (Burton et al., 2011).

Recall those proscriptive (negative) stereotypes for women—being aggressive and intimidating and the subsequent backlash faced for those violations. Women coaches may be experiencing both the "double bind" and backlash for violating gender stereotypes from their athletes (Schull, 2017). Female athletes value coaches who "tell it like it is" and act in dominant, strong, and sometimes authoritarian ways (Drago et al., 2005) and identify more stereotypical masculine traits to the head coach position (Madsen et al., 2017). However, those types of behaviours are more acceptable to athletes when they are demonstrated by male coaches. Female athletes want their female coaches to be caring, supportive, and nurturing but this contradicts what they value in coaching (Schull & Kihl, 2019). If women coaches are limited to satisfying their athletes' desires for their female coaches to be nurturing and caring, women coaches are not able to fulfil the behaviours deemed necessary to be successful coaches. Women coaches who do take on coaching behaviours that are dominant, authoritarian and "tell it like it is" are at risk of facing a backlash from their athletes (Schull & Kihl, 2019). These differential evaluations of women coaches can lead to negative evaluations of women coaches by their female athletes which may contribute to why women have been fired from head coaching positions (Burton & LaVoi, 2019).

Access to Coaching Roles

Gender stereotypes impact perceptions of who are best to serve in coaching positions, that is, men as head coaches and women as assistant coaches (Demers, 2004; Madsen et al., 2017; Schlesinger & Weigelt-Schlesinger, 2012, 2013). Furthermore, as detailed in the section to follow, gender stereotypes also impact how individuals perceive coaching roles to be available to them and how they are treated in those roles.

CONSIDERING COACHING AS A CAREER

As "girls and young women see females in coaching roles, they will be more likely to think about coaching as a legitimate and viable career, so they may aspire to become a coach" (LaVoi, 2016, p. 4). However, female college athletes, one of the most viable populations of future coaches, are reluctant to enter the profession as a result perceived challenges including, perceptions that coaching, based on gender stereotypes described in the previous section, is more appropriate for men (Burton & LaVoi, 2016; Demers, 2004; Schlesinger & Weigelt-Schlesinger, 2012, 2013). Furthermore, as a result of gender stereotypes that women are expected to be more nurturing and caring, young female college athletes are expected (by parents and family) to seek out careers that provide better work-life balance (Madsen & McGarry, 2016; Wells, 2016). Also, female college athletes witness the challenges their own female coaches face as a result of gender bias and gender stereotypes (Darvin, 2019; Madsen & McGarry, 2016; Wells, 2016) and do not want to be subject to those challenges in their own careers.

Another potential pool of applicants for head coaches are women who have worked as assistant coaches. However, the transition from assistant to head coach is neither seamless nor follows a natural progression. When compared to male assistant coaches, women had lower coaching self-efficacy and desire to advance to head coaches (Cunningham et al., 2019; Cunningham et al., 2003; Sagas et al., 2006), and greater intentions to leave coaching as an occupation (Wells et al., 2014). Recent work by Darvin (2019) highlighted a more troubling issue, a misalignment of assistant coaches' ethical and moral value systems with the perceived requirements to be a head coach.

ACCESS AND TREATMENT DISCRIMINATION

Women face both access and treatment discrimination in coaching. Considering access, women hold 6% of coaches for men's sport, while men account for 59% of head coaches for women's intercollegiate sports (Diversity Research, 2018) and the majority of all coaching positions in professional sport (Lapchick, 2019). The coaching profession must be both equitable (equal access to both men and women) and diverse (balanced representation in men's and women's sport) (Walker, 2018). However, women fail to gain access to coaching positions in men's sports (Walker & Bopp, 2011; Walker & Sartore-Baldwin, 2013).

Treatment discrimination has an insidious impact on women's experiences in coaching. Women coaches face differing expectations regarding how to best fulfil their roles (Schull & Kihl, 2019). First, women coaches are held to different standards based on gender role expectations. Female athletes perceive and male coaches possess greater human capital because "knowledge of the sport is often inherent and assumed in male coaches" (Schull & Kihl, 2019, p. 6). Furthermore, women need to be more successful athletes in the sport or have competed at a high level in order to be perceived as competent in their roles. Also, male coaches who demonstrated empathy are lauded for such expressions, while empathy is an expectation for female coaches and if not expressed, is perceived as a negative for female coaches (Schull & Kihl, 2019). These different expectations for female coaches add additional barriers to their access to and success in coaching roles.

LIMITED NETWORKING OPPORTUNITIES

Coaching opportunities in sport may be limited for women as a function of the "old boys' club" restricting women's access to be "in the know" about opportunities for coaching positions. Homologous reproduction, the practice of those in power allowing only individuals similar to them to have access to power (Kamphoff et al., 2010), exacerbates this challenge as the majority of sport leadership positions are held by men (Burton, 2015). Furthermore, women working in intercollegiate athletics have smaller informal social networks limiting their ability to advance to leadership positions in college athletics (Katz et al., 2018).

Sponsors are different from mentors, as they act to support career advancement by leveraging relationships and influence to support those individuals they are sponsoring (Wells & Hancock, 2017). Women coaches, specifically women new to the profession, recognise the critical need for formal sponsors to support their career development, yet there may be a lack of sponsors available to support women as they persist in these roles (Darvin et al., 2019).

OCCUPATIONAL TURNOVER

Occupational turnover is higher for women coaches regardless of individual- or organisational-level factors when compared to male coaches (Cunningham et al., 2019). Women coaches were younger and had less coaching experience when indicating a desire to leave the coaching profession, suggesting that occupational barriers made aspirations to continue in coaching and advance to head coaching positions less desirable for women (Cunningham et al., 2019).

Organisational-Level Practices to Support Women in Coaching

LaVoi (2016) challenged sport leaders to go beyond organisational practices that only seek to increase the number of opportunities for women to access coaching positions and instead to change sport organisation practices that will improve the experiences of women in coaching. Organisational-level strategies offered by LaVoi include revising current organisational policies and consideration of non-discrimination policies (e.g., hiring and evaluation), professional development workshops for coaches (highlighting inclusion, recognising gender bias and stereotyping, etc.), adopting policies to support work-life interface, and development of workplace cultures that support autonomy and an ethic of care. In the following section, we focus specifically on how to address biases operating within the context of organisational practices and offer best practices to minimise or reduce biases in sport organisations.

Addressing Bias in Organisations—Questioning Available Practices

Despite resources spent on well-meaning diversity training initiatives to raise awareness of and reduce bias (gender, race, etc.) in organisations, outcomes of such training do not result in long-term or substantive changes in individual levels of bias (Bohnet, 2018). When organisations with a poor history of valuing diversity and inclusion implement measures seeking to promote diversity and inclusion, their efforts can be questioned given their history (Cunningham, 2009). Organisations address surface-level diversity (race, gender, and age) by creating professional affinity groups or diversity networks based upon gender, age, and race (e.g., Women Leaders in College Sports). However, these efforts are typically centred on a single axis of one's identity, such as gender or race, failing to capture the multiplicity of one's identity (Dennissen et al., 2020). Organisations seeking to promote diversity and inclusion through diversity networks are unknowingly creating tension and frustration for employees with multiple salient identities, as these diversity networks fail to approach their inclusionary efforts through an intersectional lens (Dennissen et al., 2020). As an example, women's networks discuss women's issues solely, leading to women of non-dominant (race, ethnicity, and sexual identity) backgrounds to feel marginalised (Dennissen et al., 2020). Hence, creating affinity groups or diversity networks grounded upon single-axis identities does not necessarily create inclusionary organisations and reduce organisational biases, as biases are rooted in Whiteness, maleness, and heterosexuality. Organisations seeking to reduce biases must consider "involving privileged members of historically marginalized groups" (p. 237) to address diversity issues in coaching (Dennissen et al., 2020). This necessitates naming and reflecting on privileged status held by women in those organisations (i.e., Whiteness, heterosexuality, and ability) and then working in collaboration with those with less privilege (e.g., Black and queer) to advance opportunities for all women in the organisation, not just the heterosexual, White women.

As described earlier, biases in sport organisations persist in daily, formal, and informal workplace experiences. Addressing organisational biases means to also examine how coaches conform or alter their identity in an effort to be perceived as fitting into the organisation. For example, LGBTQ athletic administrators did not disclose their sexual orientation with colleagues in fear of their identities being perceived as unacceptable, having an adverse impact on workplace relationships (Walker & Melton, 2015). This is an important perspective to consider when organisations seek to centre diversity and inclusion through hiring practices (Bohnet, 2018). However, coaches from an under-represented group may find that "forming social connections are easier within one's [affiliated demographic] than they are across a demographic boundary" (Phillips et al., 2018, para. 3). Hence, informal cultural biases occur because our identities *can* inform our social interests, leading organisational actors to refrain from discussing interests that may be uncommon to dominant-identifying organisational peers (Phillips et al., 2018). As a result, coaches and others in sport organisations may engage in "code switching", the process of an individual (commonly practiced by Blacks) "adjusting one's style of speech, appearance, behaviour, and expression in ways that will optimize the comfort of others in exchange for fair treatment" (McCluney et al., 2019).

Reducing biases in sport organisations is not resolved merely by hiring more diverse individuals or creating diversity networks. Albeit, these are meaningful practices, but to address biases in sport organisations, leaders must also consider the multiple identities of organisational actors

(Dennissen et al., 2020) and to what extent organisational actors perceive being able to bring their full selves into their workplace (Phillips et al., 2018). Organisations can signal inclusive workplaces in many different ways, such as celebrating diverse families on websites, biographies of coaches, evaluating policies and practices that may privilege dress codes that align with White and/or male assumptions of appropriate attire, and more substantively, by debiasing recruitment, development, and evaluation policies and practices as described in the following section.

Assessing Organisational Inclusiveness

Before engaging in strategies to increase the number of women in coaching, organisations must assess how inclusive they are to under-represented groups, including women. One approach offered by Egan and Bendick (2018) encourages organisations to assess their organisational climate highlighting six "red flags" that may indicate the climate is not inclusive (see Table 8.1). An organisation can hire more women into coaching positions, but regardless of the number hired, retaining women in the organisation will be challenging if the climate is not inclusive of under-represented groups (Cunningham, 2019).

Table 8.1 Six red flags: your organisation may not be ready to recruit

Red flag #1	Has your organisation conducted multiple analyses over a period of years concerning the lack of under-represented groups? Do the reports repeatedly describe the same basic issues and outcomes?
Red flag #2	Does your organisation, for example, hire African Americans or other under-represented groups for positions or career paths that begin and end in one part of the organisation? Does the same "race matching" operate for other demographic groups? (see Borland & Bruening, 2010)
Red flag #3	Are few or no administrators trained in the skills that reduce unconscious bias and stereotyping in work functions—skills such as behavioural interviewing, basing employment decisions on explicit criteria, and writing unbiased performance appraisals?
Red flag #4	Is there no recurrent monitoring at the organisational level to find systemic differences in pay, promotions, attitudes, and job opportunities among employee groups?
Red flag #5	Is individual administrator accountability for inclusion outcomes lax or non-existent? Are there no real consequences for administrators who ignore their coach's/employer's inclusion goals? Real consequences refer to high stakes employment decisions such as promotions, bonuses, or even firing
Red flag #6	Does the recruitment strategy for increasing under-represented groups focus on entry level/assistant coach hiring without under-represented groups hiring for head coach positions?

Source: Adapted from Egan & Bendick (2018)

After reviewing and assessing organisational inclusiveness, leaders should work to address any areas that were identified as potential "red flags" and recognise that organisational-level changes will be necessary to successfully recruit and retain women coaches in their organisations.

Debiasing Recruitment of Women to Coaching

The recruitment and retention of women coaches must have leaders attuned to the historical and contemporary experiences of women coaches in their respective organisations. Meaningful recruitment and retention efforts must reflect upon the following questions: (1) How many women coaches have we had in the last 20 years? (2) What is the tenure of women coaches in our organisation? (3) How successful are women coaches in our organisation? These questions are critical for capturing retention and recruiting patterns that have adverse impact upon future women coaches hired in sport organisations. Such an approach challenges leaders to refrain from approaching retention through individual dispositions, but rather through institutional mechanisms. Thus, we suggest sport leaders assess employee well-being, in an effort to better understand contemporary workplace experiences and disaggregate such experiences between male and female coaches. By disaggregating coaches' workplace experiences, leaders apply an intersectional lens and refrain from stating "*all coaches*" and acknowledge the gendered discrepancies that exist and persist.

As noted earlier in the chapter, arguably the most qualified and likely candidates for coaching positions are former female athletes (e.g., intercollegiate, professional, and Olympian). However, female athletes report a lack of interest in coaching positions based on pressure to conform to gender stereotypes and negative perceptions of their own female coaches (Madsen, 2016). Furthermore, women assistant coaches witnessing the challenges their female head coaches faced were more likely to leave the occupation when compared to male coaches (Darvin, 2019). As a result, organisations must consider more active recruiting measures to attract women candidates for coaching positions by attending to the potential stereotypes and biases that impact recruitment (for a review, see Schlesinger & Weigelt-Schlesinger, 2013).

One such approach that has been tested in the STEM field (Carnes et al., 2015) is based on the theory of prejudice habit model (Devine et al., 2012). In this model, bias is understood to be a mental habit. The steps to "break the bias habit" begin with a person being motivated to act in less biased ways. Next, "breaking the bias habit" involves "(1) becoming aware of when one is vulnerable to unintentional bias (through bias training and education), (2) understanding the consequences of unintentional bias, and (3) learning and practicing effective strategies to reduce the impact of unintentional bias" (Carnes et al., 2015, p. 2). For a detailed discussion of the prejudice habit breaking intervention, see Devine et al., 2012. This strategy was found to be effective when used to increase hiring of female faculty in STEM positions at the University of Wisconsin–Madison (Devine et al., 2012). Given the success in STEM, a field in which women are under-represented (Moss-Racusin et al., 2010), sport organisations should consider adopting this intervention as a means to increase the number of women hired into coaching positions.

Leadership Development—Best Practices to Develop and Train Women Coaches

There is a paucity of coaching development programmes designed to support women's development in the profession (Lewis et al., 2018). Wells (2016) noted the importance of fostering the training and development of assistant coaches as critical to growing the number of women head coaches. Furthermore, women-specific coaching development programmes are necessary to develop supportive learning spaces that act "as encouraging environments in which they are not afraid to learn and sometimes fail, but have the opportunity to take the lead" (Norman, 2012, p. 232). There are programmes in the United States, Canada, and in other countries designed to develop and support the advancement of women in coaching and other areas of sport leadership. Evaluation of women's coaching development programmes demonstrated the positive impact these programmes had on women's leadership development in sport broadly. However, formal coaching development [education] programmes were perceived as less valuable for coaching development when compared to opportunities coaches had to engage in experiential learning programmes (Vinson et al., 2016). Furthermore, the provision of coaching development programmes must do more than merely attempt to increase the number of women in coaching but more importantly, address the underlying issues (see discussion earlier in this chapter) that contribute to the under-representation of women in coaching (LaVoi, 2016).

Some of the best practices for women's coaching development reported in evaluation of the Women Leadership Development Programmeme (WLDP) (Megheirkouni & Roomi, 2017), a three-year pilot programmeme designed to develop 15 selected women leaders in the UK sports organisations are listed in the following. Women who described positive changes in their development as leaders noted that the following practices were beneficial–:

1. Action learning: learning from daily tasks and learning from mistakes–.
2. Mentoring: personal attention that fosters an environment that facilitates learning and transferring knowledge faster from one person to another–.
3. Networking: in-group/out-group learning and learning from social activities.
4. Communication: voice, oral presentations, active listening, and body language.

However, participants also noted that a negative aspect of the WLDP programme was the focus only on women. This was perceived as detrimental to their leadership development as they noted working in more male-dominated organisations. Those participants were concerned that their programme was not preparing them to lead and engage with both men and women (Megheirkouni & Roomi, 2017).

Debiasing Evaluation of Women Coaches

Women coaches may also face bias in performance evaluations. In general, as a result of gender bias, women tend to receive lower performance evaluations when compared to men "even when their behaviours or skill levels are identical" (Rivera & Tilcsik, 2019, p. 250). In order to counter bias, organisations must reduce ambiguity in the evaluation of women coaches (Heilman & Caleo, 2018). Reducing ambiguity in evaluation includes clarifying performance criteria to include evaluations that are based on objective data (e.g., student-athlete graduation rate and team performance measures) and not relying on subjective ratings (e.g., student-athlete end of year evaluations). And to increase the frequency of evaluations in order to receive more timely feedback and allow opportunities for coaches to address any potential challenges or issues (e.g., pre-season, mid-season, and post-season) (Heilman & Caleo, 2018).

In addition, sport organisations must also evaluate the objective performance evaluation measures typically used. There is evidence that gender bias impacts work-based performance evaluations; a 10-point scale negatively impacts the evaluation of female faculty when compared to a 6-point scale. That is, female faculty received higher ratings for the same teaching when evaluated on a 6-point scale instead of a 10-point scale (Rivera & Tilcsik, 2019). These findings suggest that organisations, including sport organisations, using scale-based performance evaluations need to consider how the rating scale (e.g., 10 point vs. 6 point) may perpetuate gender bias in evaluation of their women coaches.

Addressing the Gendered Expectations of Familial Commitments

Sport leaders must acknowledge that coaching careers place unique but disparate stressors on the family commitments of coaches of both men and women (Bruening & Dixon, 2008; Graham & Dixon, 2017). Leaders committed to recruiting and retaining women coaches must consider how gendered familial commitments differ for female and male coaches. Male coaches' commitment to the profession of coaching was greatly influenced by their wives being committed to transient husbands and fathers during their respective sport season (Graham & Dixon, 2017). Women coaches were often not in similar familial arrangements and faced added role conflict given societal stereotypes of women and mothers (Bruening & Dixon, 2007). To recruit and retain women coaches, leaders must approach their efforts through an intersectional lens—meaning a woman is both a coach and a mother. By doing so, sport leaders transition from examining employees on a single axis of their identities and engage in "proactive diversity management" (Cunningham & Fink, 2006, p. 459). However, women coaches who are not parents are not necessarily "more available" or "more committed" to the coaching profession devoid of parental responsibilities. In fact, projecting such an attitude is enacting biases.

There are various and differing global government policies guiding maternity leave, but in what ways do implicit messages either pressure or support female coaches as parents? Language, implicit and explicit messages, and informal policies must be considered in retaining women coaches, particularly when approaching retention efforts through an intersectional lens. The stereotype of women forgoing career advancement to focus on motherhood, positions working mothers from a deficit, biased, and inaccurate lens. Leaders resist this stereotypical ideology and consider how an organisational culture of inhumane work hours layered with gendered biases, creates "locked gender inequality" in organisations (Ely & Pavadic, 2020, para 4). Both male and female coaches experience challenges balancing work and familial commitments (Bruening & Dixon, 2007, 2008; Graham & Dixon, 2017); however, organisational cultures that encourage women "to take accommodations, such as going part-time and shifting to internally facing roles" disparately hinder the career accession of women in comparison to men (Ely & Pavadic, 2020, para 4). Addressing such inequity would require organisations to address their culture of workaholism (Ely & Pavadic, 2020), but workaholism and burnout are pervasive in collegiate athletics (Taylor et al., 2019). Leaders of sport organisations need to consider the negative impacts of the culture of workaholism on both male and female coaches and the subsequent detrimental impacts on the success of the organisation. The culture of 24/7 workaholism perpetuated in sport organisations must be changed and sport organisational cultures must shift to accommodating all aspects of coaches' lives, not merely applying work–family support policies to only women coaches.

Summary

Sport organisations must recognise that women coaches face barriers in their access to coaching and biases when considering, entering, and engaging in coaching. When in coaching roles, women have fewer networking opportunities and access to sponsors to help develop in the profession. As a result of the organisational challenges and barriers that exist for women coaches working in sport, challenges and barriers that do not exist for men coaches, women are more likely to leave the profession earlier than men, resulting in a continued under-representation of women coaches. Sport leaders can enact organisational-level practices to address the challenges women coaches face. Such organisational-level practices include acknowledging biases (i.e., race, gender, and sexual orientation) within their organisations, assessing the level of inclusiveness within their organisations, and debiasing the recruitment of women to coaching positions. Furthermore, to support women to develop and thrive as coaches in their organisations, sport leaders need to provide leadership development opportunities for their women coaches, debias the performance evaluations of women coaches and consider how work–family interface policies have different impacts on female and male coaches and how such policies may perpetuate a 24/7 workaholic culture that lock female coaches in policies and positions that hinder their career development.

References

Acker, J. (1990). Hierarchies, jobs, bodies: A theory of gendered organisations. *Gender & society*, *4*(2), 139–158.
Allport, G. W. (1954/1979). *The nature of prejudice*. Addison-Wesley.
Anderson, E. D. (2009). The maintenance of masculinity among the stakeholders of sport. *Sport Management Review*, *12*(1), 3–14.
Banaji, M. R., & Greenwald, A. G. (1994). Implicit stereotyping and prejudice. In *The psychology of prejudice: The Ontario symposium* (Vol. 7, pp. 55–76).
Bohnet, I. (2018). *What work: Gender equity by design*. Harvard University Press.
Borland, J. F., & Bruening, J. E. (2010). Navigating barriers: A qualitative examination of the under-representation of Black females as head coaches in collegiate basketball. *Sport Management Review*, *13*(4), 407–420.
Brescoll, V. L., Okimoto, T. G., & Vial, A. C. (2018). You've come a long way . . . maybe: How moral emotions trigger backlash against women leaders. *Journal of Social Issues*, *74*(1), 144–164.
Brown, R., & Zagefka, H. (2005). Ingroup affiliations and prejudice. In J. F. Dovidio, P. Glick, & L. A. Rudman (Eds.), *On the nature of prejudice: Fifty years after Allport* (pp. 54–70). Blackwell Publishing. https://doi.org/10.1002/9780470773963.ch4
Bruening, J. E., & Dixon, M. A. (2007). Work—family conflict in coaching II: Managing role conflict. *Journal of Sport Management*, *21*(4), 471–496.
Bruening, J. E., & Dixon, M. A. (2008). Situating work—family negotiations within a life course perspective: Insights on the gendered experiences of NCAA Division I head coaching mothers. *Sex Roles*, *58*(1–2), 10–23.
Burton, L. J. (2015). Underrepresentation of women in sport leadership: A review of research. *Sport Management Review*, *18*(2), 155–165.
Burton, L. J., Grappendorf, H., & Henderson, A. (2011). Perceptions of gender in athletic administration: Utilizing role congruity to examine (potential) prejudice against women. *Journal of Sport Management*, *25*(1), 36–45.
Burton, L. J., & LaVoi, N. M. (2019, June). *The war on women coaches*. https://theconversation.com/the-war-on-women-coaches-116643
Burton, L. J., & LaVoi, N. M. (2016). An ecological/multisystem approach to understanding and examining women coaches. In *Women in sports coaching* (pp. 49–62). Routledge.
Carnes, M., Devine, P. G., Manwell, L. B., Byars-Winston, A., Fine, E., Ford, C. E., . . . Palta, M. (2015). Effect of an intervention to break the gender bias habit for

faculty at one institution: A cluster randomized, controlled trial. *Academic Medicine: Journal of the Association of American Medical Colleges, 90*(2), 221.

Chen, J., & Houser, D. (2019). When are women willing to lead? The effect of team gender composition and gendered tasks. *The Leadership Quarterly, 30*(6), 340.

Collins, P. H. (1991). *Black feminist thought: Knowledge, consciousness, and the politics of empowerment.* Routledge.

Collins, P. H. (2015). Intersectionality's definitional dilemmas. *Annual Review of Sociology, 41*(1), 1–20. https://doi.org/10.1146/annurev-soc-073014-112142

Crenshaw, K. (1989). Demarginalizing the intersection of race and sex: A black feminist critique of antidiscrimination doctrine, feminist theory and antiracist politics. *University of Chicago Legal Forum*, 139.

Cunningham, G. B. (2009). Understanding the diversity-related change process: A field study. *Journal of Sport Management, 23*(4), 407–428.

Cunningham, G. B. (2019). *Diversity and inclusion in sport organisations: A multilevel perspective.* Routledge.

Cunningham, G. B., & Ahn, N. Y. (2019). The role of bias in the under-representation of women in leadership positions. In N. Lough & A. Guerin (Eds.), *Routledge handbook of the business of women's sport* (pp. 83–94). Routledge.

Cunningham, G. B., Ahn, N. Y., Anderson, A. J., & Dixon, M. A. (2019). Gender, coaching, and occupational turnover. *Women in Sport and Physical Activity Journal, 27*(2), 63–72.

Cunningham, G. B., & Fink, J. S. (2006). Diversity in sport and leisure. *Journal of Sport Management, 20*, 455–564.

Cunningham, G. B., Sagas, M., & Ashley, F. B. (2003). Coaching self-efficacy, desire to head coach, and occupational turnover intent: Gender differences between NCAA assistant coaches of women's teams. *International Journal of Sport Psychology, 34*, 125–137.

Darvin, L. (2019). Voluntary occupational turnover and the experiences of former intercollegiate women assistant coaches. *Journal of Vocational Behavior.* https://doi.org/10.1016/j.jvb.2019.103349

Darvin, L., Taylor, E., & Wells, J. (2019). Get in the game through a sponsor: Initial career ambitions of former women assistant coaches. *Journal of Issues in Intercollegiate Athletics, 12*, 590–613.

Demers, G. (2004). Why female athletes decide to become coaches—or not. *Canadian Journal of Women in Coaching, 4*(5), 2–8.

Dennissen, M., Benschop, Y., & van den Brink, M. (2020). Rethinking diversity management: An intersectional analysis of diversity networks. *Organisation Studies, 41*, 219–240.

Devine, P. G., Forscher, P. S., Austin, A. J., & Cox, W. T. (2012). Long-term reduction in implicit race bias: A prejudice habit-breaking intervention. *Journal of Experimental Social Psychology, 48*(6), 1267–1278.

Diversity Research. (2018). www.ncaa.org/about/resources/research/diversity-research

Drago, R., Hennighausen, L., Rogers, J., Vescio, T., & Stauffer, K. (2005). *Final report for CAGE: The coaching and gender equity project.* http://Lsir.la.psu.edu/workfam/CAGE.htm

Eagly, A. H., & Karau, S. J. (2002). Role congruity theory of prejudice toward female leaders. *Psychological Review, 109*(3), 573–598. https://doi.org/10.1037/0033-295X.109.3.573

Egan, M. L., & Bendick, M. (2018). Increasing minority employment: Are you ready to recruit? *Employment Relations Today, 44*, 11–15. https://doi.org/10.1002/ert.21652

Ely, R., & Pavadic, I. (2020, March–April). What's really holding women back? *Harvard Business Review.* https://hbr.org/2020/03/whats-really-holding-women-back

Fink, J. S. (2016). Hiding in plain sight: The embedded nature of sexism in sport. *Journal of Sport Management, 30*(1), 1–7.

Graham, J. A., & Dixon, M. A. (2017). Work—family balance among coach-fathers: A qualitative examination of enrichment, conflict, and role management strategies. *Journal of Sport Management, 31*(3), 288–305.

Heilman, M. E., & Caleo, S. (2018). Combatting gender discrimination: A lack of fit framework. *Group Processes & Intergroup Relations, 21*(5), 725–744.

Lapchick, R. (2019). *The complete racial & gender report card (RGRC).* www.tidesport.org/complete-sport

LaVoi, N. M. (Ed.). (2016). *Women in sport coaching.* Routledge.

Lewis, C. J., Roberts, S. J., & Andrews, H. (2018). 'Why am I putting myself through this?' Women football coaches' experiences of the football association's coach education process. *Sport, Education and Society, 23*(1), 28–39.

Kamphoff, C. S., Armentrout, S. M., & Driska, A. (2010). The token female. *Journal of Intercollegiate Sport, 3*(2), 297–315.

Kane, M. J. (1995). Resistance/transformation of the oppositional binary: Exposing sport as a continuum. *Journal of Sport and Social Issues, 19*(2), 191–218.

Katz, M., Walker, N. A., & Hindman, L. (2018). Gendered leadership networks in the NCAA: Analyzing affiliation networks of senior woman administrators and athletic directors. *Journal of Sport Management, 32*(2), 135–149. https://doi.org/10.1123/jsm.2017-0306

Koenig, A. M., Eagly, A. H., Mitchell, A. A., & Ristikari, T. (2011). Are leader stereotypes masculine? A meta-analysis of three research paradigms. *Psychological Bulletin, 137*(4), 616–642. https://doi.org/10.1037/e617292010-001

Madsen, R. M., Burton, L. J., & Clark, B. S. (2017). Gender role expectations and the prevalence of women as assistant coaches. *Journal for the Study of Sports and Athletes in Education, 11*(2), 125–142. https://doi.org/10.1080/19357397.2017.1315994

Madsen, R. M., & McGarry, J. E. (2016). "Dads play basketball, moms go shopping!" Social role theory and the preference for male coaches. *Journal of Contemporary Athletics, 10*(4), 277.

McCluney, C., Robotham, K., Lee, S., Smith, R., & Durkee, M. (2019). The costs of code-switching. *Harvard Business Review.* https://hbr.org/2019/11/the-costs-of-codeswitching

McDowell, J., Cunningham, G. B., & Singer, J. N. (2009). The supply and demand side of occupational segregation: The case of an intercollegiate athletic department. *Journal of African American Studies, 13*(4), 431–454.

Megheirkouni, M., & Roomi, M. A. (2017). Women's leadership development in sport settings. *European Journal of Training and Development, 41*(5), 467–484.

Moss-Racusin, C. A., Phelan, J. E., & Rudman, L. A. (2010). When men break the gender rules: Status incongruity and backlash against modest men. *Psychology of Men & Masculinity, 11*(2), 140–151.

Norman, L. (2012). Developing female coaches: Strategies from women themselves. *Asia-Pacific Journal of Health, Sport and Physical Education, 3*(3), 227–238.

Okimoto, T. G., & Brescoll, V. L. (2010). The price of power: Power seeking and backlash against female politicians. *Personality and Social Psychology Bulletin, 36*(7), 923–936.

Pape, M. (2020). Gender segregation and trajectories of organisational change: The underrepresentation of women in sports leadership. *Gender & Society, 34*(1), 81–105.

Phillips, K., Dumas, T., & Rothbard, N. (2018, March–April). Diversity and authenticity. *Harvard Business Review.* https://hbr.org/2018/03/diversity-and-authenticity

Prentice, D. A., & Carranza, E. (2002). What women and men should be, shouldn't be, are allowed to be, and don't have to be: The contents of prescriptive gender stereotypes. *Psychology of Women Quarterly, 26*(4), 269–281. https://doi.org/10.1111/1471-6402.t01-1-00066

Ray, V. (2019). A theory of racialized organisations. *American Sociological Review, 84*(1), 26–53.

Rivera, L. A., & Tilcsik, A. (2019). Scaling down inequality: Rating scales, gender bias, and the architecture of evaluation. *American Sociological Review, 84*(2), 248–274.

Rudman, L. A., Moss-Racusin, C. A., Phelan, J. E., & Nauts, S. (2012). Status incongruity and backlash effects: Defending the gender hierarchy motivates prejudice against female leaders. *Journal of Experimental Social Psychology, 48*(1), 165–179.

Sagas, M., Cunningham, G. B., & Pastore, D. (2006). Predicting head coaching intentions of male and female assistant coaches: An application of the theory of planned behaviour. *Sex Roles, 54*(9–10), 695–705.

Schlesinger, T., & Weigelt-Schlesinger, Y. (2012). 'Poor thing' or 'wow, she knows how to do it'—gender stereotypes as barriers to women's qualification in the education of soccer coaches. *Soccer & Society, 13*(1), 56–72.

Schlesinger, T., & Weigelt-Schlesinger, Y. (2013). "Coaching soccer is a man's job!"— The influence of gender stereotypes on structures for recruiting female coaches to soccer clubs. *European Journal for Sport and Society, 10*(3), 241–265.

Schull, V. D. (2017). Young women in sport: Understanding leadership in sport. In *Women in sport leadership* (pp. 112–129). Routledge.

Schull, V. D., & Kihl, L. A. (2019). Gendered leadership expectations in sport: Constructing differences in coaches. *Women in Sport and Physical Activity Journal, 27*(1), 1–11.

Simien, E. M., & Clawson, R. A. (2004). The intersection of race and gender: An examination of Black feminist consciousness, race consciousness, and policy attitudes. *Social Science Quarterly, 85*(3), 793–810.

Taylor, E. A., Huml, M. R., & Dixon, M. A. (2019). Workaholism in sport: A mediated model of work–family conflict and burnout. *Journal of Sport Management, 33*(4), 249–260.

Vinson, D., Christian, P., Jones, V., Williams, C., & Peters, D. M. (2016). Exploring how well UK coach education meets the needs of women sports coaches. *International Sport Coaching Journal, 3*(3), 287–302.

Walker, N. A. (2018). The labyrinth of exclusion in sport and steps toward developing a culture of inclusion. *Sport and Entertainment Review, 4*(2).

Walker, N. A., & Bopp, T. (2010). The under representation of women in the male dominated sport workplace: Perspectives of female coaches. *Journal of Workplace Rights, 15,* 47–64.

Walker, N. A., & Bopp, T. (2011). The underrepresentation of women in the male-dominated sport workplace: Perspectives of female coaches. *Journal of Workplace Rights, 15*(1).

Walker, N. A., & Melton, E. N. (2015). The tipping point: The intersection of race, gender, and sexual orientation in intercollegiate sports. *Journal of Sport Management, 29*(3), 257–271.

Walker, N. A., & Sartore-Baldwin, M. L. (2013). Hegemonic masculinity and the institutionalized bias toward women in men's collegiate basketball: What do men think? *Journal of Sport Management, 27*(4), 303–315.

Wells, J. E. (2016). Female assistant coaches: Planting seeds and growing roots. In *Women in sports coaching* (pp. 139–159). Routledge.

Wells, J. E., & Hancock, M. G. (2017). Networking, mentoring, sponsoring: Strategies to support women in sport leadership. In L. J. Burton & S. Leberman (Eds.), *Women in sport leadership: Research and practice for change* (pp. 130–147). Routledge.

Wells, J. E., & Kerwin, S. (2017). Intentions to be an athletic director: Racial and gender perspectives. *Journal of Career Development, 44*(2), 127–143.

Wells, J. E., Peachey, J. W., & Walker, N. (2014). The relationship between transformational leadership, leader effectiveness, and turnover intentions. *Journal of Intercollegiate Sport, 7*(1), 64–79.

Williams, M. J., & Tiedens, L. Z. (2016). The subtle suspension of backlash: A meta-analysis of penalties for women's implicit and explicit dominance behavior. *Psychological Bulletin, 142*(2), 165–197. https://doi.org/10.1037/bul0000039

Wood, W., & Eagly, A. H. (2012). Biosocial construction of sex differences and similarities in behavior. In *Advances in experimental social psychology* (Vol. 46, pp. 55–123). Academic Press.

Part III
From Research to Practice
Evidence of Impactful Research That Has Contributed to More Gender-Inclusive Sport Coaching Contexts

9 Shared Experiences From the Margins

Culturally Diverse Women in Coaching in Aotearoa New Zealand, the United States, and the United Kingdom

Julia Symons

Introduction

The purpose of this chapter is to explore the common experiences of women coaches from culturally diverse backgrounds in Aotearoa New Zealand,[1] the United States, and the United Kingdom, by prioritising and centring their voices and stories. A second aim is to offer practical recommendations for sports practitioners to consider and create cultural safety in their coaching programme design and pathways. The research informing this chapter was undertaken during a Churchill Fellowship, which provides an opportunity for non-academic, industry-based professionals from any sector in Australia to seek out insights and experiences overseas to inform best practice around a certain topic from their field, and to apply and share these learnings locally upon completion. Whilst focusing on the experiences of culturally diverse women in elite sports environments across these three countries, there were common stories and experiences of "Otherness" articulated by the women in coaching roles. With a shared experience of being a "minority within a minority", navigating both gender and cultural diversity in traditionally White, male-dominated sports coaching environments added multiple layers of oppressions (Rankin-Wright & Norman, 2018) to their coaching journey, beyond the technical, tactical, and personal competencies and skills required of a sports coach. In addition to the gendered toll experienced by many women in coaching (Norman & Rankin-Wright, 2016), what Abney and Richey (1992) described as a "double whammy" for Black women in sport in predominantly White institutions in the US college system was often raised by women I spoke with, who had endured both racism and sexism at different times throughout their coaching careers.

Sporting organisations and administrators are often unaware of or do not consider the challenges that intersecting identities present for culturally diverse women. They may have standalone programmes for women in coaching or seek to increase cultural diversity in their coaching ranks, but seldom do they embed both gender and cultural diversity considerations in coaching programme design, development or assessment, let alone recognise the interlocking systems and impact of racism and sexism in sporting contexts (Rankin-Wright & Norman, 2018, p. 220). This absence of recognition can be attributed in part to the "Whiteness" which characterises the majority of the sporting environments navigated by the women in my research across Aotearoa New Zealand, the United States, and the United Kingdom. As a result of privileging and centring "Whiteness", experiences of inequality, oppression, and subtle discrimination have been normalised in the culture of those sports environments (Rankin-Wright et al., 2016). Understanding the impact of intersectionality is important as culturally diverse women face double or even "multiple jeopardies" when navigating their way through coaching programmes and pathway journeys, just as Carter and Hart (2010) described of the experiences of Black female collegiate athletes in the United States. Building this understanding can assist sporting organisations to create cultural safety in their environments to enable culturally diverse women to bring both their gendered and cultural identities to their coaching roles, creating opportunities to thrive as coaches, and to maximise their skills to perform their coaching responsibilities.

Women's representation in coaching is often explored through either a lens of gender, or a racial, ethnic, or cultural lens (Borland & Bruening, 2010; Norman, 2010; Rankin-Wright & Norman, 2018), but rarely does it consider the intersecting impacts of multiple identities at the same time. Available statistics reflect a lack of representation internationally across varying levels of coaching for culturally diverse women. For example, the 2019 Racial and Gender Report Card (Lapchick, 2019) showed that only 14.0% of Division I college women's basketball head coaches in the United States were African-American women, despite African-American women representing 41.9% of women basketball student athletes. In Australia, a series of studies with Aboriginal and Torres Strait Islander[2] sport coaches (Apoifis et al., 2017; Bennie et al., 2017; Marlin et al., 2020) explain that Aboriginal and Torres Strait Islander people remain largely under-represented in professional coaching roles despite being often over-represented as athletes in elite sport, with no Aboriginal or Torres Strait Islander women named as full-time, permanent head coaches in any sports. Within sports governing bodies in the United Kingdom, 99% of coaches are White, with 82% of that group being male (Sports Coach UK, 2011). In Aotearoa New Zealand, a news report in 2018 claimed that women have "more chance of running the country than coaching a national sports team", as Aotearoa New Zealand had seen three female prime ministers and yet only two out of 12 of their top team sports coaches were female at the time, both of whom were White (Caldwell, 2018). Such statistics demonstrate that across multiple continents, women from culturally diverse backgrounds are under-represented across the coaching community.

In this chapter, I will outline my Churchill Fellowship research and discuss considerations given to identifying common language and of drawing common themes from interviews in three international sporting contexts, among women with diverse identities. I will summarise the three main themes of their common experiences, being (1) the importance of cultural safety, (2) "fitting in" versus "finding belonging", and (3) the privilege, burden, and responsibility of representation. Finally, I will offer recommendations to address the challenges identified to offer sports organisations considerations and practical actions to create culturally safe coaching environments that enable culturally diverse women to bring both their gender and cultural identities to their coaching roles.

Churchill Fellowship Summary

After being awarded a Churchill Fellowship in 2017, my research across Aotearoa New Zealand, the United States, and the United Kingdom took place in 2018, investigating elite sports environments that enable culturally diverse women to thrive. As a sports administrator working on diversity and inclusion programmes in a predominantly women's sport at the time, the Fellowship provided me with a unique, industry-based research opportunity, outside of an academic context. Churchill Fellows then document their learnings and recommendations in a report that can be applied to and shared with their sector to benefit Australian communities and bring new knowledge and insights to their industry.

Through 37 meetings and attendance at three conferences, I sought to understand the common barriers and challenges experienced by culturally diverse women in those countries in elite sport as athletes, coaches, administrators and leaders, and what sports organisations, as well as other organisations and individuals, had done to address them. In addition to sharing these insights, this chapter summarises relevant research from Aotearoa New Zealand, the United States, the United Kingdom, and Australia (given the location of the industry I work in) to provide further context and understanding of the themes and recommendations identified and informed throughout my interviews.

Shared Experiences and the Language of "Otherness"

Prioritising and privileging the insights and experiences of women from cultural backgrounds that did not represent the cultural majority in their own sporting environment was critical in this research. As a White woman, I made every effort to "disrupt rather than perpetuate power structures within the research process" and to provide the culturally diverse women

I interviewed with a "platform to voice their lived experiences and perspectives, rather than be marginalised or understood through the agendas of the dominant sport coaching writers, policy makers and practitioners" (Rankin-Wright & Norman, 2018, p. 208). Whilst the White and male-dominated sporting environments in which the women worked and volunteered displayed cultural homogeneity across all three countries, the diverse gender and cultural identities of the women and the different ways in which they self-identified were anything but shared or common. Yet their journeys as "outsiders within" their sporting environments were described in common experiences, and in some cases, almost identical language to explain the ways they had navigated their gender and cultural identities in their sports. Their identities and experiences are multidimensional and should not be generalised, yet they provide a critical insight into the racialised and gendered structure of sporting organisations across different geographies and give voice to crucial counter-stories (Rankin-Wright & Norman, 2018, p. 210) that are often silenced in these sporting environments. Their counter-stories provide sports practitioners with an opportunity to critically question the cultural status quo and structures in the sports in which they operate.

Ratna and Samie (2017, p. 4) explain that "the language used to represent the heterogeneity of ethnic 'Others' is not tension-free" and that "to capture the politics of diverse groups of ethnic 'Other' girls and women is not straightforward". Hylton et al. (2015, p. 2) also recommend a cautious approach, as labels used uncritically or expediently "relating to ethnicity are likely to miss the diversity between and within ethnic groups, enforcing ideas of homogeneity". In establishing appropriate terminology for the women in my interviews, I was very conscious of these insights and the potential to homogenise the identities and experiences of such a diverse group of women. The women I met rarely used the commonly referenced collective terms from their respective countries to self-identify themselves, such as BME (Black and Minority Ethnic), BAME (Black, Asian, and Minority Ethnic), indigenous, ethnic minority, or cultural minority, which are all used interchangeably to depict non-White, culturally diverse people, and communities in the three countries I visited. Instead, they chose language and terminology that was specific to their personal connection with their own cultures, ethnicities, racial identities, religious identities, nationalities, language groups, clan groups, or tribes.

In this chapter, I have used the term "culturally diverse" to refer to women from the non-dominant cultural background within the sporting environments in which they participate, which included migrant and indigenous communities. I use this term respectfully whilst acknowledging that any collective terminology referring to such diverse individuals is inherently problematic. I also recognise that those who typically determine the use of such terminology in a sporting context are the beneficiaries of normalised, privileged "Whiteness" (Long & Hylton, 2002), including myself.

I carve out this space in this chapter to address the importance of language, for the benefit of sports practitioners who may be seeking greater engagement of women and girls from culturally diverse communities in their pathways, programmes, and activities, and to encourage consideration and recognition of the importance of language and terminology. As always, putting the "person first" and asking him/her/them of their preferences of self-identification is the best way to ensure that engagement begins from a place of respect, and leads the way for dialogue and understanding of an individual's unique view on what cultural safety means to them.

The following section of this chapter identifies three common themes from my research that reflect commonly shared experiences and insights that the culturally diverse women I interviewed were forced to navigate or negotiate in their coaching journeys. They are the importance of cultural safety, "fitting in" versus "finding belonging", and the privilege, burden, and responsibility of representation.

Importance of Cultural Safety

The most common theme of experiences shared by the culturally diverse women I interviewed was a desire to participate in culturally safe sports environments. The descriptions characterising these environments included spaces where they:

- Felt welcome
- Felt a sense of belonging
- Felt they could bring their "whole selves" to their sport
- Were trusted and respected
- Could put their views and opinions forward without fear of judgement
- Could question the status quo without feeling threatened
- Felt their family and community were also welcome in their sport
- Were supported when they were vulnerable or asked for help
- Were understood, appreciated, and accepted, as the sum of their parts

(Symons, 2018, p. 7)

Cultural safety has been defined as:

> An environment that is spiritually, socially and emotionally safe, as well as physically safe for people; where there is no assault, challenge or denial of their identity, of who they are and what they need. It is about shared respect, shared meaning, shared knowledge and experience of learning together.
>
> (Williams, 1999)

An important aspect of the definition of cultural safety is that it is determined by the recipient's experience and cannot be defined by the care giver

(Congress of Aboriginal and Torres Strait Islander Nurses and Midwives, 2014). Applying an understanding of this principle in a sporting context is important, as it centres the experiences, interpretations, and feelings of culturally diverse communities of cultural safety, as opposed to this concept being defined or intepreted by the sports organisations or administrators who are creating, running, or providing the sporting spaces or programmes. This distinction of culturally diverse women self-determining whether or not a sports coaching environment is culturally safe is important because "experiences of alienation, invisibility and 'not having a voice' provide an insight into the power relations that structure sport coaching and ultimately privilege white, able-bodied men within the system, whilst disadvantaging those considered as 'others'" (Norman & Rankin-Wright, 2016, p. 440). Environments of cultural safety place culturally diverse women at their centre, as opposed to the periphery, which they are frequently forced to inhabit, navigate, and negotiate in sports coaching. In spaces of cultural safety, the women I interviewed felt that their gender and cultural identities formed part of the fabric of the sporting spaces they occupy, as opposed to merely existing in the margins.

The concept of cultural safety has its origins in work of Māori[3] nursing in Aotearoa New Zealand (Williams, 1999) and has since been explored in different sporting contexts internationally. Cultural safety in sporting spaces is a critical factor to attracting Indigenous women in Australia to sport and physical exercise (Stronach et al., 2019) and creating places for "asserting identity, as well as maintaining culture and family links (Stronach et al., 2015, p. 23). The degree to which sporting activities feel culturally safe and comfortable was identified as a key factor influencing Pasifika community involvement in sport and recreation in Aotearoa New Zealand (Gordon et al., 2013). Similarly, Bennie et al. (2019) addressed the critical role of cultural safety in Aboriginal specific coaching programmes, which are often absent from mainstream coaching courses. In the United States, Stratta (1995, p. 54) suggested that the creation of safe spaces for African-American athletes in intercollegiate sports enabled them to "express the symbols and signs of their culture in all competitive and non-competitive sports context without being subjected to negative feedback or consequences". Taken together, each example provides an opportunity to foster a healthier cultural environment. Based on Williams' (1999) definition, as well as the descriptions provided by the women I interviewed of what characterised a culturally safe coaching space, the aspiration of creating culturally safe spaces across all sporting environments stands to benefit everyone involved in those spaces and as such, the alignment with the espoused egalitarian values and virtues of sport are clear (Symons, 2018, p. 7).

"Fitting In" Versus "Finding Belonging"

Several women reflected on the difference between "fitting in" and "finding belonging" in their sport, where they gave examples of what Jones and

Shorter-Gooden (2003) described as "shifting". This occurred when, upon entry into their sports environment, they would at times consciously (and at other times, subconsciously) alter their language and mannerisms, as well as stop themselves from talking about certain topics such as family, cultural, or religious celebrations, in order to fit into the sporting environment around them (Symons, 2018). Ratna (2011, p. 386) describes the experiences of British Asian females in football that reflected similar sentiments, where although they were part of the sporting spaces they coached in, they felt they were not necessarily accepted or valued within those spaces, and their sense of belonging and social inclusion was "engineered and negotiated at different points throughout their involvement in the sport". Borland and Bruening (2010, p. 415) described how the intersecting identities of race, gender, and sexuality forced some Black women coaches in collegiate basketball in the United States to "live double lives because they do not feel they can be themselves", which "often forces Black female assistant coaches to fit in where they are perceived by others to fit", as opposed to where they wish to. In an effort to fit in, the women I interviewed would often mould themselves to the environment rather than risking being excluded or standing out. These types of experiences share similarities to previous research, as Ratna (2017, p. 116) argued:

> being "in" a sporting space is not the same as being "of" that space: "out-siders within" have to consciously and/or subconsciously negotiate the complexities and nuances of belonging in order to progress their (sporting) careers if they decide to stay put and make claims to insiderness in those spaces.
>
> (Ratna, 2007, 2010, 2013)

The ways in which the women shared and connected with their cultural and gender identities in their sporting environments constantly evolved and changed. For some, age and experience brought increased confidence to raise issues of racism and discrimination with their sporting organisations. However, some would never raise these issues whilst still in the sporting pathway due to concerns that their allegations or complaints would not be handled well by their sporting organisation, that it would only serve to alienate them from their colleagues or teammates or potentially negatively impact their sporting career progression and opportunities (Symons, 2018). This reinforces earlier research which explored the experiences of racism of Māori sport participants, coaches, and administrators, who expressed that their experiences and feelings of discrimination were rarely discussed directly with Pākehā (a Māori term used commonly to refer to a White New Zealander of European descent) sport administrators, "for fear of ostracism or negative labels such as the stirrer or radical" (Hippolite & Bruce, 2010, p. 38). Similarly, Ahmed (2009, p. 49) addresses the pressure placed on Black women not to speak of racism, to not even mention the word, as "To speak out of anger as a Black woman is then to confirm your position as the cause of tension".

Where the coaches felt culturally safe, the sporting environment provided an opportunity to share, celebrate, and draw strength from culture and observance of cultural protocols, community, and family (Bennie et al., 2019). Some coaches described the opportunity to bring aspects of their culture into the sporting environment as a galvanising and teambuilding effect for everyone in that environment, regardless of their own cultural background (Symons, 2018). Research has provided unique examples of how culturally diverse women have brought their own cultural or religious identities to sporting spaces for the betterment of the whole environment, providing positive and practical examples of how gender and cultural identities can intersect in sports environments. Palmer and Masters (2010, p. 331) explored how Māori women in sport leadership roles in Aotearoa New Zealand incorporated their culture and values into their leadership styles and organisational culture, enabling their sporting, gendered, and ethnocultural identities to merge, with mainly positive outcomes in those environments. Whilst acknowledging significant challenges in navigating some religious and sporting requirements, several Muslim women I interviewed identified sporting environments as important places of learning and cultural exchange, as well as highlighting physical activity through sport as aligning with the requirements of their faith. Rankin-Wright and Norman (2018) also explore the encouragement of sports participation in the Qur'an and Hadith, just as Ahmad et al. (2020) summarise research demonstrating alignment between physical activity and Islamic values and norms.

The Privilege, Burden, and Responsibility of Representation

Despite their earned success, some women did not want to be more "hyper visible" than they already felt as culturally diverse women in White, male-dominated sports environments (Rankin-Wright & Norman, 2018, p. 210), nor did they wish to become a spokesperson for their race (Ratna, 2017). Women coming from cultures with collectivist value systems frequently described experiences of navigating between identities as individuals and as community members, which were frequently at odds with each other in their sporting environments (Symons, 2018). A lack of understanding of the values, social structures, and leadership styles of collectivist communities in a sports context can result in significant barriers to engagement in non-playing roles such as coaching (Ferkins et al., 2016). Alternatively, Hippolite and Bruce (2014, pp. 97–98) explored how culturally competent sporting environments guided by Māori values and fundamental beliefs could create culturally inclusive sporting environments "that are conducive to building team spirit, love and unity" for all involved. Several coaches spoke of how they knew they had become the embodiment of their sporting organisation's commitment and achievement of diversity (Ahmed, 2009). They knew their image was being used as the "face of diversity" for their sport (Symons, 2018) but as Rankin-Wright and Norman (2018, p. 211) identified, the coaches felt a "responsibility to succeed as coaches not only to represent the capabilities of Black women within coaching, but also to act as an inspiration to other women". The women sometimes had their suspicions confirmed that they were being used to further a diversity agenda or a public relations campaign, thereby enabling that organisation to "tick a box evidencing an organisational commitment to diversity" (Rankin-Wright & Norman, 2018, pp. 210–211). Despite these difficulties or their own personal feelings of discomfort, they would continue to support initiatives to drive further participation, community engagement, or connection with their communities, driven from a sense of responsibility to be a role model to the next generation to help them to "see what they could be".

Recommendations for Sport Practitioners in Coaching

The following section provides recommendations to sport practitioners for embedding cultural safety in their recruitment, engagement, and support of culturally diverse women coaches. These actions can enable the attending coaches to feel culturally safe, and to see and form connections between the coaching environment and their cultural and gender identities, rather than seeing them as separate components of themselves that cannot converge in the sporting environment. The recommendations aim to address the challenges identified in my research; however, their application and implementation will vary greatly across coaching environments, depending upon the contexts and diverse cultural backgrounds of the women involved.

Centre and Privilege Culturally Diverse Women's Voices in Coaching Programme Design

Sporting organisations should seek to centre and privilege the voices of culturally diverse women coaches by engaging them in coaching programme design. This engagement should commence from the initial design phase through to implementation, completion, and evaluation. Steps taken to prioritise the voices and insights of culturally diverse women coaches in programme design could include:

- Establishing advisory groups of women from the programme's target community.
- Appointing women from the target communities to be cultural conduits, whereby members of their community can ask questions and be provided with information about the coaching programmes on offer, as well as informing relevant cultural considerations or protocols for the

sporting organisation. Cultural conduit roles should be paid positions and may also take on the form of mentors or cultural liaison officers.
- Creating public and private feedback channels or processes to enable women to provide input throughout the phases of programme design, implementation, and evaluation.
- Researching other coaching programmes or sporting initiatives designed for the target community you are seeking to attract, engaging with the coordinators of those programmes and understanding the critical success factors of those initiatives, as well as the areas for improvement.
- Building partnerships with organisations and peak bodies that represent the target communities to help broker conversations about their specific needs and programme requirements to build trust and rapport within the community.

Taking these steps can ensure that appropriate gender and cultural considerations are built into the coaching programme from its inception, instead of retrofitting an existing programme which may have engrained systems and behaviours that are not representative or supportive of the group it seeks to attract, engage, and retain as coaches.

Creating Cultural Safety Within Coaching Programmes

This section focuses on suggested actions that may support the creation of cultural safety within coaching programmes for culturally diverse women. By prioritising cultural safety, sports organisations may better support not only the culturally diverse women it may seek to attract, but also benefit the broader inclusion of all participants through the following actions:

- Holding the activity at a time that enables participants to get carers for their children, or to have a space to bring children and other family members with them to observe the programme, in case they may also be interested in coaching opportunities in the future.
- Connecting with relevant representative cultural groups in the area to share information about the coaching programme or event, as well as seeking their support to promote the activity through their own networks, social media channels, and social events.
- Embedding relevant cultural protocol in programme agendas such as prayer, acknowledgements, or greetings from local elders or senior community leaders.
- Having sessions delivered by trainers or presenters from the target community.
- Creating formal and informal opportunities around the coaching programme for the coaches to mix and meet socially to build their coaching networks.

Shared Experiences From the Margins 169

- Ensuring the physical location of the programme is safe and accessible to the target community and, where relevant, discrete, particularly where cultural or religious requirements dictate a separation of men and women for physical activity or recreation.
- Creating a "suggestion box" that enables participants to provide confidential feedback throughout the programme to enable hosts/presenters to incorporate modifications so that the participants can see that their opinions are heard and respected.

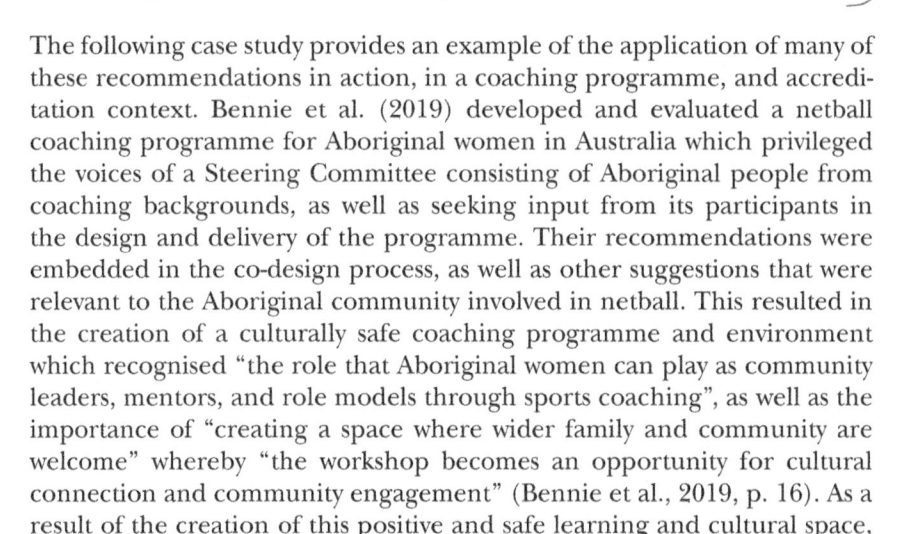

The following case study provides an example of the application of many of these recommendations in action, in a coaching programme, and accreditation context. Bennie et al. (2019) developed and evaluated a netball coaching programme for Aboriginal women in Australia which privileged the voices of a Steering Committee consisting of Aboriginal people from coaching backgrounds, as well as seeking input from its participants in the design and delivery of the programme. Their recommendations were embedded in the co-design process, as well as other suggestions that were relevant to the Aboriginal community involved in netball. This resulted in the creation of a culturally safe coaching programme and environment which recognised "the role that Aboriginal women can play as community leaders, mentors, and role models through sports coaching", as well as the importance of "creating a space where wider family and community are welcome" whereby "the workshop becomes an opportunity for cultural connection and community engagement" (Bennie et al., 2019, p. 16). As a result of the creation of this positive and safe learning and cultural space, the participants met the requirements of the coaching course and successfully received their formal coaching accreditations from the national netball governing body.

Role Models, Mentors, and Cultural Conduits

Representation and visibility of culturally diverse women are important across all areas of sport, including coaching. Women need to see themselves in various roles across the sporting landscape, should they wish to pursue them. The visibility, voices, and stories of these women as role models act as powerful tools to enable and inspire the next generation of women to "see what they can be" (Symons, 2018). Practical steps to build talent pipelines of culturally diverse women and to support the progress of those already within those pathways include the following: recruiting coaching mentors, building liaison and advocacy relationships to support future leaders, and creating strategies and development programmes for potential leaders to obtain practical experience and gain insights into leadership roles (Abney & Richey, 1992, p. 58). Specific policies and development programmes that are developed with and for culturally diverse women and communities to create concurrent and intersecting pathways to enter "mainstream" sporting environments have been found to be critical for better catering to the needs and requirements of women to feel culturally safe (Bennie et al., 2017; Borland & Bruening, 2010; Stronach et al., 2015). Creating such pathways for culturally diverse women also attracts other women from culturally diverse backgrounds to consider sports coaching as a potential opportunity in the future (Norman et al., 2014). Such pathways should be promoted through channels and forums that are freely and regularly accessed by the target audience, which may differ from traditional channels and forums used by sports organisations to promote their coaching programmes. These alternate channels can also be used to promote recruitment processes and opportunities transparently for culturally diverse coaches, as opposed to using social networks from within the sports organisation that might favour existing networks of coaches, who are already personally or professionally connected (Rankin-Wright & Norman, 2018, p. 220). Social media can also be an accessible and easy tool to promote culturally diverse women coaches as role models to a wide audience. However, the coaches should always have control over how their image and profile are used when representing a sporting organisation, as well as having approval and authority over when, where, and why they are featured.

Cultural conduit roles in sport that bridge cultural divides between sporting organisations and multicultural communities, such as cultural liaison officers or support workers, can provide critical support systems for culturally diverse women in coaching roles. They can also educate and advise sports organisations on culturally responsive practice to support people from those communities. Similarly, they can advocate for culturally diverse women in coaching roles who may themselves feel too intimidated or fearful to raise their concerns or issues with sports organisations. Past players or coaches, community elders, leaders, or mentors may take on such cultural conduit roles. Aspiring allies who may not be female or from the same cultural background as the target community can also play an important role. They can advocate for and promote the engagement and inclusion of culturally diverse women in coaching spaces and programmes where they are not represented, or do not yet have a clear or visible pathway to enter the coaching profession (Symons, 2018).

Creating connections with mentors can be an important support mechanism to enable and encourage culturally diverse women to access coaching roles. Previous research with Black women coaches in the United States (Borland & Bruening, 2010), Māori women in sports leadership in Aotearoa New Zealand (Palmer & Masters, 2010), and Aboriginal women in coaching roles in Australia (Bennie et al., 2019) described how mentoring relationships can be formal or informal, take the shape of regular or ad-hoc meetings, or simply provide a point of contact for advice and input. Any formal mentoring programme should be co-designed with women from the cultural background in focus to ensure cultural and gender requirements, as well as personal preferences for mentoring styles and engagement, are observed and catered for appropriately. For example, women from some cultural backgrounds may deem it appropriate to be paired with a male coaching mentor, whereas others may not.

Embed Cultural Safety and Diversity, Starting at the Top

To make meaningful and holistic change, sports organisations must bravely confront, discuss, and learn about racialised power relations and institutional processes that impact on their systems, structures, and culture (Rankin-Wright et al., 2016). Culturally safe coaching programmes alone, without broader cultural safety strategy and initiatives, are not enough to sustainably address the challenges regularly faced by culturally diverse women across the sporting landscape. Organisational change to create cultural safety requires a long-term, sustainable commitment from the senior management of a sporting organisation at Executive, CEO, and Board level, to insure against disruptions caused by changes in staff or funding challenges that often spell the end for programmatic diversity and inclusion activities. Too often, diversity and inclusion agendas are driven by junior or middle management staff who have limited power or influence organisationally to successfully tackle the systemic issues or embed the holistic change mechanisms required to critique and change long-held cultural norms, despite their personal commitment as champions of change (Spaaij et al., 2016, p. 288).

To ensure such change is sustained, these strategies and actions must be embedded at every level of the organisation. Each staff member must be empowered, supported, and made accountable for embedding cultural safety considerations and components of the organisation's diversity and inclusion strategy in their daily work. As Cunningham (2008, p. 142) suggests, "By making diversity a central part of the organisation, it factors into all strategic decisions, from who is hired, to the products and services offered, to the mechanisms used to market the organisation's products". This also requires the critiquing of conscious, overt actions as well as unconscious, subtle, and embedded norms and values that form the organisational cultures of sporting organisations, which Norman and Demers (2018) described as "what we stop noticing once we are three months in the organisation". Without a thorough review of the underlying culture that has informed these norms and values, any programmatic change will not address the root causes and origins that have previously prevented the creation of genuine cultural safety.

Embedding cultural awareness and responsiveness training across all areas of sporting organisations, in addition to coaching programmes, is crucial to building understanding and implementing culturally safe practices. Engaging culturally appropriate facilitators from relevant cultural backgrounds to deliver the training (Maxwell et al., 2013) is a powerful way to ensure common cultural narratives and norms are challenged and that counter-stories are centred and prioritised (Rankin-Wright & Norman, 2018), so sporting organisations are able to learn from shared storytelling and personal experiences of the people and communities that have experienced their sport from the margins.

Conclusion

This chapter aimed to prioritise and centre shared experiences of culturally diverse women in coaching across Aotearoa New Zealand, the United States, and the United Kingdom in traditionally White, male-dominated sports environments, whilst also drawing on existing research and insights from an Australian context. Despite their own unique cultural identities and localities, the common coaching experiences shared during this research told of a shared desire for cultural safety, navigating the need to "fit in" versus "finding belonging" and negotiating the privilege, burden, and responsibility of representation. Based on these themes, I have attempted to provide sports practitioners with recommendations that can assist them to better understand and support culturally diverse women in their coaching programmes, with a view to informing and creating culturally safe coaching environments at all levels of their sport. These recommendations focus on prioritising culturally diverse women's voices in the co-design of their programmes, identifying and creating role models, mentoring and cultural conduit roles, and embedding organisation-wide cultural safety and diversity under the leadership of senior management. A sports practitioner that approaches the engagement of any individual, group, or community with a mindset considerate of the impact of intersecting identities will immediately set the tone for more inclusive conversations and spaces, where culturally diverse women coaches are not forced to "shift", negotiate, or navigate their identities on a daily basis. Critically questioning and identifying "Whiteness" throughout the dominant cultural and gendered narratives and norms of mainstream sport that have led to the marginalisation of "Others" is a crucial step to inform the creation of more inclusive and culturally safe sporting spaces. Creating such spaces requires a systemic and holistic approach by sporting organisations, driven by a long-term commitment to continue to facilitate and take part in conversations with communities who have been marginalised in spaces created and governed by those sports.

The recommendations in this chapter provide sporting organisations with considerations and actions to support their progress towards creating cultural safety, but this is by no means a comprehensive list. As cultural safety is felt and defined by its recipients, sporting organisations must listen to, and work in collaboration with, women from culturally diverse communities to understand what cultural safety uniquely means to them and how it is created, from their perspective. The support and development of culturally diverse women in coaching can yield a far greater and more significant impact than just the outcomes of their immediate coaching role and responsibilities. From the community level to elite sporting environments, sporting spaces that welcome cultural and gender diversity enable participants to bring their whole selves, and therefore their whole effort, energy, and commitment, to their sporting pursuits. Everyone in the sporting community stands to benefit from the pursuit and creation of culturally safe environments.

Acknowledgment

As a sports practitioner, contributing to this collection of chapters amongst a group of extraordinary academics and authors with decades of research experience in academia was a daunting task. I am grateful to Leanne Norman for the opportunity to contribute to this book and to translate the insights of my Churchill Fellowship into tangible, practical actions, and recommendations for fellow sports practitioners. But above all else, I am thankful for the time, energy, and storytelling that were gifted to me by the women with whom I spoke during my Churchill Fellowship. I am also indebted to the fearless women I have worked with and learnt from in Australian sport, who have generously and patiently taught me by sharing their stories, experiences, and laughter.

Notes

1. Aotearoa is the Māori name for New Zealand. I have used both the Māori and English names alongside each other throughout this paper, in line with common usage of these terms and in recognition of Māori language and culture.
2. Aboriginal and Torres Strait Islander people are the Traditional Land Owners and First Nations people of Australia, having inhabited the country for more than 60,000 years. Collective terms including Aboriginal and Torres Strait Islander people, First Nations people, Indigenous Australians, First Australians and Aboriginal people are frequently used interchangeably to refer to this community and will vary in use across different contexts. When referencing themes or insights from research throughout this document, I have used the language or terminology featured in those papers to refer to those specific culturally diverse groups. I acknowledge that preferences of self-identification should always be prioritised.
3. Māori are the indigenous people of Aotearoa New Zealand. Te reo ("the language") Māori is one of the three official languages of Aotearoa New Zealand.

References

Abney, R., & Richey, D. L. (1992). Opportunities for minority women in sport—the impact of title IX. *Journal of Physical Education, Recreation & Dance, 63*(3), 56–59. https://doi.org/10.1080/07303084.1992.10604137

Ahmad, N., Thorpe, H., Richards, J., & Marfell, A. (2020). Building cultural diversity in sport: A critical dialogue with Muslim women and sports facilitators. *International Journal of Sport Policy and Politics, 12*(4), 637–653. https://doi.org/10.1080/19406940.2020.1827006

Ahmed, S. (2009). Embodying diversity: Problems and paradoxes for Black feminists. *Race Ethnicity and Education, 12*(1), 41–52. https://doi.org/10.1080/13613320802650931

Apoifis, N., Marlin, D., & Bennie, A. (2017). Noble athlete, savage coach: How racialised representations of Aboriginal athletes impede professional sport coaching opportunities for Aboriginal Australians. *International Review for the Sociology of Sport, 53*(7), 854–868. https://doi.org/10.1177/1012690216686337

Bennie, A., Apoifis, N., Marlin, D., & Caron, J. G. (2017). Cultural connections and cultural ceilings: Exploring the experiences of Aboriginal Australian sport coaches. *Qualitative Research in Sport, Exercise and Health, 11*(3), 299–315. https://doi.org/10.1080/2159676x.2017.1399924

Bennie, A., Marlin, D., Apoifis, N., & White, R. L. (2019). 'We were made to feel comfortable and . . . safe': Co-creating, delivering, and evaluating coach education and health promotion workshops with Aboriginal Australian peoples. *Annals of Leisure Research*, 1–21. https://doi.org/10.1080/11745398.2019.1622430

Borland, J. F., & Bruening, J. E. (2010). Navigating barriers: A qualitative examination of the under-representation of Black females as head coaches in collegiate basketball. *Sport Management Review, 13*(4), 407–420. https://doi.org/10.1016/j.smr.2010.05.002

Caldwell, O. (2018, June 2). *Women in charge of top New Zealand sports teams? Not likely*. www.stuff.co.nz/sport/other-sports/104112915/women-in-charge-of-top-new-zealand-sports-teams-not-likely

Carter, A. R., & Hart, A. (2010). Perspectives of mentoring: The Black female student-athlete. *Sport Management Review, 13*(4), 382–394. https://doi.org/10.1016/j.smr.2010.01.003

Congress of Aboriginal and Torres Strait Islander Nurses and Midwives. (2014). *A national summit on cultural safety in nursing and midwifery: Summary report*. www.catsinam.org.au/static/uploads/files/catsinam-national-cultural-safety-summit-report-nov-2014-final-wfkeeishbzho.pdf

Cunningham, G. B. (2008). Creating and sustaining gender diversity in sport organizations. *Sex Roles, 58*(1–2), 136–145. https://doi.org/10.1007/s11199-007-9312-3

Ferkins, L., Dee, K., Naylor, M., & Bryham, G. (2016). *Navigating two worlds: Pacific Island experiences and contribution to non-playing participation in rugby*. Auckland University of Technology Sports Performance Research Institute New Zealand. https://sprinz.aut.ac.nz/__data/assets/pdf_file/0020/72605/AUT-NZR-Report-Navigating-Two-Worlds-Pacific-Island-experirences-and-contibution-to-non-playing-particpation-in-rugby.pdf

Gordon, B., Sauni, P., & Tuagalu, C. (2013). Sport means 'family and church': Sport in New Zealand Pasifika communities. *Asia-Pacific Journal of Health, Sport and Physical Education, 4*(1), 49–63. https://doi.org/10.1080/18377122.2013.760427

Hippolite, H. R., & Bruce, T. (2010). Speaking the unspoken: Racism, sport and Maori. *Cosmopolitan Civil Societies: An Interdisciplinary Journal, 2*(2), 23–45. https://doi.org/10.5130/ccs.v2i2.1524

Hippolite, H. R., & Bruce, T. (2014). Towards cultural competence: How incorporating Māori values could benefit New Zealand sport. *Native Games: Indigenous Peoples and Sports in the Post-Colonial World (Research in the Sociology of Sport), 7*, 85–106. https://doi.org/10.1108/S1476-2854(2013)0000007009

Hylton, K., Long, J., Parnell, D., & Rankin-Wright, A. (2015). *'Race', racism and participation in sport*. Race Equality Foundation. http://eprints.leedsbeckett.ac.uk/

id/eprint/2049/1/Hylton%20et%20al%20Race%20Equality%20Foundation%20 Health%20Briefing%2040%20Final.pdf
Jones, C., & Shorter-Gooden, K. (2003). *Shifting: The double lives of Black women in America* (Reprint ed.). United States of America: HarperCollins.
Lapchick, R. (2019). *The 2019 racial and gender report card*. The Institute for Diversity and Ethics in Sport. https://43530132-36e9-4f52-811a-182c7a91933b.filesusr.com/ugd/7d86e5_517e71c07bdc45e4b9a5c053dcbe3108.pdf
Long, J., & Hylton, K. (2002). Shades of white: An examination of whiteness in sport. *Leisure Studies*, *21*(2), 87–103. https://doi.org/10.1080/02614360210152575
Marlin, D., Apoifis, N., & Bennie, A. (2020). *Aboriginal sports coaches, community, and culture (Indigenous-Settler Relations in Australia and the World)*, (1st ed.). Springer. https://doi.org/10.1007/978-981-15-8481-7
Maxwell, H., Foley, C., Taylor, T., & Burton, C. (2013). Social inclusion in community sport: A case study of Muslim women in Australia. *Journal of Sport Management*, *27*(6), 467–481. https://doi.org/10.1123/jsm.27.6.467
Norman, L. (2010). Feeling second best: Elite women coaches' experiences. *Sociology of Sport Journal*, *27*(1), 89–104. https://doi.org/10.1123/ssj.27.1.89
Norman, L., & Demers, G. (2018, April). *Changing sport organisational culture to achieve gender equity*. Symposium Presentation presented at the 2018 Social Justice Through Sport and Exercise Psychology Symposium, Minneapolis, University of Minnesota.
Norman, L., North, J., Hylton, K., Flintoff, A., & Rankin, A. J. (2014). *Sporting experiences and coaching aspirations among Black and Minority Ethnic (BME) groups: A report for Sports Coach UK* (Project Report). Sports Coach UK. http://eprints.leedsbeckett.ac.uk/id/eprint/1365/
Norman, L., & Rankin-Wright, A. (2016). Surviving rather than thriving: Understanding the experiences of women coaches using a theory of gendered social well-being. *International Review for the Sociology of Sport*, *53*(4), 424–450. https://doi.org/10.1177/1012690216660283
Palmer, F. R., & Masters, T. M. (2010). Māori feminism and sport leadership: Exploring Māori women's experiences. *Sport Management Review*, *13*(4), 331–344. https://doi.org/10.1016/j.smr.2010.06.001
Rankin-Wright, A. J., Hylton, K., & Norman, L. (2016). Off-colour landscape: Framing race equality in sport coaching. *Sociology of Sport Journal*, *33*(4), 357–368. https://doi.org/10.1123/ssj.2015-0174
Rankin-Wright, A. J., & Norman, L. (2018). Sport coaching and the inclusion of Black women in the United Kingdom. In A. Ratna & S. F. Samie (Eds.), *Race, gender and sport: The politics of ethnic 'other' girls and women* (pp. 204–224). Routledge. https://doi.org/10.4324/9781315637051-11
Ratna, A. (2007). A "fair game?": British Asian females' experiences of racism in women's football. In J. Magee, J. Caudwell, K. Liston, & S. Scraton (Eds.), *Women, football and Europe: Histories, equity and experiences* (pp. 77–96). Meyer and Meyer Sport.
Ratna, A. (2010). Taking the power back! The politics of British Asian female football players. *Young*, *18*(2), 117–132.
Ratna, A. (2011). 'Who wants to make aloo gobi when you can bend it like Beckham?' British Asian females and their racialised experiences of gender and identity in women's football. *Soccer & Society*, *12*(3), 382–401. https://doi.org/10.1080/14660970.2011.568105

Ratna, A. (2013). Intersectional plays of identity: The experiences of British Asian female footballers. *Sociological Research Online*. http://www.socresonline.org.uk/18/1/13.html

Ratna, A. (2017). Walking to and from "home": British Asian first-generation citizens, translocal identities and belonging. *Leisure Studies*. http://dx.doi.org/10.1080/02614367.2017.1285952

Ratna, A., & Samie, S. F. (2017). Introduction: Sport, race and gender—the politics of ethnic Other girls and women. In A. Ratna & S. F. Samie (Eds.), *Race, gender and sport: The politics of ethnic 'other' girls and women* (pp. 1–9). Routledge. https://doi.org/10.4324/9781315637051-1

Spaaij, R., Magee, J., Farquharson, K., Gorman, S., Jeanes, R., Lusher, D., & Storr, R. (2016). Diversity work in community sport organizations: Commitment, resistance and institutional change. *International Review for the Sociology of Sport*, 53(3), 278–295. https://doi.org/10.1177/1012690216654296

Sports Coach UK. (2011, March). *Sports coaching in the UK III: A statistical analysis of coaches and coaching in the UK*. https://issuu.com/scukres/docs/sports_coaching_in_the_uk_iii_final

Stratta, T. M. (1995). Cultural inclusiveness in sport—recommendations from African American women college athletes. *Journal of Physical Education, Recreation & Dance*, 66(7), 52–56. https://doi.org/10.1080/07303084.1995.10607118

Stronach, M., Maxwell, H., & Pearce, S. (2019). Indigenous Australian women promoting health through sport. *Sport Management Review*, 22(1), 5–20. https://doi.org/10.1016/j.smr.2018.04.007

Stronach, M., Maxwell, H., & Taylor, T. (2015). 'Sistas' and Aunties: Sport, physical activity, and Indigenous Australian women. *Annals of Leisure Research*, 19(1), 7–26. https://doi.org/10.1080/11745398.2015.1051067

Symons, J. (2018). *Investigating elite sports environments enabling culturally diverse women to thrive* (Project Report). Winston Churchill Memorial Trust. www.churchilltrust.com.au/project/to-investigate-elite-sports-environments-that-enable-culturally-diverse-women-to-thrive-new-zealand-usa-uk/

Williams, R. (1999). Cultural safety—what does it mean for our work practice? *Australian and New Zealand Journal of Public Health*, 23(2), 213–214. https://doi.org/10.1111/j.1467-842x.1999.tb01240.x

10 Supporting and Developing Women in Sport Coaching

A Lifespan Career Approach

Nicole LaVoi and Courtney J. Boucher

Introduction

Women in sport coaching are under-represented in nearly all sports, at all levels, in all positions, and in every country around the globe (LaVoi, 2016; Robertson, 2016). Currently, this issue is garnering the attention it has deserved from local, regional, national, and international governing bodies. Often the under-representation of women in sport coaching is due to the numerous, multi-faceted and well documented barriers, and lack of supports, women coaches face (Burton & LaVoi, 2016; LaVoi & Dutove, 2012; Norman & Rankin-Wright, 2018). In this chapter, we propose a new and nuanced way of conceptualising women's careers in sport coaching, by employing a career development lifespan framework. The focus of this chapter and starting point for using this new framework is women sport coaches. Women coaches are acutely under-represented and marginalised in sport, and many experience harassment, bullying, and exclusion and therefore need additional and equitable support to level the occupational playing field (LaVoi, 2016; Norman & Rankin-Wright, 2018). However, the knowledge herein can readily be applied to all coaches, including men, because—*what is good for women is good for everyone.*

Women in the Workplace: Gendered Career Development

Women's careers develop differently compared to men, yet many career development theories are grounded in classic age and stage models (see Baltes et al., 2019), which are not as applicable to women (O'Neil & Bilimoria, 2005). In addition, normal life experiences of many women (but not all)—such as pregnancy and childcare—become problematised due to incompatibility with male work models that fail to account for life course events. Feminist vocational scholars argue women's careers differ from men in three distinct ways: (1) impact of family responsibilities, (2) women's developmental psychology places greater emphasis on relational aspects in development, and (3) women's under-representation and frequent token status restrain development and advancement (O'Neil & Bilimoria, 2005).

Within sport, currently very little focus, policy, or resources exist to aid the career development or career transition of sport coaches (Knight et al., 2015), and to our knowledge, none exists specifically for women. A more nuanced, contextual, and specific way of understanding the career development of women sport coaches is needed. It is well documented that sport is a male-centred, male-dominated occupational context where male power is normalised and often invisible (Knoppers, 1987), women experience tokenism and occupational sex segregation (LaVoi, 2009), prevalent bias and stereotypes privilege White, heterosexual men (Burton & LaVoi, 2016), homophobia is rampant (Norman, 2016), mother-coaches face a gendered "mommy penalty" (Bruening et al., 2016; Schull & Kihl, 2019), and women coaches of colour experience gendered racism (Carter-Francique & Olushoga, 2016; Larsen et al., 2019; Olushola-Ogunrinde & Carter-Francique, 2020). Ageist attitudes—one of the most institutionalised forms of prejudice today—comprise stereotypical beliefs and prejudicial feelings and behavioural predispositions that affect decisions to recruit, promote, and retain employees (McCarthy et al., 2019). No research exists on lifespan ageism (those perceived to be "older", out of touch, and irrelevant, or "younger", inexperienced, and incompetent) of women sport coaches. Similarly, research about and for female para-coaches or coaches with disabilities is nearly non-existent. Resources are needed at all levels of the social-ecological system to help women of various intersectional identities enter into, develop, and progress within and across sport coaching careers. A framework for researchers, coach educators, sport administrators, and organisations—beyond an insufficient "snapshot" approach—is needed to achieve gender equity in sport.

A Multilevel Gendered System of Sport

LaVoi posited within the Ecological Intersectional Model (EIM) of Barriers and Supports for Women Coaches (LaVoi, 2016; LaVoi & Dutove, 2012), based on Bronfenbrenner's (1979) Ecological Systems Theory (EST), that coaches are nested within a system of societal, organisational, and interpersonal-relational structures, as well as continuity and change of influential temporal factors (see Figure 10.1). Each level of the environment asserts a powerful impact upon the developmental trajectories (personal and professional) of a coach and experiences in the system vary by intersectional identities. The barriers and supports women coaches face are ever changing over the life course, and EIM provides a framework for understanding and explicating the lifespan developmental perspective. Although LaVoi and Dutove (2012) explain Bronfenbrenner's EST is developmental, to date lifespan research is limited in sport coaching. One exemplar study by researchers Larsen et al. (2019) used a narrative inquiry approach to study Black assistant female collegiate basketball coaches in the United States at different points in their careers. Examination is

Supporting and Developing Women 179

warranted to more fully understand, and therefore equitably support, women in sport coaching.

Figure 10.2 depicts the proposed Stages of Career Progression Model (SCPM) for women in sports coaching. Stages of career progression are

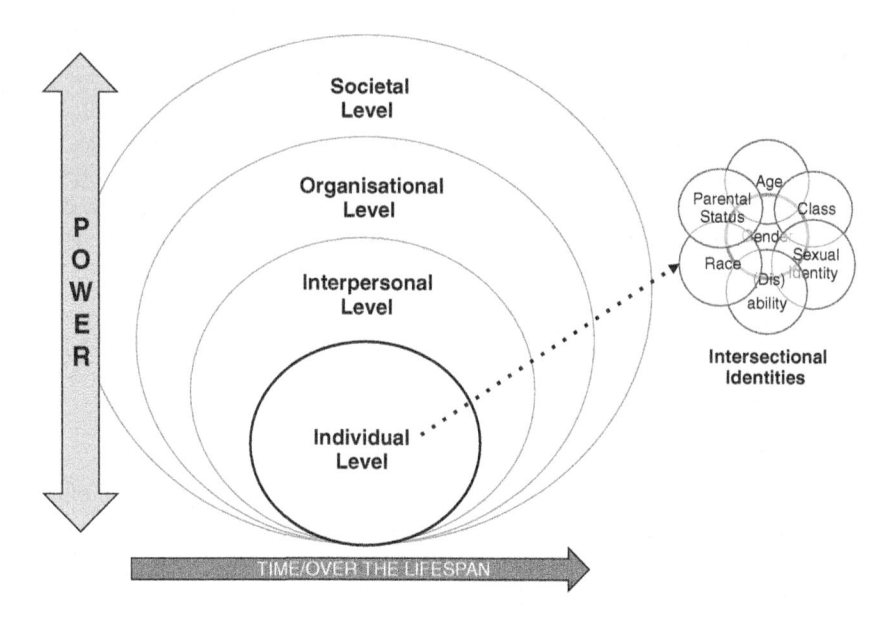

Figure 10.1 Ecological Intersectional Model of Barriers and Supports for Women in Sport Coaching

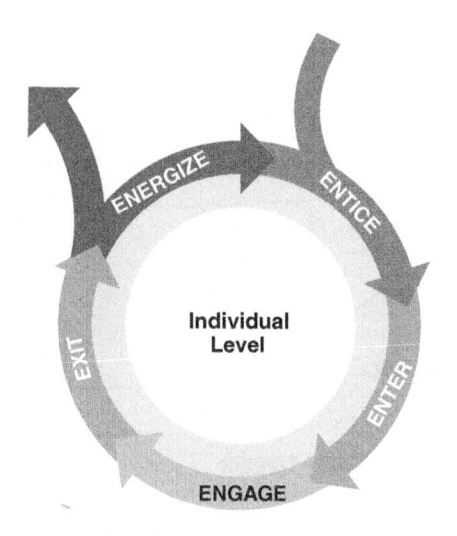

Figure 10.2 Stages of Career Progression Model

180 *Nicole LaVoi and Courtney J. Boucher*

most proximal to the individual coach, occur temporally, and are influenced by the people, networks, organisational structures, power systems, societal norms, and ideologies in which the coach is embedded. Development and experience of the coach will vary based on the intersectional identities of the coach at the individual level of the EIM, but more research is needed (Norman & Rankin-Wright, 2018). As specified in the EIM, influence across levels is bidirectional. For example, the career progression (or stagnation) of a coach may affect interpersonal relationships (i.e., the coach wants to move for a new job, but the partner does not, so the couple breaks up), just as interpersonal relationships may impact career decisions and progression (i.e., the coach wants to move for a new job, and the partner does not, so she does not accept the job offer). Offered herein, the SCPM is a hidden, additional, nuanced layer of temporal processes embedded within the EIM. The SCPM is explained in detail in the next section.

Stages of Career Progression for Women in Sports Coaching

Utility of the Stages of Career Progression Model

The proposed SCPM (see Figure 10.3) for women in sports coaching will be explained and it uses suggested. Stages were inspired by Super's (1980) lifespan, life-space approach to career development and helps to fill Roberts and Kenttä's (2019) call for research, theory, and frameworks to help understand coach career progression. Each stage can be understood as a result of experiences in the previous stage and as the launch

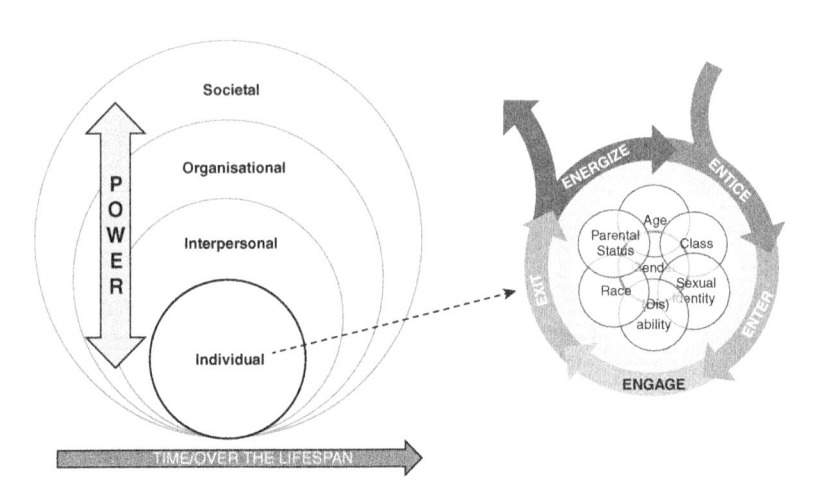

Figure 10.3 Integration of stages of career progression within the Ecological Intersectional Model of Barriers and Supports for Women in Sport Coaching

pad for subsequent experiences and stages as the individual interacts with the social, organisational, and sociocultural environments around her. The proposed stages are flexible enough to account for idiosyncrasies, challenges, and barriers women coaches face, the multiple types of coaching roles, years spent coaching, and developmental life events. The integration of a lifespan perspective to work, aging, and retirement, with other developmental lifespan theories is deficient (Rudolph et al., 2019), and sport coaching is no exception.

LaVoi's EIM combined with SCPM for women coaches (EIM + SCPM) begins to fill that deficiency. Foremost EIM + SCPM helps organisational leaders strategically pinpoint resources (at a specific EIM level *and* SCPM stage) for gender-equity initiatives. Arbitrary focused initiatives on one level or one stage, rather than using a multifocal lens of EIM + SCPM, will lead to a partial understanding of the problem and lead to an ineffective solution for gender equity. Uninformed initiatives will more likely lead to what Norman and Rankin-Wright term a "developmental dead end" which is commonplace for women coaches (2018, p. 441). Second, the model combination helps identify leverage points, useful for organisational leaders, that may help prevent coach burnout, improve physical and mental health in and through a career trajectory, and help check occupational turnover (and thereby also save money and improve programme continuity). Third, for coaches experiencing critical windows across the developmental trajectory of a coaching career (e.g., entering coaching, burnout, getting married, having children, health issues, changing jobs from assistant to head coach, coming out, being fired, and death of parent) it provides those who hire, oversee, and support women coaches, a framework of understanding of where and when to provide support. Fourth, it can be used by researchers to develop more complete knowledge along each stage that can be translated into positive applied best practices by organisational leaders. Fifth, it educates organisational leaders that women's workplace and life experiences differ from men due to gendered factors (O'Neil & Bilimoria, 2005). Sixth, the stages of career progression can be useful for those in sport governance and power, advocates, and coach educators who want to be a part of creating systems change by developing equitable programming, supports, and policies for women along the sports coaching pipeline—or who desire to build a new pipeline altogether. Seventh, this combined model will aid all stakeholders to more accurately assess and identify why and when women are leaving coaching—and how to stave off attrition. Eighth, it illuminates a specific, yet nuanced pathway for organisational leaders with power to enact change at every level to achieve gender equity. Lastly, to our knowledge, this is the first sport-specific, women-focused career progression model for sport coaches. To be transparent, much of the evidence supporting the SCPM is based on research conducted within the US intercollegiate sport system or the UK; however, learnings can be modified and applied globally. Each stage is explained in the following.

The Entice Stage is characterised by encouraging, convincing, and enticing females into sport coaching who are not currently coaching. *The Entry Stage* comprises initial movement into a coaching position via voluntary or recruitment efforts (i.e., entering the pipeline). Once an individual obtains a coaching position, the individual enters *The Engagement Stage* which contains many aspects of how women participate with, and in, their workplace and colleagues and includes support, mentorship, sponsorship, and allyship. *The Exit Stage* encompasses voluntarily or involuntarily leaving a coaching position and transitioning either to another coaching position, exiting coaching, or exiting the workforce altogether (left outgoing arrow). *The Energise Stage* is where resilience is fostered and the focus is on renewal and personal growth. For some, exiting coaching or a particular coaching position can be energising, but for many who get fired or are burned out, recovery, resilience, and renewal may take time. During *The Energise Stage*, coaches may be energised and/or enticed back to the profession, choose to re-enter coaching and if so, the stages of career progression is regenerated. Depending on the individual-situational interaction, the time spent at any stage varies and the "push-and-pull" of negative and positive factors—or barriers and supports—that influence career progression decision points along the way will also vary (Knight et al., 2015; Super, 1980). Decision or leverage points occur at all stages and are influenced by the multiple levels of the ecological environment, for example, taking on a new role, moving organisations, declining a job offer, earning a degree or coaching certification, or starting a family may impact decision-making. Existing evidence and suggestions for application at each stage are summarised with more depth in the following sections.

The Entice Stage

How do we get former female athletes, adolescent girls and young women (AGYW), mothers, retiring professional female athletes, encore career women, and grandmothers interested in sport coaching? Little is known about effective strategies pertaining to the recruitment of females into coaching across the lifespan. Strategies, programmes, and initiatives to encourage, convince, excite, entice, and enlist more females into coaching has observably been ineffective, or perhaps more accurate—non-existent—in many contexts. Data are clear that young women who are former athletes and possess knowledge and athletic capital are not pursuing coaching careers (Drago et al., 2005). And given under-representation, women are not seen as coaching role models (LaVoi, 2016), and young women may see sport leadership in a way that does not match self-perceptions (Schull, 2017). A greater number of visible same-sex and same-identity role models is proven to positively improve girls' and women's self-perceptions in male-dominated professions (Lockwood, 2006), and recent data show that female athletes are inspired by successful women in sport as it provides proof that coaching is a viable career pathway and negative stereotypes can be overcome (Midgley et al., 2020).

According the Social Cognitive Career Theory (SCCT; Lent et al., 1994), individuals are likely to become interested in, choose to pursue, and perform better at activities in which they have strong self-efficacy beliefs, as long as they also have necessary skills and environmental supports to pursue these activities. To entice girls and women into coaching, they need to be exposed to similar others performing successfully in coaching, be given opportunity to develop competence, and be placed in situations where success can be experienced.

Wasend and LaVoi (2019) used SCCT to examine influence of female athletes' exposure to female coaches (i.e., salient same-identity role models) and found they were four times more likely to *currently* be coaching than athletes coached by a male head coach. Data indicate that women coaches may be modelling effective ways to navigate the occupational gendered landscape, provide proof coaching can be a career goal and that women can achieve, manage work–family conflict, and may provide active mentoring, social support, and a network for their athletes who enter and helps them subsequently stay in coaching (Wasend & LaVoi, 2019). Based on SCCT, organisations need to strategically target every level of the EIM to help entice—provide skill development opportunities to help females feel efficacious, provide visible female role models in positions of power, leverage women within all communication materials (e.g., print, social, and digital), and regularly highlight and celebrate the accomplishments of women, which helps to counter damaging and false gender-biased and stereotypical societal messages.

Many AGYW and adult women love sport, and a convincing communication campaign that taps into their love of the game, passion, desire to give back, opportunity to be a role model, make a difference in the lives of others, and stay involved in a sport they love, is a largely untapped and under-utilised recruitment strategy. For an example, see The Tucker Centre's #SHECANCOACH inspirational campaign and *Game On: Women Can Coach* toolkit materials. Evidence-based strategies to recruit mother-coaches exist (LaVoi & Leberman, 2015; Leberman & LaVoi, 2011) but additional knowledge is needed on how to entice and recruit different demographic profiles of females into sport coaching (LaVoi et al., 2019b). One simple, cost-effective strategy is to simply *ask her and/or invite her* to think about or consider coaching. Sport leaders can leverage women and those with social and athletic capital (e.g., elite female athletes and coaches) to perform "The Ask" which provides the social encouragement and motivational direction towards a goal, and positively influences self-efficacy and outcome expectations about the consequences of engagement in coaching—the three tenants of SCCT (Bandura, 1986).

Opportunity exists for coaching associations, national governing (NGB/Os) bodies/organisations (e.g., Sport Canada and USPOC), and international governing bodies and federations (e.g., IOC and FIFA) to support and develop initiatives to help entice girls and women to enter coaching. More can, and should be, done.

The Entry Stage

The Entry Stage involves moving into a coaching position via voluntary or recruitment efforts. Entry may be a tentative choice that is being explored and this stage is about "trying on" coaching. Educational programming is needed for novice coaches or coaches in new positions, at every level and age, to develop skills necessary to survive and thrive, including increasing awareness of, and exposure to, the realities of the (biased) sporting world they will face (Leberman, 2017). Entry-level coaches over-rely on previous athletic experiences, available role models, and apprenticeship to prepare them, which leaves them unprepared (Callary & Gearity, 2020). Given the scarcity of women coaching role models, this is particularly salient for females.

In *The Entry Stage*, it is important to keep in mind that women and girls are not a monolith. Employing the EIM, intersectional identities, environmental context, and interpersonal supports will shape variant needs and experiences of oppression (LaVoi, 2016) across one's career. For example, a new volunteer mother coach who will coach her child has different needs than a high school student coaching summer camp, than a high-performance coach moving from an assistant to a head coach position, than a newly retired professional athlete who has never coached but wants to enter the profession. Once women have entered coaching, support is needed to keep them engaged within the coaching pathway. When women have positive experiences upon entry where they feel nurtured, valued, safe, and supported, the more likely she will sustain engagement in coaching (Knight et al., 2015; LaVoi & Wasend, 2018). Interestingly, UK women coaches at the grassroots level in female-dominated sports report greater acceptance and support from male colleagues, which suggests women who display "coaching feminities" may experience more support (Murray et al., 2020). Organisational leaders must create a positive and supportive climate *for all women regardless of identities, level or sport type*, upon entry to coaching.

The Engagement Stage

The Engagement Stage contains many aspects of how women participate with colleagues and experience their workplace. *Development* and *Support* (including mentorship, sponsorship, and gender allyship) are the two primary hallmarks of engagement where serious skill building, excitement about one's career, networking, stabilisation, establishing oneself, and adjustment to improve one's position is undertaken. In short, for women it is about obtaining the right skills and finding an inclusive, "goodness-of-fit" environment where she can succeed. For sport organisations, this means providing a workplace culture where women feel competent, safe (psychologically and physically), valued, and supported (LaVoi & Wasend, 2018), as data suggests coaches who do not feel appreciated or fail to have their basic needs met are more likely to leave the job, and perhaps coaching altogether (Knight et al., 2015).

The Career Self-Management Model (CSM; Lent & Brown, 2013), grounded in the SCCT mentioned earlier, focuses on process and actions (i.e., how people make choices) of career development. The CSM was developed to predict how people make school- and work-related choices and manage other important developmental tasks, challenges, and crises, regardless of the occupations they enter (Brown & Lent, 2019).

Within *The Engagement Stage*, coaches stay engaged and manage their career through a series of actions and decisions (Brown & Lent, 2019). A few examples of career self-management actions relevant to sport coaching are negotiating the contemporary work world including cross-generational challenges, managing school-to-work and work-to-work transitions, searching for and attaining employment, coping with negative career events (e.g., getting fired, being under investigation, scandals, and a losing season), coping with lifespan events (e.g., marriage, childbirth, divorce, eldercare, and personal health), refining networking skills, preparing for expected and unexpected career related changes, updating skills, building job niches, and planning retirement (Brown & Lent, 2019). Normalised and common life experiences of female coaches, such as marriage, pregnancy, and childcare, become problematised due to their incompatibility with male work models that do not take life course events into account (O'Neil & Bilimoria, 2005). Better understanding of these processes by organisational leaders may help more effective engagement and development women in sport coaching.

Development

Unfortunately, a longitudinal body of evidence on how to optimise coach preparation and development does not exist (Callary & Gearity, 2020). Many programmes worldwide focus on developing AGYW as leaders in and through sport (Leberman, 2017), but not specifically or explicitly through coaching. Development typically includes taking on critical job assignments and professional development opportunities that are important for career progression. However, as Larsen et al. (2019) noted, Black women assistant coaches are often pigeonholed into positions that limits development of essential knowledge and skills necessary to be becoming a head coach.

Based on recent data, women-only professional development opportunities appear to be effective in keeping women coaches engaged. Specifically, the Tucker Center's longitudinal study of women graduates of the WeCOACH NCAA Women Coaches Academy (WCA) in the United States indicates that 88% of 700+ women are still coaching up to five years after attending the WCA (LaVoi et al., 2020), lending support for the impact and need for women-only or women-focused coach development opportunities. A key finding from a qualitative study conducted by Leberman and LaVoi (2011) was women expressed a desire for single-sex coach education and mentorship programmes as opposed to the established co-educational structure, a finding that was recently supported as women coaches in a separate study vocalised a clear desire for a single-sex option (Vinson et al., 2016). One key component to empowering women coaches is to educate and help them interrogate, and subsequently navigate, the gendered system and gender bias inherent in leadership that unarguably affects their careers (Schull & Kihl, 2019). Another is to challenge those in power—who create the unfavourable environments in which women desire, need, and opt into single-sex programmes—to both self-asses bias and make cultural organisational change.

A single-sex, women-focused, coach education programme can be a crucial step in sustained engagement because it recognises the simple fact that women are positioned, advantaged, evaluated, and constrained differently, and therefore need additional resources for gender equality to be achieved (Subrahmanian, 2005). Researchers have stressed the idea of that male hegemony is present in the sporting world, and coach education programmes are no exception (Sartore & Cunningham, 2007; Schell & Rodriguez, 2000; Whisenant, 2008; Whisenant et al., 2002). Women report it difficult to navigate and integrate themselves within the traditional male-focused coaching hierarchy and have reported issues with the sexist, derogatory and bigoted nature of coach educators and male peers within coach education programmes (Lewis et al., 2015). In these formal learning settings, female coaches were often excluded, unwelcomed, and described the atmosphere as intimidating, awkward, and often uncomfortable, due in part because very few coach developers are women and the few that exist experience rampant gendered discrimination (Norman, 2020).

To combat this problem, many organisations are developing women-only professional development, similar to the WeCOACH Women Coaches Academy. The WCA is a single-sex coach education programme, led by women with specific curriculum designed for women that provides education, professional development, and networking, with the goal of supporting and retaining women in the coaching profession (LaVoi, 2020; LaVoi et al., 2019b). Single-sex or women-focused coach education programmes are becoming popular around the globe. The biggest target of opportunity, however, is for sport organisations to develop a culture where women feel equitably treated, valued, and supported.

Levels of Systems Support

Based on a meta-analysis on women in sport coaching research, far more research exists on barriers, than supports (Burton & LaVoi, 2016; LaVoi &

Dutove, 2012)—more research on supports is needed and warranted. For gender equity to occur, organisational leaders must develop targeted and much needed supports at all levels of the EIM across every career stage.

INDIVIDUAL-INTERPERSONAL LEVEL SUPPORT

Researchers have reported that coaches rely on various social supports (family, friends, and staff) to help cope with job-related stressors (Norris et al., 2017). Women need support throughout their career trajectory, but some researchers argue critical windows exist, when important career shaping events tend to occur and where burnout or exit are more likely. Some argue the "make or break" years for women are between the ages of 28 and 45 (Wichert, 2014), others argue the age is 36–45 (O'Neil & Bilimoria, 2005). LaVoi et al. (2020) noted a dramatic decline in the number of female assistant collegiate coaches after the age of 27. Regardless of the critical age window, it is clear that women within an organisational culture that provides women the same career support as men (Wichert, 2014) and meets her essential human needs of belongingness, competence, and autonomy will feel supported (including tangible resources, professional development, equitable pay, and emotional support) and be more successful in keeping women in the pipeline (Knight et al., 2015; LaVoi & Wasend, 2018; Zakrajsek et al., 2020). In short—*happy coaches do not leave.* It is also likely if coaches feel supported and socially well (Norman & Rankin-Wright, 2018) at every level of the EIM, they may have more positive psychosocial and occupational outcomes, be less likely to burnout and in turn, leave coaching. Organisational leaders should explicitly ASK women what they need to feel supported—listen—and then strategically act.

Sport science researchers have predominantly focused on athlete well-being, mental health, and burnout. Attention to these same important factors for sport coaches has grown over the last decade (Durand-Bush et al., 2012; Norman & Rankin-Wright, 2018; Norris et al., 2017; Olusoga et al., 2019). Recently researchers called for a greater understanding of female coaches' stressors, social support, and coping (which they argued are different from men) as it relates to well-being and reducing the likelihood of burnout (Norris et al., 2017). In one cross-sectional sample of US collegiate women coaches, 18% (76 of 420) reported they "agreed" or "strongly agreed" they currently felt burned out from coaching (LaVoi, 2020), but in a retrospective sample of eight high performance female Canadian coaches 75% reported experiencing burnout at least once in her career (Durand-Bush et al., 2012). Burnout for women in sport coaching is commonplace.

Based on the data, burnout is a major concern for female coaches as they report more emotional labour compared to male peers, but research lags behind. Examining burnout is imperative because coaches who experience burnout are more likely to withdraw from the profession entirely, explaining in part, why on average one in three coaching positions turns over every year (Raedeke, 2004). Given the individual, organisational, and financial costs of burnout, early detection and intervention are imperative, helping coaches develop individual positive coping skills and social supports are key strategies for prevention (Olusoga et al., 2019). Yet burnout, coping and well-being are not just individual-level issues, they are influenced by gendered organisational culture and societal ideologies surrounding the coach (Norman & Rankin-Wright, 2018), as specified in the EIM.

INTERPERSONAL AND ORGANISATIONAL-LEVEL SUPPORT

Three ways to explicitly support women coaches at the interpersonal and organisational levels include mentoring, sponsorship, and gender allyship. These support functions are outlined next. *Mentoring* is a relationship between an experienced individual and a (usually) more junior person seeking career assistance, and personal and professional support (Fowler et al., 2007), making it a form of intergenerational-shared leadership. Sustained mentors can notice signs of ill health or ill-being, and intervene (Norman & Rankin-Wright, 2018). Mentoring has the potential to empower women as both mentees and mentors within masculine organisational contexts (Dashper, 2019). *Mentors provide support, talk with you and give advice* (Ang, 2018) and mentoring programmes that challenge gender stereotypes, gender inequality, the status quo, and dominant ideals of what is means "to coach" and helps change thinking around the masculine model on which ideas of success are based, are likely more impactful for women (Dashper, 2019). Research pertaining specifically to sports mentoring is not new (Bloom, 2013; Nash, 2003), but a more in-depth and comprehensive attention to coach mentoring (see Chambers, 2018; Leeder et al., 2019) and specifically women coaches (Allen & Reid, 2019; Banwell, Kerr et al., 2019; Banwell, Stirling et al., 2019; LaVoi, 2020) has increased recently. Related to *The Entice Stage*, Madsen and McGarry (2016) argued active mentoring of female athletes into coaching careers—by coaches of either gender—is more likely to lead female athletes to become coaches than mere exposure to female coaches.

Organisations who desire to create a theoretically based, rigorously evaluated mentorship programme for women coaches should review the collaborative Canadian venture—the Female Coach Mentorship Model (FCMM; Banwell, Kerr et al., 2019; Banwell, Stirling et al., 2019). Another, more recent programme currently being evaluated in the United States, is the WeCOACH Mentor Trio Programme, comprising a *Gold Mentor* (the trio leader, more than ten years of coaching experience, with at least five years head coach experience), *Silver Mentor/Mentee* (more than five years of coaching experience, less than ten years as assistant, associate, or head coach) and a *Bronze Mentee* (less than five years coaching experience) (LaVoi, 2020). While traditional mentor programmes consist of a mentor–mentee, the Mentor Trio approach includes Silver-level coaches who are at a pivotal decision point and critical zone in their career trajectory and statistically leave the profession at the highest rate (LaVoi, 2020). Women leave to a greater degree than men, due in part, because they are younger and less experienced, and for those who want to have families they often perceive and have internalised the false narrative that coaching is incompatible with starting a family (LaVoi et al., 2020).

The function of mentorship is important to support and develop women coaches, but contemporary thinking also includes the important role of sponsors, alongside with mentors. *Sponsors are influential senior leaders with organisational power who are political advocates to get you where you want to go.* Sponsors drive career progression, open doors, invest time, effort, and resources to prepare you for a top role, put you in the right place and the right time, protect you from negative career influences, give career breaks and challenging assignments, and provide networking opportunities to access people in positions of power (Ang, 2018; Banwell et al., 2019). Sponsors use their power and capital to help the career progression of the protégé, and it is believed to be the solution to counter the under-representation of women in leadership positions (Ang, 2018). Organisational leaders should all be sponsors of, and for, women.

Allyship is when an individual of a dominant social group *purposely aligns with a marginalised social group to combat systemic oppression and strives to change organisational systems of power to become more equitable.* Allyship is not a new concept, but its application to sport leadership and organisations in terms of gender allyship is innovative. In her ground-breaking work, Heffernan (2018) claimed correctly that male dominance in sport contexts is often argued by sport feminist scholars to be a major and problematic barrier to women's inclusion in the occupational landscape. However, in her work, she defines *gender allyship* in a way that assumes men to be part of the solution, through whom organisational change can occur, as men's power affords them the ability to introduce initiatives designed to disrupt gendered social practices in sport organisations (Heffernan, 2018). Heffernan also argues women are also gender allies. The applications of gender allyship for women in sport coaching are numerous, salient, and much needed. Ally strategies fall within two categories: (1) creating positions for women, through hiring processes that embody increasing the number of women in their sport organisations and (2) creating an organisational culture that values gender equity and developing an organisational culture to retain women already in the organisation (Heffernan, 2018), whereby both may also entice women into the organisation—the first stage of the SCPM.

What is clear, and emerging research and evaluation supports, is that women in sport coaching need supports at all levels of the EIM. Given men hold a majority of the power in sport, change will not occur until a critical mass of men mentor women, become sponsors, and learn to become gender allies by changing organisational culture. It is simply not enough to develop women coaches and form women-focused networks and female mentorship models. *The gendered system that privileges men must change, and that change must be driven by men.* And more resources are needed pertaining to women in later stages of the career lifespan, including *The Exit Stage.*

The Exit Stage

The Exit Stage encompasses voluntary (e.g., childbirth, job transfer, resignation, retirement, and desire to spend more time with family) or involuntary (e.g., fired, contract not renewed, elder care, and illness) occupational turnover, and transitioning either to another coaching position, exiting coaching altogether, or exiting the workforce (i.e., retirement). Roberts and Kenttä (2019) argue, due to the prominence of a coach identity and the often public nature of the role, coupled with lack of career or retirement planning, that transitioning and/or existing is easier said than done. Data exist as to why women across all intersectional identities leave coaching due to a plethora of barriers and deleterious effects of psychological health and occupational satisfaction (Kamphoff, 2010; Larsen et al., 2019; LaVoi, 2016; LaVoi & Dutove, 2012). However, research on coach career transitions and occupational turnover behaviours, including retirement, is "embryonic" (Roberts & Kenttä, 2019, p. 407), and to our knowledge *very little* exists specific to women in sport coaching.

In one of the few existing studies (Darvin, 2019), the US female assistant collegiate coaches who experienced voluntary and purposeful occupational turnover were interviewed. These women, all single with no children, reported leaving coaching due to a toxic or hostile culture or one that did not fit personal ethics or values, feelings of burnout, experiences of destructive, narcissistic, and controlling head coaches, a desire to have a balanced life and freedom to engage with friends and non-nuclear family members (Darvin, 2019). Based on limited data for the small cohort ($n = 81$) of approximately 700 WCA graduates who are no longer coaching, two-thirds of those not coaching entered non-sport related careers, one-fourth transitioned into athletic administration positions, and four individuals retired (LaVoi et al., 2019). Longitudinal data from the *Women in College Coaching Report Card* demonstrate that head coach occupational turnover rates year-to-year for NCAA D-I head coaches of women's teams has varied from 7% to 13% over time (LaVoi, 2019), and reasons for turnover vary. Currently analysis of this data by gender, age, sexual identity, and current coaching status is underway (LaVoi et al., 2020). These data will extend findings that show when women (compared to men) do not perceive inclusivity, women express greater occupational turnover intentions, and intention to leave their coaching roles sooner, likely due to anticipating or experiencing negative outcomes due to gender bias in the workplace (Cunningham, 2016).

Age-based fault-lines and discrimination processes are institutionalised in most all workplaces and as cross-generations of coaches, athletes, staff, and parents interact with each other on a daily basis, pressure to deal with the presence and impact of ageist attitudes in the workplace is increasing (McCarthy et al., 2019). Advocates of gender equity in sport suspect and some researchers have uncovered (Norman & Rankin-Wright, 2018) gendered ageist discrimination. Limited data suggest that "older"[1] veteran women coaches who are fired have a lesser likelihood of returning into the coaching carousel compared to their male counterparts (LaVoi et al., 2020). In a longitudinal data set of NCAA D-I coaches, positional turnover (i.e., fired, retired, and took another position) is being examined and for whose current occupational status could be discerned ($n = 501$)—excluding those that cannot be found, who retired, or passed away—the men and women did not differ significantly by age, but nearly *twice as many men* (42%, $M_{age} = 43.6$) were still coaching, compared to women (23%, $M_{age} = 41.9$) (LaVoi et al., 2020). While this analysis is preliminary, a gendered age bias appears to be emerging. Additional research is needed to explore occupational turnover patterns and if age-based stereotypes, prejudice, and discrimination exists. Organisational leaders should be aware of gender and age-related biases in the recruitment and hiring process.

Throughout the retirement process, coaches have physical, cognitive, motivational, financial, and socioemotional needs (Zhan et al., 2019). Research is needed to ascertain what women need as they transition from work-to-retirement either voluntarily or involuntarily. The global workforce is aging, including sport coaches. Within all head coaches of women's NCAA D-I teams, 11.2% (401 of 3,561) will reach or surpass the average US retirement age of 62 in the next five years (LaVoi et al., 2019a). For some, retirement from a non-coaching job means they can enter coaching . . . perhaps as a grandparent-coach! No research exists pertaining to enticing females, especially an "older" untapped talent pool of individuals, looking for an encore career, with a great deal of life experiences, into sport coaching. Organisational leaders should consider non-traditional women as viable, knowledgeable, and available coaches.

The Energise Stage

The Energise Stage is characterised by renewal, resilience, and a focus on personal growth. As evidenced in the previous section, literature around coach burnout exists, but far less attention is given strategies for coping (Norris et al., 2017) or personal growth that can result (Olusoga & Kenttä, 2017). Very recently, a turn to self-care for coaches and a recognition that the mental health, well-being, and resilience of coaches warrant equal attention to that given to athletes, has taken place. While coaches take care of athletes, a realisation that a weak or non-existent system of care exists for most coaches. During *The Energise Stage*, the unique talents and abilities of women in this reinventive career phase where women are often looking to "give back" and serve others should be recognised and utilised (O'Neil & Bilimoria, 2005), yet for women in sport coaching this is often not the reality. Based on limited data, to energise coaches, the focus should be on psychological need satisfaction (belongingness, competence, and autonomy), and if returning, to choose an organisational culture that facilitates need satisfaction and does not actively thwart needs (Norris et al., 2017). For women to re-enter coaching, especially when older and she was fired, it likely requires an actively engaged sponsor or gender ally. Future research is needed.

Conclusion

In this chapter, we proposed a new way of conceptualising the career pathway for women coaches, what is needed to support them, and proposed solutions and supports for women in sport coaching at every level of the EIM using a career progression lifespan framework. The proposed SCPM for women in sports coaching and each stage was explained, and gaps in knowledge were highlighted and applications were suggested. Equitable resources are needed to help women of various intersectional identities, levels and sport types enter into, develop and progress within and across the career progression of sport coaching, and we hope the SCPM will forward this agenda. It provides a roadmap to help decision-makers within sport organisational target resources. Without a systems + developmental lifespan career approach, nuanced understanding of the interplay of barriers and women's intersectional identities, and the equitable supports needed across the career trajectory, the scarcity of women in sports coaching will endure. The lifespan career approach is well-suited to serve as an overarching theoretical framework to advance "support" investigation of women coaches as well as provides a strategic resource roadmap for organisational leaders to follow who care about, and desire to achieve, gender equity for women coaches. In short, those in positions of power (who are mostly men) must and should use their power to enact change and support women. Much work remains!

Note

1. It is generally accepted that this categorisation of "older" tends to come into effect from the age of 50 years onward (McCarthy et al., 2014).

References

Allen, J. B., & Reid, C. (2019). Scaffolding women coaches' development: A program to build coaches' competence and confidence. *Women in Sport and Physical Activity Journal*, 27(2), 101–109. https://doi.org/10.1123/wspaj.2018-0047

Ang, J. (2018). Why career sponsorship matters for advancing women. *Women and Business*, 1(4), 36–43.

Baltes, B., Rudolph, C. W., & Zacher, H. (Eds.). (2019). *Work across the lifespan*. Academic Press.

Bandura, A. (1986). *Social foundations of thought and action: A social cognitive theory*. Prentice-Hall.

Banwell, J., Kerr, G., & Stirling, A. (2019). Key considerations for advancing women in coaching. *Women in Sport & Physical Activity Journal, 27*(2), 128–135. https://doi.org/10.1123/wspaj.2018-0069

Banwell, J., Stirling, A., & Kerr, G. (2019). Towards a process for advancing women in coaching through mentorship. *International Journal of Sports Science & Coaching, 14*(6), 703–713. https://doi.org/10.1177/1747954119883108

Bloom, G. A. (2013). Mentoring for sport coaches. In P. Potrac, W. Gilbert, & J. Denison (Eds.), *Routledge handbook of sports coaching* (pp. 494–503). Routledge.

Bronfenbrenner, U. (1979). *The ecology of human development*. Harvard University Press.

Brown, S. D., & Lent, R. W. (2019). Social cognitive career theory at 25: Progress in studying the domain satisfaction and career self-management models. *Journal of Career Assessment, 27*(4), 563–578. https://doi.org/10.1177/1069072719852736

Bruening, J. E., Dixon, M. A., & Eason, C. M. (2016). Coaching and motherhood. In N. M. LaVoi (Ed.), *Women in sports coaching* (pp. 95–110). Routledge.

Burton, L. J., & LaVoi, N. M. (2016). An ecological/multisystem approach to understanding and examining women coaches. In N. M. LaVoi (Ed.), *Women in sports coaching* (pp. 49–62). Routledge.

Callary, B., & Gearity, B. (2020). *Coach education and development in sport: Instructional strategies*. Routledge. https://doi.org/10.4324/9780429351037

Carter-Francique, A., & Olushoga, J. (2016). Women coaches of color: Examining the effects of intersectionality. In N. M. LaVoi (Ed.), *Women in sports coaching* (pp. 81–94). Routledge.

Chambers, F. C. (Ed.). (2018). *Learning to mentor in sports coaching*. Routledge.

Cunningham, G. B. (2016). Women in coaching: Theoretical underpinnings among quantitative analyses. In N. M. LaVoi (Ed.), *Women in sports coaching* (pp. 223–233). Routledge.

Darvin, L. (2019). Voluntary occupational turnover and the experiences of former intercollegiate women assistant coaches. *Journal of Vocational Behavior, 116*. https://doi.org/10.1016/j.jvb.2019.103349

Dashper, K. (2019). Challenging the gendered rhetoric of success? The limitations of women only mentoring for tackling gender inequality in the workplace. *Gender, Work & Organization, 26*(4), 541–557. https://doi.org/10.1016/j.jvb.2019.103349

Drago, R., Hennighausen, L., Rogers, J., Vescio, T., & Stauffer, K. D. (2005). *The coaching and gender equity report*. http://lsir.la.psu.edu/workfam/cage.htm

Durand-Bush, N., Collins, J., & McNeill, K. (2012). Women coaches' experiences of stress and self-regulation: A multiple case study. *International Journal of Coaching Science, 6*(2), 21–43.

Fowler, J. L., Gudmundsson, A. J., & O'Gorman, J. G. (2007). The relationship between mentee mentor gender combination and the provision of distinct mentoring functions. *Women in Management Review, 2*(8), 666–681. https://doi.org/10.1108/09649420710836335

Heffernan, C. (2018). *Gender allyship: Considering the role of men in addressing the gender leadership gap in sport organizations*. The University of Minnesota Digital Conservancy. http://hdl.handle.net/11299/201034

Kamphoff, C. S. (2010). Bargaining with patriarchy: Former female coaches' experiences and their decision to leave collegiate coaching. *Research Quarterly for Exercise and Sport*, *81*(3), 360–372. https://doi.org/10.1080/02701367.2010.10599684

Knight, C. J., Rodgers, W. M., Reade, I. L., Mrak, J. M., & Hall, C. R. (2015). Coach transitions: Influence of interpersonal and work environment factors. *Sport, Exercise, and Performance Psychology*, *4*(3), 170–187. https://doi.org/10.1037/spy0000036

Knoppers, A. (1987). Gender and the coaching profession. *Quest*, *39*(1), 9–22. https://doi.org/10.1080/00336297.1987.10483853

Larsen, L. K., Fisher, L., & Moret, L. (2019). The coach's journal: Experiences of Black female assistant coaches in NCAA division I women's basketball. *The Qualitative Report*, *24*(3), 632–658. https://nsuworks.nova.edu/tqr/vol24/iss3/16/

LaVoi, N. M. (2009). Occupational sex segregation in a youth soccer organization: Females in positions of power. *Women in Sport & Physical Activity Journal*, *18*(2), 25–37. https://doi.org/10.1123/wspaj.18.2.25

LaVoi, N. M. (2016). A framework to understand experiences of women coaches around the globe. In N. M. LaVoi (Ed.), *Women in sports coaching* (pp. 13–34). Routledge.

LaVoi, N. M. (2019). *Head coaches of women's collegiate teams: A report on seven select NCAA Division-I institutions, 2018–19*. The Tucker Center for Research on Girls & Women in Sport. www.cehd.umn.edu/tuckercenter/library/docs/research/WCCRC_Head-Coaches_2018-19_D-I_Select-7.pdf

LaVoi, N. M. (2020). Sport coach development: Education and mentorship for women. In B. Callary & B. Gearity (Eds.), *Coach education and development in sport: Instructional strategies* (pp. 203–214). Routledge.

LaVoi, N. M., Boucher, C., & Silbert, S. (2019a). *Head coaches of women's collegiate teams: A comprehensive report on NCAA division-I institutions, 2018–19*. The Tucker Center for Research on Girls & Women in Sport. www.cehd.umn.edu/tuckercenter/library/docs/research/WCCRC-Head-Coaches_All-NCAA-DI-Head-Coaches_2018-19.pdf

LaVoi, N. M., Boucher, C., & Sirek, G. (2020, August). *Head coaches of women's collegiate teams: A comprehensive report on NCAA division-I institutions, 2019–20*. The Tucker Center for Research on Girls & Women in Sport. www.cehd.umn.edu/tuckercenter/library/docs/research/WCCRC_2019-20_Head-Coaches_All-NCAA-DI-Head-Coaches_2020-September.pdf

LaVoi, N. M., & Dutove, J. K. (2012). Barriers and supports for female coaches: An ecological model. *Sports Coaching Review*, *1*(1), 17–37. https://doi:10.1080/21640629.2012.695891

LaVoi, N. M., & Leberman, S. (2015). A rationale for encouraging mothers to coach youth sport. *Canadian Journal for Women in Coaching*, *15*(1), 1–4.

LaVoi, N. M., McGarry, J., & Fisher, L. (2019b). Final thoughts on women in sport coaching: Fighting the war. *Women in Sport and Physical Activity Journal*, *27*(2), 136–140. https://doi.org/10.1123/wspaj.2019-0030

LaVoi, N. M., Schad, N., & Kaufmann, C. (2019). *NCAA women coaches academy: Longitudinal career trajectory*. The Tucker Center for Research on Girls & Women in Sport.

LaVoi, N. M., Silva-Breen, H., & Richmond, P. (2020). *Occupational turnover patterns of NCAA D-I head coaches of women's teams: A longitudinal analysis by gender, age, and sexual identity*. Manuscript in preparation.

LaVoi, N. M., & Wasend, M. K. (2018). *Athletic administration best practices of recruitment, hiring and retention of female collegiate coaches.* Tucker Center for Research on Girls & Women in Sport. www.cehd.umn.edu/tuckercenter/library/docs/research/ADReport-Best-Practices.pdf

Leberman, S. (2017). Future sport leaders: Developing young women to lead. In L. J. Burton & S. Leberman (Eds.), *Women in sport leadership* (pp. 130–143). Routledge.

Leberman, S. I., & LaVoi, N. M. (2011). Juggling balls and roles, working mother-coaches in youth sport: Beyond the dualistic worker-mother identity. *Journal of Sport Management, 25*(5), 474–488.

Leeder, T. M., Russell, K., & Beaumont, L. C. (2019). "Learning the hard way": Understanding the workplace learning of sports coach mentors. *International Sport Coaching Journal, 6*(3), 263–273. https://doi.org/10.1123/iscj.2018-0069

Lent, R. W., & Brown, S. D. (2013). Social cognitive model of career self-management: Toward a unifying view of adaptive career behavior across the life span. *Journal of Counseling Psychology, 60*(4), 557. https://doi.org/10.1037/a0033446

Lent, R. W., Brown, S. D., & Hackett, G. (1994). Toward a unifying social cognitive theory of career and academic interest, choice, and performance. *Journal of Vocational Behavior, 45*(1), 79–122. https://doi.org/10.1006/jvbe.1994.1027

Lewis, C. J., Roberts, S. J., & Andrews, H. (2015). 'Why am I putting myself through this?' Women football coaches' experiences of the Football Association's coach education process. *Sport, Education and Society, 23*(1), 28–39. https://doi.org/10.1080/13573322.2015.1118030

Lockwood, P. (2006). "Someone like me can be successful": Do college students need same gender role models? *Psychology of Women Quarterly, 30*(1), 36–46. https://doi.org/10.1111/j.1471-6402.2006.00260.x

Madsen, R. M., & McGarry, J. E. (2016). "Dads play basketball and moms go shopping!" Social role theory and the preference for male coaches. *Journal of Contemporary Athletics, 10*(4), 277–292.

McCarthy, J., Heraty, N., & Bamberg, A. (2019). Lifespan perspectives on age-related stereotypes, prejudice, and discrimination at work (and beyond). In B. B. Baltes, C. W. Rudolph, & H. Zacher (Eds.), *Work across the lifespan* (pp. 417–435). Academic Press. https://doi.org/10.1016/B978-0-12-812756-8.00017-7

Midgley, C., DeBues-Stafford, G., Lockwood, P., & Thai, S. (2020). She needs to see it to be it: The importance of same-gender athletic role models. *Sex Roles*, 1–19. https://doi.org/10.1007/s11199-020-01209-y

Murray, P., Lord, R., & Lorimer, R. (2020). 'It's just a case of chipping away': A postfeminist analysis of female coaches' gendered experiences in grassroots sport. *Sport, Education and Society*, 1–14. https://doi.org/10.1080/13573322.2020.1867527

Nash, C. (2003). Development of a mentoring system within coaching practice. *Journal of Hospitality, Leisure, Sport and Tourism Education, 2*(2), 39–47. https://doi.org/10.3794/johlste.22.37

Norman, L. (2016). The impact of an "equal opportunities" ideological framework on coaches' knowledge and practice. *International Review for the Sociology of Sport, 51*(8), 975–1004. https://doi.org/10.1177/1012690214565377

Norman, L. (2020). "I don't really know what the magic wand is to get yourself in there": Women's sense of organizational fit as coach developers. *Women in Sport and Physical Activity Journal, 28*, 119–130. https://doi.org/10.1123/wspaj.2019-0020

Norman, L., & Rankin-Wright, A. (2018). Surviving rather than thriving: Understanding the experiences of women coaches using a theory of gendered social well being. *International Review for the Sociology of Sport*, *53*(4), 424–450. https://doi.org/10.1177/1012690216660283

Norris, L. A., Didymus, F. F., & Kaiseler, M. (2017). Stressors, coping, and well-being among sports coaches: A systematic review. *Psychology of Sport and Exercise*, *33*, 93–112. https://doi.org/10.1016/j.psychsport.2017.08.005

Olushola-Ogunrinde, J., & Carter-Francique, A. R. (2020). Beyond the Xs and Os. In S. Bradbury, J. Lusted, & J. van Sterkenburg (Eds.), *'Race', ethnicity and racism in sports coaching* (pp. 142–156). Routledge.

Olusoga, P., Bentzen, M., & Kenttä, G. (2019). Coach burnout: A scoping review. *International Sport Coaching Journal*, *6*(1), 42–62. https://doi.org/10.1123/iscj.2017-0094

Olusoga, P., & Kenttä, G. (2017). Desperate to quit: A narrative analysis of burnout and recovery in high-performance sports coaching. *Sport Psychologist*, *31*(3), 237–248. https://doi.org/10.1123/tsp.2016-0010

O'Neil, D. A., & Bilimoria, D. (2005). Women's career development phases: Idealism, endurance and reinvention. *Career Development International*, *10*(3), 168–189. https://doi.org/10.1108/13620430510598300

Raedeke, T. D. (2004). Coach commitment and burnout: A one-year follow-up. *Journal of Applied Sport Psychology*, *16*(4), 333–349. https://doi.org/10.1080/10413200490517995

Roberts, C. M., & Kenttä, G. (2019). Knowing when, and how, to step out: Coach retirement. In R. Thelwell & M. Dicks (Eds.), *Professional advance in sports coaching: Research to practice* (pp. 397–414). Routledge.

Robertson, S. (2016). Hear their voices: Suggestions for developing and supporting women coaches from around the world. In N. M. LaVoi (Ed.), *Women in sports coaching* (pp. 177–223). Routledge.

Rudolph, C. W., Zacher, H., & Baltes, B. B. (2019). Looking forward: A new agenda for studying work across the lifespan. In B. B. Baltes, C. W. Rudolph, & H. Zacher (Eds.), *Work across the lifespan* (pp. 605–623). Academic Press. https://doi.org/10.1016/B978-0-12-812756-8.00026-8

Sartore, M. L., & Cunningham, G. B. (2007). Explaining the under-representation of women in leadership positions of sport organizations: A symbolic interactionist perspective. *Quest*, *59*(2), 244–265. https://doi.org/10.1080/00336297.2007.10483551

Schell, L. A. B., & Rodriguez, S. (2000). Our sporting sisters: How male hegemony stratifies women in sport. *Women in Sport and Physical Activity Journal*, *9*(1), 15–34. https://doi.org/10.1123/wspaj.9.1.15

Schull, V. D. (2017). Young women in sport: Understanding leadership in sport. In L. J. Burton & S. Leberman (Eds.), *Women in sport leadership* (pp. 112–129). Routledge.

Schull, V. D., & Kihl, L. A. (2019). Gendered leadership expectations in sport: Constructing differences in coaches. *Women in Sport and Physical Activity Journal*, *27*(1), 1–11. https://doi.org/10.1123/wspaj.2018-0011

Subrahmanian, R. (2005). Gender equality in education: Definitions and measurements. *International Journal of Educational Development*, *25*(4), 395–407. https://doi.org/10.1016/j.ijedudev.2005.04.003

Super, D. E. (1980). A life-span, life-space approach to career development. *Journal of Vocational Behavior, 16*(3), 282–298. https://doi.org/10.1016/0001-8791(80)90056-1

Vinson, D., Christian, P., Jones, V., Williams, C., & Peters, D. M. (2016). Exploring how well UK coach education meets the needs of women sports coaches. *International Sport Coaching Journal, 3*(3), 287–302. https://doi.org/10.1123/iscj.2016-0004

Wasend, M., & LaVoi, N. M. (2019). Are women coached by women more likely to become sport coaches? Head coach gender and female collegiate athletes' entry into the coaching profession. *Women Sport and Physical Activity Journal, 27,* 85–93. https://doi.org/10.1123/wspaj.2018-0043

Whisenant, W. A. (2008). Sustaining male dominance in interscholastic athletics: A case of homologous reproduction . . . or not? *Sex Roles, 58*(11–12), 768–775. https://doi.org/10.1007/s11199-008-9397-3

Whisenant, W. A., Pedersen, P. M., & Obenour, B. L. (2002). Success and gender: Determining the rate of advancement for intercollegiate athletic directors. *Sex Roles, 47*(9–10), 485–491. https://doi.org/10.1023/A:1021656628604

Wichert, I. (2014). *Why organizations should support women's career development and what can be done to help women reach senior roles.* IBM Working Paper.

Zakrajsek, R. A., Raabe, J., Readdy, T., Erdner, S., & Bass, A. (2020). Collegiate assistantcoaches' perceptions of basic psychological need satisfaction and thwarting from head coaches: A qualitative investigation. *Journal of Applied Sport Psychology, 32*(1), 28–47. https://doi.org/10.1080/10413200.2019.1581855

Zhan, Y., Wang, M., & Daniel, V. (2019). Lifespan perspectives on the work-to-retirement transition. In B. B. Baltes, C. W. Rudolph, & H. Zacher (Eds.), *Work across the lifespan* (pp. 581–604). Academic Press. https://doi.org/10.1016/B978-0-12-812756-8.00025-6

11 An Evaluation of a Mentoring Programme to Support High-Performance Women Coaches

Luke Norris, Nicola Clarke and Leanne Norman

Challenges for Women Coaches

Sport has historically been a context of constraint for women as both athletes and coaches, restricting agency and choices (Theberge & Birrell, 1994). However, sport can also be a site for transformation, as shown with increased participation and opportunities for women across multiple sports (Acosta & Carpenter, 2012). Women's lack of presence and political voice at high-performance levels is concerning for the potential impact on women at all stages of leadership and participation inside sport and the wider context. Sport plays a significant role in Western society in reinforcing gender distinctions, marginalising femininity, and promoting masculinity, and thus perpetuating unequal gendered relations (Saavedra, 2009).

Over the past decade, there has been a significant increase in the interest of football (soccer) worldwide for women (see Figure 11.1). As a result,

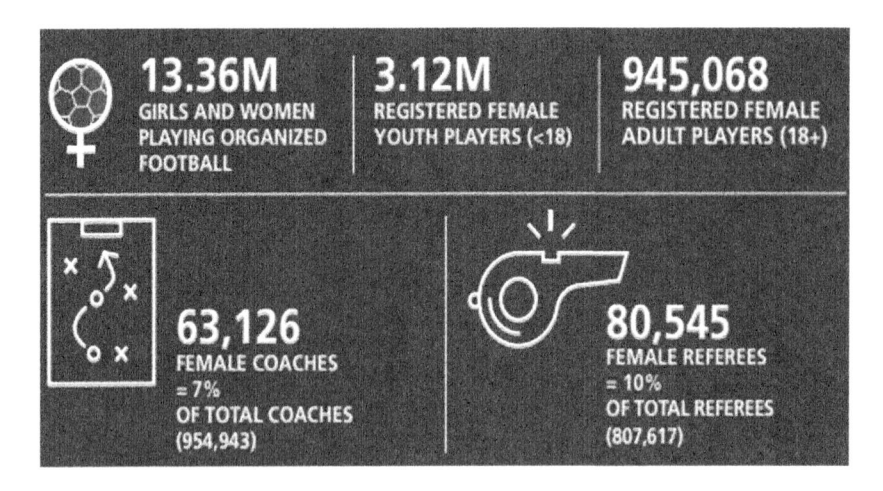

```
13.36M          3.12M                  945,068
GIRLS AND WOMEN REGISTERED FEMALE      REGISTERED FEMALE
PLAYING ORGANIZED YOUTH PLAYERS (<18)  ADULT PLAYERS (18+)
FOOTBALL

63,126                          80,545
FEMALE COACHES                  FEMALE REFEREES
= 7%                            = 10%
OF TOTAL COACHES                OF TOTAL REFEREES
(954,943)                       (807,617)
```

Figure 11.1 Number of women involved in football worldwide from the Women's Football Member Association's Survey Report 2019

Source: FIFA (2019)

UEFA (Union of European Football Associations, 2017) reported that football is the number one participation team sport for women in various countries including England, Norway, and Germany. However, whilst there is a growth in the number of women playing football, the same growth has not been mirrored with women coaches. Whilst FIFA (Federation Internationale de Football Association) reported in 2019 that England had the highest number of women coaches (3,520) in Europe, there are still only nine women coaches for every 91 male coaches in England. The gap is even more noteworthy when considering qualified coaches as demonstrated by there being approximately 10,033 UEFA B qualified male coaches in England, compared to only 301 UEFA B qualified women coaches. This translates to a lack of women coaches in high-performance roles with only 13 being head coaches/managers currently at Barclays FA (The English Football Association) WSL (Women's Super League) and FA Women's Championship clubs in the UK (The FA, 2020).

Women's Experiences of Social and Educational Coaching Environments

Beyond the statistics, research that has been conducted with women coaches has found that they frequently feel under-valued, isolated, and discriminated (Norman, 2008; Norman & Rankin-Wright, 2016; Schlesinger & Weigelt-Schlesinger, 2012). The feelings of exclusion can stem from the perceived informal "closed" social networks within coaching. This is important as coaches use their social support to gain knowledge, sustain self-esteem, increase sense of mattering, and assist with career development (Norris et al., 2020). Therefore, closed networks create an environment that can be restrictive for many women who wish to progress to a high-performance setting through lack of opportunities and an informal appointment system that favours men (Norman, 2008). Senior women coaches based in the UK have discussed the difficulty of developing and maintaining coaching relationships because of the perceived hostility of coaching environments and networks dominated by men (Norman, 2014). This leads to women feeling removed from the coaching community and as though they have to "prove themselves" as coaches to a greater extent than their male counterparts, reducing their intentions to develop or continue in the profession (Norman, 2010).

Coach education programmes can play an integral part of the journey for a coach to feel belonging, develop as a coach, and remain in the coaching profession (Erickson et al., 2007). Education programmes should aim to provide positive social environments for learning that creates equal opportunities for women coaches to enhance their skills, progress in coaching roles, and feel part of the coaching community. However, this is often not the case for women as coach education provisions tend to be dominated by men with course tutors often demonstrating a predisposition towards associated male attributes, orientations, and characteristics (Lewis et al., 2018). Therefore, a challenge that exists for sports organisations—if they wish to retain and develop their women coaches—is to ensure women feel a sense of belonging and inclusion within the profession and organisation.

In response to the deficit of women coaches in football, the FA have created various initiatives to upskill women coaches to enable women to progress within the coaching community. This chapter will provide an evaluation of one of those initiatives—the "Elite Coach Menteeship Programme"—in order to share good practice and lessons learned in relation to establishing and delivering programmes designed to support the career development of high-performance women coaches. To begin with, the menteeship programme is outlined, including its purpose and context. Next, the research evaluation process is highlighted, encompassing the objectives and methods used to collect data, followed by coaches' experiences of the programme. The chapter closes with some recommendations and implications for coaches, other sports organisations, and NGBs to effectively develop diversity and inclusion initiatives and improve gender equity.

FA Elite Coach Menteeship Programme

The challenge remains in sporting environments to develop diverse and inclusive initiatives that support under-represented populations, including women. To try and provide women coaches with additional skills and experiences in high-performance settings, the FA created the Elite Coach Menteeship Programme. This section will provide an overview of the programme.

Purpose and Context

As part of the FA's commitment to enhancing the diversity of the coaching workforce in England, the primary intention of the Elite Coach Menteeship programme was to address the under-representation of women, and Black, Asian, and Minoritised Ethnic (BAME) coaches at the elite level in football. Women and BAME coaches continue to be significantly under-represented at the top levels of men and women's football. The chairman of FA's England Commission Report from 2014 highlighted a need for long-term investment to redress this imbalance (The FA, 2014). The report stated that the FA aimed to create further opportunities to ensure that more women and BAME coaches obtain relevant qualifications and gain essential experiences to challenge for high-performance coaching and technical roles in football. It is important to address this imbalance to provide role models for future generations. To help create further opportunities for women coaches, the FA allocated funds towards initiatives with the primary intention of addressing the under-representation of BAME male and women coaches at the elite level. Introduced in 2016, the menteeship programme offered employment at the FA for one year, to a select group of talented women and BAME football coaches. The role provided coaches with opportunities to work within different FA departments and experience placements with national and regional coaches in high-performance, talent development, and grassroots environments.

Elite Menteeship Programme Overview

The Elite Coach Menteeship Programme was developed for women and BAME coaches to experience formal and informal learning opportunities and a range of placements to gain exposure to elite experiences within the game of football. The coaches became full-time employees of the FA for a 12-month period and completed internal placements (e.g., national and international camps), additional learning opportunities (e.g., gaining additional qualifications), and employability workshops (e.g., presenting, interview skills, and developing curriculum vitae). In the first cohort of coaches and subsequently since, four coaches a year completed five internal work-based placements in eight-week blocks: Regional Physical Education and Coaching in Education Co-Ordinator (PE), County Coach Developer (CCD), Youth Coach Developer (YCD), Regional Coach Developer (RCD), and National Coach Developer (NCD). Whilst on these placements, coaches worked alongside a placement lead to complete a variety of relevant activities.

Each placement offered different opportunities for coaches to develop their knowledge, skills, and experience. The PE placement encompassed coaches helping to develop FA resources and courses as well as supporting teachers, those within initial teacher education, and coaches in delivering football activities within curriculum and extra-curriculum time. Second, the coaches' role during the CCD placement was to support FA tutors on local and national courses, deliver in-service programmes for local FA accredited clubs, and help develop coaching resources. YCD involved coaches supporting in-club continuous personal development and mentoring, and providing regional and on-site coach support to professional club coaches. The RCD placement involved supporting the delivery of FA Level 1, 2, and FA Youth Module qualifications regionally. Finally, the NCD placement included observing and contributing to UEFA B, A License, and Pro License courses. Coaches were also encouraged to continue any existing coaching commitments alongside the programme where possible, to allow coaches to apply their learning in a practical setting.

Research Programme

The programme of research was one of the three integrated projects led by Leeds Beckett University under a broad title of the "Evaluation of the Changing Experiences of Women Football Coaches" commissioned by the

FA for three years. The following will highlight the aims and objectives of the research and the methods used to collect data.

Aims and Objectives

The purpose of the research was to track the women coaches' experiences who had been accepted on the Elite Coach Menteeship Programme (i.e. cohorts 1, 2, and 3) over the first three years of the programme and report on the coaches' and key stakeholders' experiences. The aims of the project were as follows:

- To understand, follow, and evaluate the changing experiences of three cohorts of women football coaches participating in the FA Mentoring Programme.
- To analyse the perspectives of the key stakeholders involved in the provision of the FA mentoring programme.
- To evaluate the provision of the menteeship programme in collaboration with key stakeholders and women coaches.

Methodology

The research commenced in autumn 2016 and ran for three years: year 1 (2016/2017, cohort 1), year 2 (2017/2018, cohort 2 and stakeholders), and year 3 (2018/2019, cohort 3 and stakeholders). To evaluate the programme and collect the experiences of the coaches, interviews were conducted with coaches over a three-year period and key stakeholders during the second and third years. Women coaches from all three cohorts (age range = 26–31; see demographic information, Table 11.1) were interviewed at three points during each menteeship scheme: at the start, mid-point, and end of the programme. The purpose of the interviews was to understand the coaches' current position in football, their experiences of the programme, their expectations of the programme, and the perceived impact of the programme on their coaching. Follow-up interviews were also conducted a year

Table 11.1 Coach characteristics

Pseudonym	Ethnicity	Disability	Qualification	Cohort
Annabel	British Asian	Non-disabled	UEFA B	One
Alice	Black British	Non-disabled	UEFA B	One
Kaylee	White British	Non-disabled	UEFA B	Two
Sasha	White British	Non-disabled	UEFA B	Two
Steph	White British	Non-disabled	UEFA B	Three

Note: Coaching qualification accurate at time of first interview.

after the completion of the menteeship scheme with coaches from cohorts 1 and 2 to track their subsequent experiences and career progression.

Research Findings

This section provides an overview of the key findings from the research as evidence for the future programme recommendations that concludes this chapter. Together, the four findings present the coaches' experiences of their work-based placements and how these experiences were shaped by the following: coaches' relationships with key stakeholders; coaches' expectations of the programme; and how coaches' perceived the programme was viewed by significant stakeholders.

Coaches' Experiences of Work-Based Placements

Overall, the women coaches reported positive feedback across all of the placements and believed they gained valuable knowledge, skills, and experiences from engaging in the observation, design, and delivery of football coach-tutor and mentor-related work. There was a unanimous agreement among the coaches that the NCD placement and national camps significantly exceeded expectations. It was cited that this was because it offered unique and powerful learning experiences and the trust that was demonstrated by the placement lead enabled the coaches to take an active role during the placement:

ALICE: Probably national coach developers [was the best] because we got to live the... [experience], it was just let them get on with it. That's probably the best one.
STEPH: Yeah, it [national camps] was an amazing experience. It was tiring but it was so good! Like, I'll remember it forever, if you know what I mean, once in a lifetime [experience].

Coaches acknowledged the benefits of taking part in a variety of placements to help widen their understanding of working in different environments. However, some coaches questioned if having such a wide range of placements gave them the best career development and expressed a preference to have a more bespoke approach. Coaches discussed that allowing more choice and inclusivity in the placement selection may be more beneficial for their development:

ALICE: So for me, they [FA] couldn't understand at the beginning that I didn't want to do national coach [NCD], I wanted to do further education [PE]. The programme should have allowed me to delve a little bit deeper into it [PE] and really got to grips with it. So it didn't... it gave me holistic development but it didn't give me exactly what I wanted.

KATIE: So, for example, on my CV, as an elite coach mentee, I'll highlight the coaching stuff, I won't highlight the school stuff because they don't see too much value in it if I'm going for a head coach position with a ladies team.

The opportunity to engage in a variety of placements for a significant length of time was made possible by the one-year employment offered by the programme. However, a challenge of the full-time nature of the programme was that the women coaches across all cohorts mentioned the difficulty balancing the FA menteeship role and existing coaching commitments at their clubs. In particular, Sasha highlighted that finding the time to be able to commit to both roles was challenging:

So from the club's perspective they're like, "well, we've got you as a coach but you can only do one night a week?!" So that affects my coaching context, and, if I'm honest, I'm at a bit of a crossroads now where I'm like, right, I need to either give up some of the stuff I'm doing on placement so I can fit this is, or I need to find another club that will allow me to be flexible. So, it's just difficult to get that, you know, which one do you focus on? . . . For me there's no point in me doing this programme if I'm not coaching two, three times a week.

Overall, all of the placements seemed to be beneficial to the coaches and were facilitated by the unique full-time employment the menteeship programme offered. Yet, there were discussions about whether the programme could be more bespoke to align with the women coaches' chosen career path within football.

Coach–Stakeholder Relationships

Most of the coaches' experiences with the internal stakeholders (e.g., mentors, placement leads, and programme manager) were positive. Coaches highlighted that if the relationship with the stakeholders were positive, the benefits gained from the placement increased. This was principally because the coaches were made to feel valued, an included member of the department team, and were trusted with more responsibility. Kaylee described how one placement lead provided her with more freedom and respect:

They [placement lead] gave me a lot of freedom to do what I wanted, so I was able . . . because I already had an existing relationship with them, I was able to do more in terms of the delivery, and I guess they respect and they trust me.

However, Alice highlighted that this was not always the case:

It isn't necessary for me to be there [placement], so like meetings and stuff, or courses that I've been delivered, some aspects where it's just, okay, I want

> *to get involved but you're not really let be involved. Yes, there's two [placements] . . . from January to June, I worked with really good people who were really nice, helpful, but there were little bits of it, just looking back, [placement lead] didn't fully trust me.*

A lack of communication about the broader purpose of the programme was perceived to influence the relationship between some of the coaches and placement leads. Annabel discussed how she felt the relationship with some of the placement leads was strained because of the perception that the coaches would eventually take over their job:

> *And that's always an issue, because everyone's scared, everyone's very insecure about their own skill set, that they'll be like "Oh am I going to lose my job if she's better than me and she's more experienced than me?" So we just piped down in the corner, "tell her to make the tea and coffee" . . . but I don't do that.*

Highlighting the importance of relationships with peers to woman coaches' experiences, the individual coaches' busy schedules meant that sometimes, the time coaches were able to spend together was limited because of the programme schedule. A consistent theme from cohort 3 was for more communication and connection with the other coaches in their cohort. For example, Steph highlighted that this would potentially provide opportunities to share experiences of the placements and learn from each other:

> *So, like, we're [coaches] meant to have, we were meant to have like meetings quite frequent throughout the year but we haven't really ever had them and, if we have, they're like, they're not meetings to talk about your stuff, they're more meetings like . . . So, for example, we'd have a date booked in and it's not really a meeting, it's more like we're doing the presentation workshop that day, so you don't really have a chance to speak about anything because as soon as you arrive, obviously you're doing the workshop. And I think it's a bit of a shame because we haven't had one really, all year, where it's just been about let's all meet up, have a good time together, and actually just chat about how everything's going.*

These findings suggest that relationships with stakeholders (notably peers and those in mentoring roles) significantly influenced the coaches' satisfaction with and perceived benefits from the programme. In contrast, a lack of trust and/or communication in these key relationships had a detrimental effect on coaches' experiences of the programme and at times, led to feelings of isolation.

Coaches' Expectations of the Menteeship Programme

The main expectation highlighted pre-programme by all three cohorts of coaches was the opportunity to work in high-performance settings within football, both during and post-programme. This was preferably full-time and at a higher level than they were coaching at before they entered the programme:

KAYLEE: I think the main part of it [the programme] is employability, because it said, I remember on the booklet that we got, that the aim of it is to become more employable within football at a higher level. So I'm hoping that I'm going to be employable now at [women's] championship level. If I get that then I guess that's a success.

In part, these expectations arose from the marketing and pre-course materials shared with coaches during the recruitment stage of the programme. For example, coaches perceived the reference to "elite" in the title of the programme differently. Some interpreted this wording negatively because they felt it doesn't promote the right message, raised coaches' expectations of the programme, and caused uncertainty about the overall purpose of the programme:

SASHA: In terms of [expectations] I'm not [sure] . . . it's really because it's called an elite coach menteeship. So does that mean we're expected to become elite coaches by the end? I don't know. I'm not sure.

Both coaches and stakeholders questioned whether the coaches were meant to become elite by the end of the programme. There was a feeling that using this word was misleading in creating expectations that this programme would immediately lead to a role at elite level. At times, this caused frustrations for coaches, some of whom had left paid roles to complete the menteeship and expressed concerns that there was no "exit strategy" post-programme. One such coach was Steph, who was unsure of her next steps after the menteeship programme:

> *If they could add on something at the end a bit more, about like the exit strategies, I think it would be even more empowering for people. So, like they're going to see me now, go from six years' full-time to . . . I don't know what I'm going to do really. And that's probably not motivational to people, seeing someone like that in those roles. Because people are leaving full-time roles for this, aren't they?*

The different interpretations regarding the programme was not confined to the title but included the objectives. The prospectus set out that: "The long-term aim is to create the opportunity for more BAME male and women coaches to challenge for employment in elite men's and women's football". However, the coaches felt there was a lack of clarity on whether the programme was in place to develop women coaches holistically with a view of progressing into elite roles in the long-term or to help them gain employment in a high-performance setting as the next step in their career. Sasha, who was more focused on self-development, thought the programme had exceeded expectations because of the different experiences encountered during the placements:

> [The menteeship programme has] exceeded my expectations even more, if that makes sense? So, and it's just been kind of like a stair, like a staircase kind of, you know, can I do the next one? Okay, can I do the next one and just gradually get to that point? And I think that's basically what the programme largely is, you come very low and then gradually you climb the stairs at the end of the programme.

In contrast, Alice felt that her expectations of gaining employment in a high-performance setting post-programme had not been -fulfilled:

> If you call me in one year or in 18 months' time when I've got the job I want then the programme's been useful, but if we have the conversation and I'm out of football or nowhere near where I want to be then it isn't... So, it's... I know other guys [coaches] are probably thinking the same thing, actually they are thinking the same thing, they're thinking what's the point of the programme if you're not being shortlisted. The whole point was to shortlist us. If the issue is females and BAMEs representation, we're still not being represented because we can't get jobs, and if we can't the people that are similar to us in terms of ethnicity, they definitely won't. So it hasn't changed anything.

During her follow up interview, Kaylee discussed applying for employment post-programme and her frustrations of not being offered interviews, despite her skills and experiences:

> Ultimately the best person is going to get the job, and I don't think sometimes, when I've applied for jobs in the men's game or the boy's game, I don't believe that I'm not good enough to get an interview, the amount of jobs I apply for, because what skills have other people got above me for what was required... maybe a foundation for the boy's team?... Do they have a better understanding of player development, what experience? Boy's maybe, but do they manage players better, are they a better coach? How do you know until you've had an interview with someone?... It's got to be [gender], that's got to be the only reason, what else is there that stands in the way? If I'm ticking their requirements on a piece of paper, they might as well have a box that says "Are you female or male?"

In summary, these findings suggest that initiatives designed to address the under-representation of women coaches would benefit from clarity regarding both the short- and long-term programme aims. Without this, women coaches in this study experienced frustration and questioned the effectiveness of the programme. Notably, Kaylee's experience of applying for coaching roles following the menteeship also highlights the limitations of the programme in addressing wider socio-cultural inequalities that individuals may face, and supports Banwell et al. (2020) recommendation to build organisational change objectives into future mentoring initiatives.

Coaches' Perceived Stakeholder Programme Perceptions

The coaches emphasised the importance of the perception of the programme from stakeholders both internally (e.g., mentors, placement leads, programme manager, and organisation) and externally (e.g., football clubs, other coaches, and organisations). For example, coaches perceived that the FA demonstrated that the programme was highly valued through a rigorous application process, significant financial investment into programme resources, and the provision of opportunities to access coaching environments at the elite level (national and international training camps):

KAYLEE: I think they [FA] did a good job in terms of bursaries and things. You also don't want people just passing the qualifications. You want to make sure they're actually good enough to be promoting females and then giving them something, and then they're actually doing that. So, I guess I quite like the fact that obviously our role, I guess it's a prestigious role, but the fact that we had to apply for it.

The time and resources put in by the FA was important to increase the positivity and effectiveness of the programmes visibility:

ALICE: At this present moment in time, I believe it [menteeship programme] is important, yes. It has a massive opportunity to impact the game in a positive way. How it's done . . . because the stigma attached with it can enhance or be detrimental to your career, because you're in the spotlight.

However, some coaches were apprehensive as to whether the programme was seen by others only as a diversity tick-box exercise, and as a consequence, felt a sense of responsibility to perform both in their role and upon graduating from the programme, due to the perceived additional attention on their careers. The concern that the programme was performed for perfunctory purposes to serve a bureaucratic expediency was accentuated by the perceived lack of diversity within the organisation:

ANNABEL: There are women coaches, but there's no one that "looks like me" I was like, "Where do I belong? Do I belong anywhere?" . . . Yes, [I think I've just been a tick-box] and that's always been my concern . . . If you think, out of 800 people, I was the only one that looked like me. That is scary . . . that is a scary statistic.

This suggests that an unintended consequence of the high-profile nature of the programme was to reinforce the commonly reported experience that women coaches feel an additional pressure to prove themselves to be competent in their role (Norman, 2010). Overall, the coaches appreciated the opportunity to develop their knowledge, skills, and experience through the programme and were keen for the extent of their learning to be highlighted both internally and externally to the organisation, in order to reduce any negative perception of the programme as a "hand out" or tick box exercise.

Programme Evaluation

We would like to take this moment to thank the FA for allowing us to conduct this research. It is brave for an organisation to take on research that requires them to look at themselves critically and "lift the lid" on the culture and processes within the organisation to expose any gaps between the aspirations for programme participants and the reality of how participants experienced the programme. It is important to note that the matter of diversity and inclusion is not confined to sports and the following recommendations can be related to organisations in the wider context.

Recommendations

The coaches and stakeholders involved in the Elite Coach Menteeship Programme recognised the positive steps of creating an initiative such as this and the FA's willingness to tackle the issue of under-representation of women and BAME coaches in the UK. Arising from this are recommendations for organisations to effectively develop diversity and inclusion initiatives. These recommendations are useful for the FA, other sports organisations, and NGBs to consider when constructing effective initiatives to support women coaches and create a genuine level playing field. Furthermore, the recommendations are useful for coaches of the menteeship programme as changes have been implemented as a direct result of the research findings (see operational lessons learnt), providing future coaches with a more efficacious experience.

Clarity of Programme Objectives

When developing initiatives to enhance diversity and inclusion, a critical aspect to consider is the clarity of the strategic objectives (Nishii & Özbilgin, 2007). A lack of clarity from the organisation and internal stakeholders can be a significant concern for the coaches, leading to unrealistic expectations and questioning of the overall intention of the programme. The lack of clarity of "elite menteeship" in practice led to expectations of employment in an elite setting and questions as to whether the programme was positive or a "tick-box" exercise that provided a detrimental effect on the perceptions of women coaches. While there was an appreciation that the FA is taking "positive action" in implementing a programme to develop women coaches and is one of the few organisations in the sector to do so, this incredulity came in part from the fact that the programme capacity was only four coaches for each cohort and that none of the coaches have since been employed by the FA, despite the FA investing significant sums of money in their development. There is concern that this poses a message to the outside world that these coaches are "not good enough".

Clearly defining "success" and creating a greater sign-on and ownership of the programme across the organisation is more likely to lead to positive outcomes (Doyle & George, 2008). Organisations should consistently revisit and evaluate the purpose and intent of diversity and inclusion programmes to ensure that the objectives are clear and the approach and content is reflective of those aims (Nishii & Özbilgin, 2007). For example, some of the coaches highlighted that they were unsure what the overall purpose of the programme was and so were unsure of the effectiveness of the programme. One of the challenges with creating a diversity and inclusion programme of this nature is evaluation. The risk with using solely quantitative (e.g., numbers and figures) measures is that it only tells one part of the story (Rankin-Wright et al., 2016): the diversity piece. Unless organisations recognise the dual role that the programme can play in not just increasing numbers, but also in building a culture of inclusiveness, the programme is unlikely to affect sustainable longer-term change. Organisations should ensure that there are quantitative and qualitative (e.g., individuals experiences) criteria to measure the effectiveness on both diversity and inclusiveness dimensions, thereby increasing the opportunity to reduce the statistics around under-representation (Snow & Hambrick, 1980).

Moreover, consistent improvement and enhancement of the programme, to ensure it meets the short- and longer-term outcomes, will help to further upskill women coaches, providing them with increased opportunity of employment in high-performance football. Overall, while there is common ground between internal and external stakeholders and a willingness to tackle the issue of under-representation of women in organisations, there often seems to be no common vision on how the interventions translate into outcomes. According to the coaches and internal stakeholders, this often comes from a lack of communication between the organisation and internal stakeholders. Therefore, organisations must incorporate different systematic means of measuring progress in diversity integration, ensuring that the results of evaluation and assessment are shared with all constituencies, as well as taking accountability for ensuring progressive change (Doyle & George, 2008). A lack of clarity and communication means that, while people recognise and support the need for interventions such as this, there are very different views around measuring the efficacy of the programme.

Organisational Culture Towards Inclusion

A major discussion point from the coaches was the culture of the organisation towards inclusion. Inclusion is about creating belonging, connection, and enabling participation and contribution (Roberson, 2006). Hence, there is an argument that there is an important success criterion around the extent to which the coaches are valued for their diversity of thinking and embraced within the organisation. This can help promote collaboration and increase the perceptions of women coaches within and outside of the organisation. If the predominant organisational culture is reflected in departments and teams working in silo, this can culminate with a low level of collaboration across the organisation (Roberson, 2006). This can lead to a lack of awareness of the opportunities the programme presents in enabling coaches to contribute to challenge the thinking in the organisation and bring diversity to the conversation. This is important as cultural awareness is required for diversity and inclusion programmes to succeed (Miller, 1998).

Whilst it was acknowledged that the FA had taken positive steps towards increasing diversity and inclusion, it is important that a programme such as this does not operate in isolation and is embedded within the organisation (Kanter et al., 1992), leading to systemic behavioural and cultural change. On occasions, programme participants experienced exclusion which undermines the very purpose of these programmes. For example, the lack of communication about the broader purpose of the initiative to the programme leads, often led to coaches not being fully included in the placement, meaning they did not feel organisational belonging. This links to the evaluation of such programmes. Organisations often focus on diversity and increasing the numbers but do not derive the full benefits of the programme as they fail to build inclusion. Inclusion unlocks the benefits of diversity and without inclusion, an organisation will not achieve the desired programme outcomes and the longer-term benefits that diversity brings (Stevens et al., 2008).

Programme Ownership

Previous organisational research demonstrates that change initiatives often fail due to the absence of sponsorship and lack of sign-on from key stakeholders (Ang, 2018; Rao & Kelleher, 2003). Although the menteeship programme has been running for a few years, there is still a significant degree of resistance from some stakeholders within the organisation. The coaches perceived that part of this was stakeholders believing that the coaches would eventually take over their job. The resistance towards the initiative emanates in the form of questioning why this programme exists. A stakeholder described how ongoing internal resistance can take up a significant percentage of time. Internal stakeholders who have not been consulted effectively about the purpose of the change programmes often perceive that they have a lack of ownership in acquiring the programme outcomes, which can impede change.

A programme of this nature may benefit from more visible executive sponsorship that sets out a clear vision to ensure the programme achieves what was intended (Ang, 2019). Including a diversity and inclusion programme in wider communications and marketing strategies (both internally and externally) would increase visibility. Furthermore, including stakeholders in the design and implementation of the programme could also lead to a more collaborative approach between departments and other initiatives within the diversity and inclusion programme. Sharing the initiative would help give women a platform to develop themselves and progress in the organisational hierarchy, whilst also giving the organisation a key role in solving this perennial issue (Ang, 2018). A positive organisational culture often provides a sense of security and stability (Sopow, 2006). With regards to the FA menteeship programme, it was acknowledged that it has the potential to be "world leading". However, this will only happen if there is commitment to take a collaborative approach both internally and externally. This programme is an example of a powerful initiative that could be even more impactful if a best practice change management approach was applied.

Variety Versus Bespoke Approach to Placements

An area that produced differences in opinions between the coaches was the structure of the programme. Some of the coaches acknowledged the potential value of completing a variety of different workshops to gain experiences and knowledge in a diverse range of areas, but also questioned whether this approach optimised their development. Coaches were relatively clear about their career aspirations, so the opportunity to choose their preferred placements would create greater clarity for both coach and stakeholders. Therefore, a more bespoke approach that greater aligns the placements with the coaches' personal goals and assists them in getting employment post-programme may be more beneficial (Gravenhorst et al., 2003). Consequently, this approach would create the opportunity to build a personal development plan that could form part of a comprehensive feedback process which could incorporate the coaching competency framework. The coach would leave the programme having achieved clear outcomes, have a better understanding of potential gaps between their current stage of development and desired goals and have the potential to deliver an increased return on investment. This can be directly associated back to the clarity of the objectives. If the aim of the programme is to develop women's skill base, then a variety approach may be more beneficial. However, if the aim is focused on employment, a bespoke approach may be more effective. The structure should adapt to and not undermine the vision of the programme (Kotter, 2007).

Operational Lessons Learnt

Changes have already been made by the current programme manager for future cohorts of coaches following recommendations provided by the research. The first step that has been taken is to develop a marketing and communications strategy to increase the visibility of the programme across the organisation to try and increase collaboration across FA departments. This will be helpful in engaging people in understanding the coaches' journeys and to mainstream the programme within the core activities of the organisation (Roberson, 2006). Time has also been spent before the inductions speaking to the coaches and building relationships with each one of them, such as getting to know their aspirations and concerns. A new induction process has been developed with a range of internal stakeholders invited to take part (e.g., placement leads) to increase collaboration, implement improved planning processes to minimise overlap with camps, and provide other additional learning activities. In response to feedback from the women coaches who participated in the research, it was felt they were left unsupported once they left the programme, but options are now being considered to create an alumni community. This is important to ensure a sense of connection, integration, and belonging for coaches through higher-quality working relationships (Norris et al., 2020).

Concluding Thoughts

Women who pursue careers in coaching, and other sectors, are still under-represented and under-valued (Norman & Rankin-Wright, 2016). Organisations, such as the FA, are creating initiatives to try and reduce this imbalance and increase representation. However, the coordination of these programmes by stakeholders and organisations can heavily impact on the effectiveness and perceptions of women and BAME coaches. If programmes are not designed and implemented effectively, this can have a detrimental effect on inclusion and perceptions of women coaches. For equality programmes to run effectively, clear communication is key. It is recommended to provide internal communication from the organisation to the internal stakeholders to clarify the purpose of the programme and reduce any perceived threats between the stakeholders and coaches. External communication to enhance programme visibility is also vital to increase the positive perceptions and value of the programme by upskilling and providing experiences to women coaches at elite levels. To ensure the programme is consistently developing and providing the best support for women, constant reflections in relation to the approach and aims are required.

Overall, the FA have taken significant steps towards tackling the issue of under-representation of women coaches in the UK but there are still substantial improvements that can be made to support women in organisational settings. Programmes designed to enhance diversity and inclusion are being developed and are important to enhance equality but should systemically include diversity and inclusion within their culture to create opportunities for all to reach high-performance levels.

References

Acosta, R. V., & Carpenter, L. J. (2012). *Women in intercollegiate sport: A longitudinal, national study. Thirty-five year update, 1977–2012 (No. ED570883)*. https://eric.ed.gov/?id=ED570883

Ang, J. (2018). Why career sponsorship matters for advancing women. *Women and Business, 1*(4), 36–43. https://ssl-kolegia.sgh.waw.pl/pl/KGS/publikacje/Documents/Why_career_sponsorship_matters_for_advancing_women.pdf

Ang, J. (2019). The sponsorship game plan for the organisation. In J. Ang (Ed.), *The game plan of successful career sponsorship* (pp. 117–124). Emerald Publishing Limited. https://doi.org/10.1108/978-1-78756-295-020191014

Banwell, J., Kerr, G., & Stirling, A. (2020). Benefits of a female coach mentorship programme on women coaches' development: An ecological perspective. *Sports Coaching Review*. https://doi.org/10.1080/21640629.2020.1764266

Doyle, R., & George, U. (2008). Achieving and measuring diversity: An organizational change approach. *Social Work Education, 27*, 97–110. https://doi.org/10.1080/02615470601141235

Erickson, K., Côté, J., & Fraser-Thomas, J. (2007). Sport experiences, milestones, and educational activities associated with high performance coaches' development. *The Sport Psychologist, 21*(3), 302–316. https://doi.org/10.1123/tsp.21.3.302

The FA. (2014). *The FA Chairman's England commission report*. www.thefa.com/the-fa-chairmans-england-commission-report%20.pdf

The FA. (2020). *The gameplan for growth. The FA's strategy for women's and girls' football: 2017–2020. Final review and report*. www.thefa.com/the-gameplan-for-growth-final-review-and-report.pdf

FIFA. (2019). *Women's football member associations survey report 2019*. https://img.fifa.com/image/upload/nq3ensohyxpuxovcovj0.pdf

Gravenhorst, K. M. B., Werkman, R. A., & Boonstra, J. J. (2003). The change capacity of organisations: General assessment and five configurations. *Applied Psychology, 52*, 83–105. https://doi.org/10.1111/1464-0597.00125

Kanter, R. M., Stein, B. A., & Jick, T. D. (1992). *The challenge of organizational change: How companies experience it and leaders guide it*. Free Press.

Kotter, J. P. (2007). Leading change: Why transformation efforts fail. *Harvard Business Review, 73*(2), 59–67. www.mcrhrdi.gov.in/91fc/coursematerial/management/20%20Leading%20Change%20-%20Why%20Transformation%20Efforts%20Fail%20by%20JP%20Kotter.pdf

Lewis, C. J., Roberts, S. J., & Andrews, H. (2018). 'Why am I putting myself through this?' Women football coaches' experiences of the football association's coach education process. *Sport, Education, and Society, 23*, 28–39. https://doi.org/10.1080/13573322.2015.1118030

Miller, F. A. (1998). Strategic culture change: The door to achieving high performance and inclusion. *Public Personnel Management, 27*(2), 151–160. https://doi.org/10.1177/009102609802700203

Nishii, L. H., & Özbilgin, M. F. (2007). Global diversity management: Towards a conceptual framework. *The International Journal of Human Resource Management*, *18*(11), 1883–1894. https://doi.org/10.1080/09585190701638077

Norman, L. (2008). The UK coaching system is failing women coaches. *International Journal of Sports Science and Coaching*, *3*(4), 447–476. https://doi.org/10.1260/174795408787186431

Norman, L. (2010). Feeling second best: Elite women coaches' experiences. *Sociology of Sport Journal*, *27*, 89–104. https://doi.org/10.1123/ssj.27.1.89

Norman, L. (2014). A crisis of confidence: Women coaches' responses to their engagement in resistance. *Sport, Education and Society*, *19*(5), 532–551. https://doi.org/10.1080/13573322.2012.689975

Norman, L., & Rankin-Wright, A. J. (2016). Surviving rather than thriving: Understanding the experiences of women coaches using a theory of gendered social well-being. *International Review for the Sociology of Sport*, *54*(4), 424–450. https://doi.org/10.1177/1012690216660283

Norris, L. A., Didymus, F. F., & Kaiseler, M. (2020). Understanding social networks and social support resources with sports coaches. *Psychology of Sport and Exercise*, *48*, 101665. https://doi.org/10.1016/j.psychsport.2020.101665

Rankin-Wright, A. J., Hylton, K., & Norman, L. (2016). Off-colour landscape: Framing race equality in sport coaching. *Sociology of Sport Journal*, *33*(4), 357–368. https://doi.org/10.1123/ssj.2015-0174

Rao, A., & Kelleher, D. (2003). Institutions, organisations and gender equality in an era of globalisation. *Gender and Development*, *11*, 142–149. https://doi.org/10.1080/741954264

Roberson, Q. M. (2006). Disentangling the meanings of diversity and inclusion in organizations. *Group and Organization Management*, *31*(2), 212–236. https://doi.org/10.1177/1059601104273064

Saavedra, M. (2009). Dilemmas and opportunities in gender and sport-in-development. In R. Levermore & A. Beacom (Eds.), *Sport and international development* (pp. 124–155). Palgrave Macmillan. https://doi.org/10.1057/9780230584402_6

Schlesinger, T., & Weigelt-Schlesinger, Y. (2012). 'Poor thing' or 'Wow, she knows how to do it'—gender stereotypes as barriers to women's qualification in the education of soccer coaches. *Soccer and Society*, *13*, 56–72. https://doi.org/10.1080/14660970.2012.627167

Snow, C. C., & Hambrick, D. C. (1980). Measuring organizational strategies: Some theoretical and methodological problems. *Academy of Management Review*, *5*(4), 527–538. https://doi.org/10.5465/amr.1980.4288955

Sopow, E. (2006). The impact of culture and climate on change programs. *Strategic Communication Management*, *10*(6), 14–17. www.proquest.com/scholarly-journals/impact-culture-climate-on-change-programs/docview/203574588/se-2?accountid=10792

Stevens, F. G., Plaut, V. C., & Sanchez-Burks, J. (2008). Unlocking the benefits of diversity. All-inclusive multiculturalism and positive organizational change. *Journal of Applied Behavioral Science*, *44*, 116–133. https://doi.org/10.1177/0021886308314460

Theberge, N., & Birrell, S. (1994). The sociological study of women and sport. In D. M. Costa & S. R Guthrie (Eds.), *Women and sport: Interdisciplinary perspectives* (pp. 323–330). Human Kinetics. https://doi.org/10.1080/17460263.2012.654629

UEFA. (2017). *Women's soccer across the national associations 2016/17*. www.uefa.com/MultimediaFiles/Download/OfficialDocument/uefaorg/Women%27sfootball/02/43/13/56/2431356_DOWNLOAD.pdf

12 Reflections on Career Development From Women Who Coach Canadian Elite Track and Field Athletes

Larena Hoeber and Laura Dahlstrom

Background

The picture of Canadian women coaches is usually ones who are young, single, without a family, leave the profession within five years or continue at the community or introductory levels, hold part-time positions, and most likely work with women or girls (Kerr, 2010; Reade et al., 2009; Robertson, 2016). The picture is also informed by research about barriers to coaching or negative experiences in the role (LaVoi, 2016a; Kerr & Marshall, 2007; Norman, 2010a, 2010b; Reade et al., 2009; Robertson, 2010). One such barrier for some is that the Canadian sport system does not adequately support women's entry into and retention in elite coaching positions (Kerr & Ali, 2012; Robertson, 2016). However, missing from the picture are the experiences of women who do enter, succeed, and stay in the coaching profession, especially at the elite level. Norman (2013, p. 5) noted "what is absent within this research is the voice of the woman coach and an analysis of what it means to work within an under-resourced system where men are consistently recruited over women into coaching roles".

Our focus is on keeping women coaches at the elite level of amateur sport and ensuring that other women experience a developmental system that is supportive of them. While women are coaching in the Canadian sport system, we do not see enough of them at the elite level. For example, during the 2016–2017 season, women accounted for 16% of head coaches in the Canadian university system, which is down from 19% in the 2010–2011 season (Norman et al., 2020). Furthermore, only 10% of the coaches on the 2018 Canadian Winter Olympics team were women, while women accounted for 13% of coaches at the 2014 Winter Olympics (Szklarski, 2018). These figures demonstrate that there are opportunities to be a head coach in elite sport, but the number of women in these positions is decreasing. One way to understand this situation was to explore the career development of women coaches who were in the system and identify strategies that kept them in the profession.

For this chapter, we discussed the career development of Canadian women who coached high performance track and field athletes using an ecological framework (Burton & LaVoi, 2016; LaVoi, 2016b). First, we shared their reflections on initiatives to support them as coaches at the system, organisational, and interpersonal levels of sport. Next, we highlighted some of the personal strategies they used to remain coaching within the sport system. For each of these levels, we offered some suggestions to foster women's development as elite coaches. Finally, we provided some ideas for future research in this area.

Ecological Framework

To understand women's coaching experiences throughout their career, we deemed an ecological framework to be appropriate (LaVoi, 2016b). This framework considered influences and supports for one's experiences from macro to micro levels (Burton & LaVoi, 2016). In our study, women commented on four levels of support in relation to their development and involvement as elite coaches. At the *system level*, support included opportunities for women to coach and favourable societal attitudes about women in these roles. *Organisational-level* support for women in coaching included policy development and the establishment of training, mentorship, and networking programmes. At the *interpersonal level*, supports included relationships and connections that women coaches had with those around them, such as family, friends, athletes, and peers. At the *personal level*, we considered how women's emotions, interests, and perceptions impacted their willingness to coach.

Support in the Canadian System

Given the focus of this book, we chose to highlight some of the programmes and initiatives available to women coaches in Canada at the time of the study (for more details, see Marshall & Sharp, 2010; Misener & Danylchuk, 2009; Safai, 2013; Werthner, 2005). As noted by Robertson (2016), this list illustrated that the Canadian approach to the development of women coaches is one "focus[ed] on encouragement as opposed to legislation" (p. 217). Many of the programmes and initiatives are presented as options, rather than requirements, for women and sport organisations to participate in or implement.

- Established in 1974, the *National Coaching Certification Program* (NCCP) is a coach education and training programme sponsored by the Coaching Association of Canada (CAC) with the assistance of national, provincial, and territorial sport organisations. It is typically delivered as workshops for individuals coaching at the entry to elite levels of sport in Canada.
- The *Women in Coaching Program* is a CAC initiative that provided professional development grants, apprenticeship grants, and National Coaching Institute scholarships to women.

- Since 2000, the CAC, in partnership with the Women in Coaching Program, has offered the *Online Mentor Program* to match less-experienced women coaches with mentors.
- The *Women in Coaching Apprenticeship Program* was established in 1999 as part of the *National Team Apprentice Program* (NTAP). The NTAP provided women opportunities to gain coaching experience with their national teams leading up to Olympic Games and major international events. The programme also provided them with financial support and time to complete NCCP certification required to be hired in a full-time position.
- Although not specific to women, the *Canada Games Apprenticeship Program* was developed to assist coaches in obtaining higher levels of NCCP certification and extending their coaching network.
- In 1986, Sport Canada created the *Policy on Women in Sport*. The policy advocated for, rather than mandated, equal opportunities for women as athletes, coaches, officials, and managers in sport.

Participants and Methodology

We used a phenomenological approach to understand women's lived experiences as elite coaches (Marshall & Rossman, 2011; Moustakas, 1994). Since the second author was a former track athlete on a co-ed sport team and given the scant amount of research on women who coach men and women (Walker, 2016), we recruited coaches from this sport. Track and field teams often have 5–10 volunteer assistant coaches who specialise in particular events. Head coaches rely on event coaches' expertise and require them research, plan, and implement training programmes for their athletes.

With the assistance of a key informant, we used snowball sampling to recruit participants in Canada. Our sample was different from the usual picture of Canadian women coaches (cf. Kerr, 2010; Reade et al., 2009; Robertson, 2016). The six women in our study (Mary, Cheryl, Sarah, Tracy, Kelly, and Lisa—all pseudonyms) had 12 to 40 plus years of coaching experience. At the time of data collection, all were coaching, mostly as an assistant coach, for university track and field teams or the national athletics team. In terms of NCCP qualifications, one had Level 2, one had Level 3, and the other four had obtained Level 5 (the highest level), with two of them serving as NCCP instructors. Five were married, three had children, and five had completed at least one post-secondary degree. Given the small population of Canadian women coaching track and field at elite levels, we did not ask them to comment on their ethnicity or if they had a disability, as this additional information could reveal their identities.

We conducted semi-structured interviews using Norman's (2010b) interview guide. She examined elite women coaches' career development in four areas: (1) entry to coaching and early coaching experiences, (2) career challenges and successes, (3) relationships with others in their sport, and

(4) development ideas for aspiring coaches. The interviews ran between 90 and 120 minutes with an average of 110 minutes. All but one interview was conducted via telephone as the participants lived and worked in different communities across Canada. The second author conducted a manual content analysis (Berg, 2009) to examine each woman's experiences individually (within case analysis) followed by a cross-case analysis (Creswell, 2007).

Findings

Participants provided insight into the realities of being a woman coaching high-performance track and field athletes, men and women, in Canada. While they recounted some of their struggles, frustrations, and difficulties as coaches, for the purpose of this chapter we focused on their reflections of the strategies available to them and the impact of those on their coaching careers. At the system level, they commented on elite coaching opportunities within Canada. At the organisational level, some talked about how specific coaching initiatives and programmes impacted their career development. At the interpersonal level, they discussed the support they received from mentors and sponsors.

Reflections on Support at the System Level

Based on the conversations with the participants, it was evident that there were many volunteer opportunities to coach track and field athletes at high schools, private track clubs, provincial teams, and some university teams. In contrast, there were few full-time paid head coaching positions in the sport for women (and men) in Canada.

As volunteer part-time assistant coaches with university, provincial, and club teams, Tracy and Sarah received honorariums for their time. To supplement their income, both had jobs outside of coaching. While Sarah accepted that coaching was a hobby for her, the Canadian head coach job market was a source of frustration for Tracy. She spoke about the difficulties of advancing in the sport system, even though she had earned the highest NCCP certification and two post-secondary degrees (one being a masters in coaching), was an instructor for the NCCP programme, and invested several years volunteering as a coach with the intention to pursue it as a full-time occupation. She always felt supported by her provincial sport organisation but suggested that "once you start putting [coaches] on national teams that's when things get weird". Her comment suggested that coaching decisions at the national level were not always informed by principles of gender equity or transparency. Tracy recounted several negative experiences where she had been appointed as a coach to national teams and was removed at the last minute without an explanation. She later discovered she had been replaced with a man or a non-Canadian coach. For her, it appeared that one's qualifications did not matter; some women were consistently passed over in hiring decisions at the national level.

Some participants suggested that the Canadian amateur sport system had a history of devaluing women as leaders, by paying them less than men and offering them less prominent positions. Mary noted that while her national sport organisation had done a better job in recent years of providing national-level coaching opportunities for women, for many years they hired women as team managers and administrative assistants rather than as coaches. Interestingly, Cheryl felt that being the team manager held a level of prestige as part of the coaching staff. But she encountered a different situation when she began her most recent appointment as a coordinator for with one of the national training centres. She recounted:

> They created a new position . . . and I got that position to be an assistant working with the lead coach and director of the center . . . it kind of led me to feel like a second-class citizen. I felt left out that I didn't really have anything to do and found that my job was more just to do clerical [work]. I was emailed with something to do and expected to do it but there was no input. My expertise was not valued. So just last year they revised my role and took everything to do with the national centre away from me and instead they cut my salary in half again [laugh].

Although it is not clear if her negative experience was specifically related to being a woman or to the position as a coordinator, nonetheless she felt that she was deceived, having been gradually pushed out of a leadership position and forced to accept less pay and power to continue as part of the elite sport system. Mary came to the same conclusion regarding her experience with wage inequality. She recognised that:

> My salary is nowhere near what some of my male counterparts are [making] who have [fewer] credentials than I . . . but then again . . . I like coaching not because I do it for the money because if I did I would be in totally different occupation for sure.

Action item: While there are opportunities to coach elite athletes in Canada, there are barriers in the hiring process, including political decision-making and pay inequalities. To address these barriers, sport governing bodies, university athletic departments, and sport clubs could establish (if they have not already done so) system-wide policies requiring women be interviewed for head coach positions, greater transparency and accountability in hiring decisions, and pay equality for these positions. Ensuring that men and women are paid the same as head coaches could attract more women to these positions. Similarly, women may be more inclined to apply for head coaching positions if they were assured that the hiring process was fair.

Reflections on Organisational Support

At the organisational level, participants commented on the accessibility of coaching certification workshops and adaptations made by their employers to address work-life balance. Additionally, they spoke of the benefits of formal policies and programmes aimed specifically at women, but also highlighted some of the problems with them.

The participants reported varying levels of access to NCCP workshops across Canada. For example, Kelly experienced difficulties completing NCCP certifications due to limited offerings in her province and a lack of information about such opportunities from her provincial sport governing body. Sarah travelled to another province to get her Level 3 technical because it was not offered in her home province, yet it was a requirement to coach her team. It is not surprising that lower levels of the NCCP programme were more readily accessible than higher, specialised levels, since more individuals require entry levels of coaching certification. However, the fact that higher levels were less accessible may explain why some women coaches did not continue beyond entry-level coaching positions. Although this situation impacts men as well, with some women having a greater share of domestic responsibilities, it can be more challenging for them to travel and take time off to access higher levels of training in other provinces.

Managing work-life balance is a commonly identified reason for women leaving the coaching profession (Kamphoff, 2010; Kerr & Ali, 2012; Robertson, 2010). Many participants in this study felt it was crucial for employers and supervisors to find creative ways to retain women interested in coaching during their parenthood years. Cheryl identified several examples of women coaching at the university level who benefitted from flexible work options, such as job sharing, when they started a family. Lisa was the head coach (albeit as a volunteer) of a university team when she was pregnant. She approached her employer (the Dean) to determine how her pregnancy would impact her job:

> We are the biggest team. We have the biggest female team on campus and I'm pregnant. So we have a choice now. Either when I have this baby I'm going back to [my old profession] or I am going to come here full time and you will pay a full-time position.

She was given a full-time coaching position when she completed her maternity leave. Additionally, her direct supervisor (the athletic director) supported her request to take her children along when the team travelled to meets and provided per diems for them. She made similar arrangements with her current employer in the sport system. She felt quite strongly that "if anybody had come up to me and said 'You can't bring this baby with you' I would have walked away". She believed that if sport organisations wanted to keep women coaches they needed to "think out of the box of how to allow children to be with their mothers as much as possible". Lisa's comments are in line with Shaw and Allen's (2009) recommendation that sport organisations establish cultures that value motherhood and work-life balance.

Some participants commented on how women-specific policies, programmes, and initiatives benefited them. For Sarah, the Women in Coaching grants allowed her to attend elite competitions to further her learning in a practical setting at the beginning of her career. The Women in Coaching Programme supported childcare costs, which was particularly important for younger women. Lisa explained "with the apprenticeship programme and the push to keep women in coaching there are a lot of adjustments made for women with babies to continue". While participating in it, Lisa was permitted to use some of the grant to bring a nanny with her when travelling. This flexibility in spending grant money allowed her to travel to gain experience, shadow her mentor, and maintain her relationship with her child.

Interestingly, participants also shared some apprehensions about the women-specific initiatives. Cheryl suggested that quota requirements put women at a disadvantage because they are labelled as a token:

> Like sitting on an [international] cross-country committee where there's now a rule that there has to be two women. So, people think that it is because you are a woman on the committee you must be a token woman and you are not really supposed to have an opinion.

Similarly, Mary felt that being associated with a coaching programme directed towards women altered people's perceptions of her coaching credibility. She recalled:

> I had won nationals in [two track and field events]. And then later on in that summer I was part of the Women in Coaching Programme. People saying, "Well you know because of the Women in Coaching Programme you got pulled into this". Really, I had a coaching degree and coaching portfolio since like 1983. So there [was this] perception that I was a token coach and people really wouldn't really listen to what I had to say. Then when I got the [head coach position] job people [assumed] "Oh well you know this just is another kind of token thing". But they didn't see the work that I had done with the programme the year before [or] the work that I had been doing with the athletes that I was working with.

Women's-only initiatives are often recommended by women as an improvement in their development as coaches (see Lewis et al., 2018). However, organisations should be mindful that there are some disadvantages to them, including the perception of tokenism (see Clarkson et al., 2019), which could contribute to further marginalisation of women coaches.

Action item: The Coaching Association of Canada have proposed many initiatives, policies, and programmes to support the recruitment and retention of women coaches, including those with children. These suggestions include the provision of babysitting services during competitions, flexible work schedules, scheduling practices at mid-day, and establishing co-coaching positions. We recommend that sport governing bodies, university athletic departments, and clubs implement these ideas, which would demonstrate their commitment to women coaches. In turn, it will be easier to recruit and retain women coaches if these initiatives already exist in the organisations.

We recommend that organisations, such as coaching associations, sport governing bodies, and women's advocacy groups, continue to offer women-specific initiatives and programmes. These initiatives are necessary in order to develop a critical mass or a community of elite women coaches. However, these women-specific initiatives need to exist alongside other programmes, such as coach education, networking opportunities, and mentorships, which are offered for all coaches.

Reflections on Support at the Interpersonal Level

Some participants commented on formal mentorships and sponsorships, while others described informal relationships established at coaching clinics and track and field meets. Although some of these relationships were created through organisational programmes, the benefits were experienced at the interpersonal level, and thus are discussed in this section.

Participants noted that their mentors and sponsors were critical to their development as coaches because they were a source of encouragement, knowledge, and expertise. Most mentors were established coaches whom they shadowed or corresponded with on a regular basis. The participants felt comfortable going to them for any coaching questions or concerns they had. Sarah stated:

> I go to the others that I trust . . . when I was in Moncton during an NCCP course [I met a male coach from a Canadian university who I have] learned so much from. I still do because he's got a lot of knowledge. He explains things in a way that I understand them and that makes a huge difference. I had [a] run in [with another male coach who I] learned a lot. I learned a lot from both of them. Never been formally mentored by anybody but I definitely took a lot of positives from them and learned a lot from them . . . I know that I can go to either of them pretty much at any time . . . My abilities to coach my athletes definitely have a lot [to do with] what I have learned from them.

Another benefit of mentors, especially women in those roles, was the opportunity to learn from those who were already succeeding as coaches. Lisa reflected:

> I had two babies at home and a very busy husband. I needed to hook up with people who [had] been there to know that it was possible because some days it seemed impossible. So you need to have someone to call when it feels impossible.

Lisa commented on the advice she received from her women mentors:

> When I got my [national sport organisation] contracts [one mentor] took it. She tore it apart. She fixed it. She made suggestions. [Another mentor] re-wrote it. I mean they made me ask for more money. They just helped me to believe in my worth and not be scared to go and ask for it and they were right every time!

Some participants discussed the availability of men and women as mentors and sponsors. Tracy's sponsor was a paid employee of a national sport organisation and part of his job was to communicate with her regarding coaching. He was a "good sounding board" for her. Tracy appreciated all that he had done for her and for the collegial relationships she had with several male coaches over the course of her career but admitted that "it would be nice to have [a] female [mentor] though".

Our findings showed that mentors and sponsors were an important part of women's development as coaches, but some would have appreciated access to more women in these roles. In contrast, other research (Clarkson et al., 2019; Kerr & Marshall, 2007) has found that relying on men as mentors recognised and leveraged the male-dominated system in sport. Banwell et al. (2019) and Wells and Hancock (2017) have also argued for sponsorship of women coaches in addition to mentorship. Sponsorship implies a concerted effort by someone with power (e.g., connections, high-ranking position, and resources) to advocate for and draw attention to the sponsoree (Wells & Hancock, 2017). While mentors provide valuable advice on careers, sponsors can "open doors of opportunities and raise the visibility of mentees" (Wells & Hancock, p. 141).

Action item: We recommend that new women coaches be paired with men and women mentors and sponsors. This could be accomplished through formal mentorship or sponsorship programmes. Additionally, we recommend that more established women and men coaches connect with new women coaches. Other women coaches serve as role models and can help navigate the male-dominated sport system. Men can use their power and advantage in the sport system to serve as allies to women coaches. Of note, the Coaching Association of Canada has developed guides for mentors,

Personal Strategies Used to Stay in the Sport System

In addition to initiatives at the system, organisational, and interpersonal levels, participants shared personal strategies they used to stay in their coaching positions. The three most commonly used strategies were highlighting their passion for coaching, mentoring athletes to be coaches, and establishing a support system with peers. These strategies illustrated the additional work done by women to remain in the coaching field.

Valuing Coaching as Their Passion

All the women in this study shared that coaching was their passion. Sarah indicated "I have two passions in life: [my job] and then coaching". Tracy took on a part-time job to support her passion of coaching. In contrast, Cheryl deliberately took on less paid work so she could continue coaching while raising her children. Kelly said that her friends envied her for pursuing her passion full time.

> I love this stuff and I love doing it. In fact, a lot of my friends are just going "You are so lucky because you are doing what you love". I know I have a dream job. It's great I just wish I [were] being paid for it [laugh]. That would be great! If I could make a living doing my dream job that would be amazing!

Similarly, Norman (2013) commented that the women coaches in her study were "surviving coaching on a diet of 'love for the game'" (p. 12). She concluded that those who stayed in the system "are reliant on the perceived intrinsic values of their sport to maintain their interest and motivations for coaching" (p. 12).

There is a strong similarity between these participants' pursuit of their passion as coaches and Stebbins' (2007) concept of serious leisure:

> Serious leisure is the systematic pursuit of an amateur, hobbyist, or volunteer core activity that people find so substantial, interesting, and fulfilling that, in the typical case, they launch themselves on a (leisure) career centered on acquiring and expressing a combination of its special skills, knowledge, and experience.
>
> (p. 5)

Although not always by choice, some participants in our study pursued coaching as a form of serious leisure activity. They dedicated many hours a week to practices and competitions. They invested time and money to further their coaching knowledge. They regularly travelled to events to gain experience, network with others, share their coaching knowledge, and observe other coaches. They were passionate about giving back to their sport and were invested in the development and overall well-being of their athletes. It appeared that their passion for coaching contributed to their acceptance of the type of coaching career they had, even if it was not under ideal conditions (e.g., full-time employment or equal pay to their male counterparts).

Action item: We recommend that marketing campaigns and communications directed at women and girls should emphasise passion as a motivation for entering the coaching profession. This approach could, at least, attract and keep some women in coaching while other changes, such as equal pay, childcare provisions, and full-time positions, are widely established in the sport system.

Mentoring Athletes to Become Coaches (3) mentoring

In addition to their passion for coaching, several of the women talked about their joy in mentoring athletes to become coaches. They shared their coaching knowledge with their athletes and encouraged them to pursue coaching once they finished their competitive careers. Sarah felt it was important to educate her athletes about the coaching knowledge they have acquired as they train with her:

> It's letting them know that I'm teaching them things that they are going to be able to go and teach other people at some point if they are interested. Then those leaders automatically come help out at every track meet and are helping... [the] little kids at track meets... if I do my job and what I feel is important to me as a coach [I am] making them good people.

A few coaches commented on mentoring male athletes in their coaching journey. Mary appointed a former male athlete to be her co-head coach. She reflected:

> I think one of my proudest things as a coach so far in my career... [is] bringing new coaches into the mix. I've had a few athletes that competed for me in my first few years at [the university] and they had such a great experience that they wanted to coach. They wanted to give back to the sport. One of those athletes, he graduated like 5 or 6 years ago now, is my assistant coach at the university. He is a teacher. There is no full-time job as far as track goes other than mine but I made him my assistant head coach and he has been able to do amazing things... I helped him a little... in his earlier part of his career but I think

I became more of a friend and a mentor for him and we've struck up more of a great friendship . . . he has become a definite friend and supporter, a confidant. . . . he is a great coach and I have been able to mentor him and help further his career.

Mentorship, for some participants, was not just about being mentored, but also about sharing their knowledge and experience with the next generation of coaches. These mentorship situations provided women with opportunities to be respected and valued for their knowledge and skills, thus contributing to their confidence and worth as coaches. Although mentorship was a strategy that kept them engaged as coaches, it also illustrated to younger athletes that women can be mentors and leaders.

Action item: We encourage women coaches to educate their athletes (both men and women) about the possibility of coaching in the future. They could encourage athletes to start taking and earning coaching certification while still in their competitive careers. They could provide opportunities for their athletes to develop coaching skills, such as working with younger athletes. On a practical side, having women mentor athletes helps to create a critical mass of coaches in the sport system. Additionally, this process helps to establish succession plans for coaching in clubs and organisations.

Networking With Peers

Several participants discussed the importance of social support from family members, close friends, and colleagues, a point that has been noted in previous research (Kamphoff et al., 2010; Kilty, 2006). Norman and colleagues (2018) referred to these as horizontal relationships, as opposed to vertical relationships with supervisors or mentors.

Many participants recognised that networking was a means to building a support system and feeling less isolated or marginalised, which in turn helped to keep them in the profession. One of the benefits of the NCCP workshops, beyond learning specific coaching techniques and skills, was the opportunity to network with and learn from peers. Tracy shared that "speaking with people who are willing to talk to you" about coaching had been important to her development. Tracy, Cheryl, and Sarah liked the approach used within some workshops that acknowledged the wealth of coaching knowledge already present in the group (i.e., among peers). Sarah explained that "the instructor was one of my old coaches . . . I had already learned all that I could learn from him. But the other coaches that were there taught me sooo much and I appreciated that". In Mary's experience, building relationships within the coaching community was valuable to her continued development as a coach.

Being able to have time to sit down with other coaches not just female coaches, but other coaches, other colleagues and just [be] able to vent and discuss the different things that you go through . . . that you have those people to talk to and lean on as far as a resource. It's great to be able to pick up the phone and talk to other . . . female and male coaches alike. You know about different things that we all go through as coaches. There are some things that happen to coaches universally.

When Cheryl instructed NCCP courses she advised new coaches to take advantage of opportunities to network. She explained:

> It's how you get ahead . . . I say to the coaches "Take the NCCP levels. Join the Coaching Association of Canada. Join the provincial coaches association or whether it is Coaches of BC [British Columbia] or Coaches of Alberta or whatever. Read the magazines. Find out about the workshops they give. Sign up for them. That's how you network" . . . wouldn't you want the head coach of that organisation to be that kind of person? Wouldn't you have want them to have met with the other coaches and have gone to workshops?

Many participants in this study acknowledged the importance in surrounding themselves with people who supported and encouraged them to pursue their passion rather than dropping out of coaching. One caution, however, with informal networking is that it can contribute to or be viewed as cliquey, exclusive, or territorial (Shaw & Allen, 2009). The existence of formal networking opportunities, where organisations have control over attendees and match-ups, can alleviate some of the problems associated with informal networking.

Action item: Within the sport system, we recommend that organisations provide formal mentoring programmes and offer a variety of opportunities to network and establish a community of coaches (e.g., social events, workshops, and conferences). The establishment of these programmes and networking opportunities demonstrates organisational commitment to the success of women. In turn, this commitment contributes to a working culture where women are valued. If women feel included and supported in their working environment, they more likely to stay.

Conclusions

The findings from this study may suggest that our participants were thriving as coaches because they were supported at various levels within the coaching ecosystem in Canada. However, the reality was more likely characterised as one of surviving in the current system (Norman & Rankin-Wright, 2018). Until larger-scale changes are established at the system level, such as more opportunities to coach full-time, pay equality for men and women coaches, and improved societal attitudes towards women in leadership roles, women coaches need development pathways and support at all levels in the sport system to be successful (Burton & LaVoi, 2016; LaVoi, 2016b). Sport organisations, governing bodies, and clubs have responsibility for establishing and maintaining working conditions that are attractive to women. These include women-only coaching programmes, networking opportunities, and formal mentorship—sponsorship strategies, which operate alongside other programmes to support all coaches. Organisations and clubs that value and support women are more likely to keep them.

Implications for Future Research

The intent of this chapter was to share strategies that women used to develop as coaches and stay in the field of coaching. As such, we did not go into much detail about the challenges and barriers they faced. One of the challenges that many of them mentioned was the negative attitudes that people had about them as coaches. The women in our study commented that after gaining the trust and confidence of their athletes, they continued to deal with stereotypes and skepticism from athletes' parents and other coaches. For some women coaches, the constant need to prove oneself to other people in the sport system can be a source of frustration and another reason to leave the profession. To address this problem, one area of future research could explore attitudes towards women coaches, through interviews with athletes' family members, sport organisation staff, and sport media. Alternatively, researchers could monitor social media sites (e.g., Twitter, Instagram, and Facebook) for reactions and comments about elite women coaches. Both avenues of research can highlight current perceptions of women coaches and identify areas that need changing. Understanding where the problems lie and with whom can inform the creation of social marketing campaigns, by sport organisations, women advocacy groups, and coach educator programmes, to develop more positive and supportive attitudes and beliefs about women coaches.

At the organisational level, we know that some programmes and initiatives have been established to support women's development as coaches (see the Coaching Association of Canada). Despite this information, there continues to be a low percentage of women coaching at the elite levels in the Canadian sport system (see Norman et al., 2020). This information suggests that other systemic problems exist. To build on Shaw and Allen's work (2009) examining how organisational values impact the experience of women coaches, we recommend conducting ethnographies in sport organisations, clubs, sport governing bodies, and coach education programmes. This avenue of research could provide insight into the everyday life in sport, specifically how elements of culture, such as ceremonies, artefacts, and language, impact women's experiences as coaches. For example, are there informal practices, such as after-work get together, that exclude women? Are women's accomplishments recognised in organisational spaces with plaques, trophies, or awards? Are women's successes as coaches highlighted in daily conversations and communications, like social media?

At the interpersonal level, since men as mentors and sponsors were mentioned by participants, future research could explore men's experiences as allies for women coaches. Additionally, some of the women in our study mentored their athletes to become coaches. We recommend that research examine the experiences of athletes, who were coached and mentored by women coaches. Based on this work, sport organisations can develop strategies to encourage more men and athletes to advocate for women coaches, thus contributing to more inclusive and diverse working environments.

References

Banwell, J., Kerr, G., & Stirling, A. (2019). Key considerations for advancing women in coaching. *Women in Sport and Physical Activity Journal, 27*(2), 128–135. https://doi.org/10.1123/wspaj.2018-0069

Berg, B. L. (2009). *Qualitative research methods for the social sciences* (7th ed.). Pearson Education.

Burton, L., & LaVoi, N. M. (2016). An ecological/multisystem approach to understanding and examining women coaches. In N. M. LaVoi (Ed.), *Women in coaching* (pp. 49–62). Routledge.

Clarkson, B. G., Cox, E., & Thelwell, R. C. (2019). Negotiating gender in the English football workplace: Composite vignettes of women head coaches' experiences. *Women in Sport and Physical Activity Journal, 27*(2), 73–84. https://doi.org/10.1123/wspaj.2018-0052

Creswell, J. W. (2007). *Qualitative inquiry & research design: Choosing among the five approaches* (2nd ed.). Sage.

Kamphoff, C. S. (2010). Bargaining with patriarchy: Former female coaches' experiences and their decision to leave coaching. *Research Quarterly for Exercise and Sport, 81*(3), 360–372. https://doi.org/10.1080/02701367.2010.10599684

Kamphoff, C. S., Armentrout, S., & Driska, A. (2010). The token female: Women's experiences coaching men at the Division I level. *The Journal of Intercollegiate Sport, 3*, 297–315. https://doi.org/10.1123/jis.3.2.297

Kerr, G. (2010). Female coaches' experience of harassment and bullying. In S. Robertson (Ed.), *Taking the lead: Strategies and solutions from female coaches* (pp. 57–72). The University Press.

Kerr, G., & Ali, B. (2012). Perceived barriers to achieving gender equity in Canadian interuniversity sport: Perspectives of athletic directors. *Canadian Journal for Women in Coaching, 12*(2), 1–7. https://coach.ca/sites/default/files/2020-05/CJWC_APRIL2012_EN_1.pdf

Kerr, G., & Marshall, D. (2007). Shifting the culture: Implications for female coaches. *Canadian Journal for Women in Coaching, 7*(4), 1–4. https://coach.ca/sites/default/files/2020-04/WiC_Journal_October_2007_Vol_7_No_4.pdf

Kilty, K. (2006). Women in coaching. *The Sport Psychologist, 20*, 222–234. https://doi.org/10.1123/tsp.20.2.222

LaVoi, N. M. (Ed.). (2016a). *Women in coaching*. Routledge.

LaVoi, N. M. (2016b). A framework to understand experiences of women coaches around the globe: The ecological-intersectional model. In N. M. LaVoi (Ed.), *Women in coaching* (pp. 13–34). Routledge.

Lewis, C. J., Roberts, S. J., & Andrews, H. (2018). 'Why am I putting myself through this?' Women football coaches' experiences of the Football Association's coach education process. *Sport, Education and Society, 23*(1), 28–39. https://doi.org/10.1080/13573322.2015.1118030

Marshall, C., & Rossman, G. B. (2011). *Designing qualitative research* (5th ed.). Sage.

Marshall, D., & Sharp, D. M. (2010). Understanding mentoring as a development tool for female coaches. In S. Robertson (Ed.), *Taking the lead: Strategies and solutions from female coaches* (pp. 117–145). The University Press.

Misener, K., & Danylchuk, K. E. (2009). Coaches' perceptions of Canada's national certification program (NCCP): Awareness and value. *International Journal of Sport Science & Coaching, 4*(2), 233–243. https://doi.org/10.1260/174795409788549580

Moustakas, C. (1994). *Phenomenological research methods*. Sage.

Norman, L. (2010a). Bearing the burden of doubt: Female coaches' experiences of gender relations. *Research Quarterly for Exercise and Sport, 81*(4), 506–517. https://doi:10.1080/02701367.2010.10599712

Norman, L. (2010b). Feeling second best: Elite women coaches experiences. *Sociology of Sport Journal, 27*(1), 89–104. https://doi.org/10.1123/ssj.27.1.89

Norman, L. (2013). The challenges facing women coaches and the contributions they can make to the profession. *International Journal of Coaching Science, 7*(2), 3–23.

Norman, L., & Rankin-Wright, A. L. (2018). Surviving rather than thriving: Understanding the experiences of women coaches using a theory of gendered social well-being. *Sociology of Sport, 53*(4), 424–450. https://doi.org/10.1177/1012690216660283

Norman, L., Rankin-Wright, A. J., & Allison, W. (2018). "It's a concrete ceiling; it's not even glass": Understanding tenets of organizational culture that supports the progression of women as coaches and coach developers. *Journal of Sport and Social Issues, 42*(5), 393–414. https://doi.org/10.1177/0193723518790086

Norman, M., Donnelly, P., & Kidd, B. (2020). Gender inequality in Canadian interuniversity sport: Participation opportunities and leadership positions from 2010–11 to 2016–17. *Journal of Sport Policy and Politics*. https://doi.org/10.1080/19406940.2020.1834433

Reade, I., Rodgers, W., & Norman, L. (2009). The underrepresentation of women in coaching: A comparison of male and female Canadian coaches at low and high levels of coaching. *International Journal of Sport Science and Coaching, 4*(4), 505–520. https://doi.org/10.1260/174795409790291439

Robertson, S. (2010). *Taking the lead: Strategies and solutions from female coaches*. The University Press.

Robertson, S. (2016). Hear their voices: Suggestions for developing and supporting women coaches from around the world. In N. M. LaVoi (Ed.), *Women in coaching* (pp. 177–222). Routledge.

Safai, P. (2013). Women in sport policy. In L. Thibault & J. Harvey (Eds.), *Sport policy in Canada* (pp. 317–349). University of Ottawa Press. https://books.openedition.org/uop/720

Shaw, S., & Allen, J. B. (2009). The experiences of high performance women coaches: A case study of two Regional Sport Organisations. *Sport Management Review, 12*(4), 217–228. https://doi.org/10.1016/j.smr.2009.03.005

Stebbins, R. (2007). *Serious leisure: A perspective for our time*. Transaction Publishers.

Szklarski, C. (2018, February 2). Women coaches in Canadian sport far and few between. *The Star*. www.thestar.com/news/canada/2018/02/02/women-coaches-in-canadian-sport-far-and-few-between.html

Walker, N. (2016). Cross-gender coaching: Women coaching men. In N. M. LaVoi (Ed.), *Women in coaching* (pp. 111–125). Routledge.

Wells, J. E., & Hancock, M. G. (2017). Networking, mentoring, sponsorship: Strategies to support women in sport leadership. In L. J. Burton & S. Leberman (Eds.), *Women in sport leadership: Research and practice for change* (pp. 130–147). Routledge.

Werthner, P. (2005). Making the case coaching as a viable career path for women. *Canadian Journal for Women in Coaching*, 5(3), 1–9. https://coach.ca/sites/default/files/2020-04/WiC_Journal_May_2005_Vol_5_No_3.pdf

13 'If There Were More Women Coaches Around, I Think Things Would Be Different' Women Boxing Coaches

Struggles to Challenge and Change a Male-Dominated Sport Environment

Jorid Hovden and Anne Tjønndal

Introduction

The current research body on the gendering of coaching shows that women coaches still experience discrimination, harassment, and unfair working conditions compared to their male counterparts (de Haan & Knoppers, 2019; Hovden, 2012; Norman, 2010a, 2010b; Tjønndal & Hovden, 2016). Even in Norway, a nation celebrated as a 'champion of gender equality', over 80% of elite level coaches are men (Fasting, Sisjord & Sand, 2017). Thus, coaching remains one of the most gender unequal leadership roles in sport (Hovden, 2014). Especially in male dominated sports, there are few women coaches. For instance, 24% of the members of the Norwegian Boxing Federation (NBF) are women, but only 9% of boxing coaches are women (Hovden & Tjønndal, 2019). Male dominance in boxing is perhaps not surprising, since the best possible outcome of a competition is to render your opponent unconscious through repetitive punches to the head—an achievement that is mostly associated with male aggressiveness rather than femininity (Rana, 2017). Nevertheless, women's involvement in boxing is increasing both globally and in Norway, especially since the inclusion of women's boxing in the Olympic Games in 2012 (Smith, 2014). However, while the number of women boxers in Norway has been steadily increasing since 2016, the number of women coaches remains low (Tjønndal, 2019a).

Training sessions in Norwegian boxing clubs are often in gender-mixed groups, which means that men and women train together and have the same coaches. Hence, most women coach both male and female athletes in boxing. Still, recruiting female coaches has proven to be a major challenge. It is therefore essential to ask the following questions: Why do so few women make the transition from athletes to coaches? What kind of mastering and challenges do they face in their daily coaching practices?

How does the NBF understand and respond to this situation? This chapter aims to address these issues. More concretely, it explores how women boxing coaches experience their everyday lives in that role, and how the NBF's intervention, the "Norway Female Box" (NFB), aims to address their situation. Against this background, the research questions guiding the chapter are given as follows:

1. How do women coaches experience their daily situations and the opportunities for career development in a male-dominated environment?
2. How does the NFB intervention facilitate motivation and ensure better conditions and support for women to engage in coaching?
3. What kinds of recommendations can be suggested for similar women-centred programmes in other sports?

In order to explore these research questions, we have adopted an exploratory research strategy consisting of visual methods in combination with qualitative interviews. Our analysis addresses the gendered, everyday situation of women boxing coaches and how they conceive and experience the NFB intervention as a source of empowerment and support in their career development. At the end of the chapter, we reflect on NFB as a best practice intervention and make some suggestions and recommendations for how sports organisations can enhance the recruitment of women coaches and improve their careers. In the following, and as a backdrop, we briefly describe the objectives and implementation of the NFB project.

Norway Female Box

The intervention was initiated in 2017, as a national project organised and funded by the NBF, which represents a boxing space for and by women. This can be exemplified by the story of the origins of the NFB logo. To determine a logo, the NBF held a competition in which girls and women from all Norwegian boxing clubs were encouraged to submit their own designs. The athletes then voted for their favourite proposal at the first NFB event. Thus, the logo (Figure 13.1) was designed by an athlete and chosen by the athletes themselves.

The aim of NFB is twofold. First, the intervention aims to support female athletes by providing more possibilities for them to develop their boxing skills together with other women boxers and women coaches. This is important, because many female boxers train in local clubs where the majority of the members are boys and men. In other words, they experience being in the minority in their daily sporting environments. Although training with men can be good practice, it does not simulate a realistic boxing situation in the same way as sparring with other women. The long-term goal is therefore to develop more female Norwegian boxers who can compete at an

Figure 13.1 The Norway Female Box logo

internationally high level. Second, NFB aims to recruit, empower, and support female boxing coaches. It does this by arranging training camps 3–4 times a year in different parts of Norway. Additionally, NFB travels to international tournaments with athletes and coaches to give them international competition experience.

The aim to support, develop, and recruit women coaches is implemented in several ways. First, all NFB activities (training camps, competition trips, and educational courses) are planned and organised by local women coaches in cooperation with two female head coaches as the overall leaders. Thus, the coaches gain experience in planning, leading, and coordinating NFB activities and have opportunities to practise and assume a head coach role in groups of 40–70 athletes; a role that most female coaches rarely experience in their local clubs. In addition, women coaches gain experience in coaching athletes in competitions and in practising team roles like cutman (responsible for preventing and treating physical damage to a fighter during the breaks between rounds) and coach. NFB also provides financial support for women coaches who want to go abroad and gain their international coaching degrees with the International Boxing Association (AIBA), and through hosting all-women coaching and referee courses. One of the main objectives is to make female coaches feel more capable of dealing with the various situations that can arise in competition settings, where injuries and knockouts can occur in a split second.

Theoretical Framework: A Practice Approach to Doing Gender in Sport Organisations

A practice approach to doing gender in sport organisations pays attention to the various actors, relationships, and activities and enables us to visualise people's practices in everyday social relations (Kvande, 2007; Smith, 1987). We find this approach to be a fruitful and analytical way of understanding the gendering of coaching practices. Smith (1987) argues that social relationships have power over subjects and reproduce practices independently of individual objectives. This study of how gender relationships are experienced in coaching may thus enable us to show how the structural framework of male dominance works and which relationships and organisational infrastructures are essential in the process of changing dominant relationships.

The practice approach reflects an open understanding of gender, in that it is the activities in different social relationships that decide what will be the meanings of gender. Accordingly, Acker (1997) talks about gendered practices as those requiring knowledge about the specific context in which they take place. This perspective maintains that organisational systems, such as boxing clubs, should be studied through the local activities in which people are engaged (Smith, 1987; Kvande, 2007). Explorations of gendered practices include identifying how concrete relationships and activities are gendered, what people do and say, and how they think about these activities (Acker, 1997). This point of entry facilitates an exploration of how everyday coaching is experienced as gendered, for example, how practices reflect assumptions about inequalities between women and men, and how social relationships are shaped by variations in the relational construction of masculinities and femininities. In this way, the approach also shows how practices and social relationships are shaped by power asymmetries between women and men.

Based on these assumptions, the practice approach offers a lens for identifying how the gendering of coaching in boxing take place by asking who does what, how, where, when, and under which circumstances. The gendered experiences and challenges in women's everyday coaching practices shed further light on how the NFB intervention can respond to these challenges and contribute to develop their coaching careers.

Methods

In order to explore the gendered challenges and experiences of women boxing coaches, we used an exploratory research strategy. First, we asked five coaches engaged in NFB to use their smartphones to each take five photographs that reflected their everyday lives as boxing coaches. For each photograph, the participants described in words what it symbolised in their everyday lives. Parallel to this process, we asked them to write about their joys and challenges of being a woman boxing coach. This type of approach draws heavily on established ethnographic approaches and visual qualitative methodologies (Rose, 2016; Mitchell, 2011). This first step in our data collection led to material consisting of 25 photographs accompanied by brief descriptions and five journal-style reflective notes on their everyday lives as boxing coaches. The second stage in our data collection consisted of qualitative interviews with each coach. In the interviews, we used the photographs and the reflective notes as the basis for the conversation. Each interview was conducted face-to-face in a location chosen by the participants. The interviews lasted between one and two hours and were transcribed. In our presentation of the material, we use a combination of photos (with descriptions) and quotes from the participants' notes and interviews.

The participants were five women engaged as coaches in NFB from four different Norwegian cities (see Table 13.1). The youngest was 23 years of age and the oldest was 45. Two of the women had children and were in a position in which their everyday lives included managing motherhood together with a coaching career. Three of the women coaches had formal coaching education. Four of the five coaches had backgrounds as athletes. None of the women were professional coaches, that is, they were not able to support themselves financially as coaches. Some of the participants' characteristics are summarised in the following table. All the participants have been given pseudonyms to protect their identities.

Visual Methods and Ethical Considerations

All projects based on visual methodologies need ethical considerations in terms of consent. In our study, the data include photographs of people. In some cases, the coaches submitted photographs of themselves, and

Table 13.1 Description of the sample

Name	Age	Coach education	Former athlete career	Children	Vocation	Ethnicity
Hilde	23	National coach education	4 years	None	Engineering student	Norwegian
Tina	43	International coach education	15 years	None	Cleaner	Norwegian
Andrea	45	None	14 years	Two boys	Small business owner	Norwegian
Malika	37	None	None	None	Actress and poet	Non-Norwegian
Charlotte	36	National coach education	11 years	One girl	Associate professor	Non-Norwegian

in other cases, photographs of family members, friends, and athletes in their clubs. Publishing this type of research data has its problems. In our research, we have gone to great lengths to secure informed consent and have provided the participants (the coaches and the people included in their photographs) with written information about the research project and how the photographs will be used. In the case of children, we gathered additional consent from their parents. Our work to secure consent in this project was approved by the Norwegian Centre for Research Data and the Norwegian National Research Ethics Committee. Even though we have been given the legal right to publish the photographs, there is always an issue when it comes to viewing research ethics as something related to law, or as something related to morality. Especially when it comes to photos of children and youth, we have been sensitive as to which photographs have been chosen in order to ensure that publication does not harm the participants.

Joy and Mastering in Women's Everyday Coaching Practices

Boxing—My Life's Passion

Like athletes, coaches often express a deep passion for their sport. Feminist studies have linked girls' and women's passion for sport to feelings of mastering, empowerment, and belonging, also when engaging in male-dominated sports (Hovden, 2014). Sports like boxing allow women to demonstrate hegemonic masculine skills and capacities such as strength, determination, and aggression (Alsarve & Tjønndal, 2019). In this study, through their photographs and interviews (see Figures 13.2, 13.3, 13.4, 13.5), the boxing coaches expressed in various ways a passionate relationship with boxing and the boxing community. In the interviews, one of the coaches expressed it like this: "Boxing has been very passionate for many years, I hardly do other activities". Another stated: "I was hooked already at the first practice and am still unable to quit". Their passion for boxing was reported as one of the main reasons for engaging in coaching. Accordingly, one of the coaches submitted the following photograph with the comment: "As a coach, I seldom have time to practice, but devote myself to sparring whenever I can. I just love to box".

Another participant talked about the boxing club as her family, because as an immigrant she had no family members in Norway. She expressed a feeling of belonging to the boxing community in one of her notes:

> The expression that friends are the family you choose yourself, hit me a lot. I lost my father when I was eleven and my mother nine years ago. My siblings live abroad. I have no family in Norway, but the members of the boxing club are my closest friends, and I like to call them my family.

Figure 13.2 A coach sparring with her athlete

Recruitment and the Mastering of Coaching

The informants were introduced to coaching by older, experienced male coaches in their clubs and were often asked to help with the youngest athletes, mostly children between eight and 13 years of age and sometimes with special responsibility for the girls in the group. Two of the coaches explained this in the following way: "He asked me if I would like to be a coach, he wanted to start a boxing group for girls" and "He asked me to be involved and to go pads with the girls. As a woman and an immigrant, I was someone with whom many of them could identify".

If There Were More Women Coaches 241

This may indicate that women's entry into coaching is based on a relationship that is shaped by gender and by differences in coaching experiences, which may in turn reflect dominant assumptions about men and women in coaching (Tjønndal, 2019b; Hovden, 2004; Norman, 2010b). Nevertheless, despite their roles as assistants coaching children, the interviewees found the coaching role rewarding. They felt mastery and/or that their involvement could make a difference. One of them expressed it like this:

> If I had to state three things that made me happy as a boxing coach, I would say: the feeling of community, the feeling of teamwork, and the feeling of self-confidence that I develop during the boxing practices.

She then added:

> It feels especially rewarding when you know that some of them (youth boxers) have been bullied, are unsuccessful at school and are unable to express themselves when they come to the gym. After only six months you realise how many of them are blossoming—and seem to be quite another person.

In this regard, several of the coaches submitted photographs of themselves together with happy athletes:

Figure 13.3 Coaches and athletes posing for a group photo after training

Other interviewees expressed similar experiences and talked about their mastery and how they were making a difference:

> My strength is that I am good as seeing them . . . how they are. I am also able to motivate them and see their skills . . . to lift them up.
>
> It means a lot to me to see that I can make things possible for them . . . that they have a sense of belonging. I also think that I am a role model for these kids, and that this is something I like to be.

After many years of coaching, most of the interviewees were still in an assistant coaching role, with a main responsibility for the girls or the youngest athletes in the club. Only one of them had become a head coach. It therefore seemed that many of them had developed an image of themselves as a "second-best" coach (Norman, 2010b). But why this image? What kind of social relationships, attributions, gendered practices, and power relations characterised their daily conditions? In the next section, we illustrate how the organising, tasks, and attitudes in their surroundings are gendered.

The Gendering of Dilemmas and Challenges in Everyday Practices

The interviewees talked about the many gendered challenges highlighted in their photographs and stories about their daily coaching practices, and why these led to frustration, reflection, and a lack of career development. Their narratives pointed to dilemmas and relationships shaped by complexity, authority and gendered power.

Tasks, Responsibilities, and Recognition

The feeling of being a second-best coach was dominant amongst most of the interviewees. Several of them talked about a gendered distribution of tasks and responsibilities, and how a continuous questioning of their boxing skills and competences limited their opportunities to develop as coaches. One of the more experienced interviewees had the following reflections:

> In the beginning I never felt I was a real coach . . . but a kind of assistant coach. And I have often wondered if it is because I am a woman. I also have this feeling today, even though I have been in it for a long time. The athletes always ask me questions about the trips, their injuries, advice about how to improve their self-confidence and cope with nerves before competitions. All of this always comes to me . . . I still do not feel worthy to be a head coach . . . I do not feel as competent as

the male coaches when it comes to physical boxing skills . . . but it is not because I not master them . . . I would also like to go pads and lead the athletes in competitions. I don't think I am less competent to go pads and do technical drills. But I never get the chance to do that and improve, because I must do all the other things and it gets too much . . . It is about the gendered thing . . . that women must take on all kinds of responsibility. This is how the vicious circle goes . . . that you try to make everyone satisfied all the time.

Another expressed similar feelings:

I have a feeling that as a woman I have to be in all the vulnerable roles . . . that I must identify with the losers so they can come to me and cry and that kind of thing. In this way I fulfil the expectations of a women coach as the kind, comforting and caring person. The one who serves coffee instead of being on the mat and telling the boys: "Up with your guard".

The coaches with children also mentioned other tasks or responsibilities that mostly fell on their shoulders. In one of the photographs and the attached comment, one of them described the situation like this:

My daughter Veronica (one year old) is with us at boxing practice almost every day. As my husband and I are both coaches, we take it in turns to look after her.

"However, it is always me who takes her home when she gets tired. It has never been the other way around . . . we know that these are social norms we follow . . . so I absolutely experience that I am the woman". The other coaching mother commented on her experiences in this way: "as women we have more of a bad conscience about the children than men".

These gendered practices indicate how women coaches are given tasks and responsibilities that are not directly associated with the core tasks of coaching (Tjønndal & Hovden, 2016). They are rather given responsibility for most of the support services and are thus excluded from tasks and responsibilities that give them status as a head coach and that can promote their coaching careers, such as responsibility for the technical and tactical development of the best boxers. This points to how the everyday practices and social relationships in a male-dominated boxing gym still give men the power to decide which tasks and responsibilities are the most suitable for women, which according to Smith (1987) reproduce the gendered structures in the boxing gym regardless of women's objectives and ambitions as coaches.

Coping With Less Authority, Respect, and "Mansplaining"

One of the main challenges for the interviewees was the feeling of having less authority and respect as women. Several of them highlighted situations of being exposed to "mansplaining":

> I feel I must have more pointed elbows and cannot be myself 100% as my male counterparts can. I must toughen up, empower myself, put on a mask and try to behave like them. It's a pity that you have to put on a mask and play a role to be accepted and respected as a woman . . . If there were more women coaches around, I think things would be different.

The coaches also mentioned situations in which their authority and competence were questioned:

> It is very unpleasant when I have taken responsibility for the female athletes and a male coach comes along and overrides me, telling me that I should do something else. I would never have done that to a male colleague. And fuck . . . what is this about?
>
> I am always somewhat dumbstruck in such situations. Such behaviour is also disturbing to the athletes.

One of the youngest coaches experienced "mansplaining" from male athletes. She described how male athletes interrupted her and told her how to do the sparring. It was obvious that such episodes triggered displeasure, but she said that she had made up her mind to face such situations by offensively thinking: "I'll show you I know what I'm talking about . . . I'm as good as everybody else". Such experiences highlight how the gendering of coaching is visible through expectations of who does what, where, and under what circumstances (Acker, 1997; Kvande, 2007). Situations in which women's authority as coaches is questioned point to asymmetric gender relationships, where male coaches are seen as boxing experts.

Women Coaches for Women Athletes?

Most of the interviewees talked about why they were most comfortable when coaching women athletes:

> I think it is better for me to coach girls, I have more self-confidence here . . . I get angry at myself, being a radical feminist and thinking that men are better suited to coaching men. But that is because I am much more afraid of them (male athletes) . . . and that is also something with boxing. It is much easier to talk to the girls when you spar with them,

you know you take them. When you spar with boys, they might knock you out.

It was also argued that female athletes could benefit from being coached by a woman. As former boxers, the women coaches emphasised their abilities to share gendered experiences of fight situations between women. The coaches emphasised that sparring with men was something quite different and did not always reflect the fight situation faced by female athletes in the ring.

Figure 13.4 Female coach and female cutman at work during a boxing tournament

The advantage of having women coaches for women athletes in competitions was more concretely expressed in connection with the following photo and accompanying note:

> As a woman I have been in this situation and felt it in my body several times . . . felt the nervousness and fear the girls have before entering the ring. As I can easily identify with the situation, I can help them to calm down and focus on the tasks ahead.

However, some of the interviewees experienced that male coaches did not appreciate and understand the value of having a female coach for female athletes. One of the episodes mentioned in the interviews illustrates this:

> I was in a clinch with the male coach so to speak. He did not understand the resource and significance of having separate practices for girls/women or of having a women's group in the club. So, after a while I was no longer allowed to organise such practices. But when I left, most of the female athletes also dropped out. They obviously had a need for these women-only practices.

As other recent studies have suggested (Siegele et al., 2020; de Haan & Knoppers, 2019; Hovden, 2012; Tjønndal & Hovden, 2016), this episode illustrates that a male-dominated coaching environment makes it possible for male coaches to have the power and authority to define what is best for female athletes and female coaches.

In the following section, we shed light on how the NFB intervention responded to some of the aforementioned challenges and how the intervention empowered women coaches and promote their careers.

Norway Female Box: A Space for Female Community, Empowerment, and Career Development

As previously indicated, the NFB intervention aimed to empower and develop the careers of female boxing coaches and help more women to make the transition from athletes to coaches. During the three years of the intervention, the female coaches involved participated in training camps, competition trips, and educational coaching programmes and were actively involved in the planning, organising, and implementation of these activities. In the following, we give some glimpses as to how the interviewees experienced being part of NFB.

A Meeting Point for Sharing, Cooperation, and Community

The interviewees talked a lot about the importance of NFB as a place for meeting other female coaches and sharing experiences in a safe and special atmosphere:

> It is so special . . . both in the boxing practices with only female athletes and when we are eating pizza together. We are, so to speak: "high

on life" . . . it shows that we share something together that we love. In the club we are a lot more alone in our everyday practices. In Female Box, it is the team feeling that dominates. For me this is magic and something I miss in my club . . . I feel a lot more included here. I think women are better at supporting, cheering and cooperating.

Another narrative maintained that the NFB practices were different from those of the club in other ways:

If it had been male boxing instead of female, I would never have dared to take on the responsibility for an entire programme . . . Coaching males would at least take one week to prepare, because I had to show a perfect programme. I think . . . for boxing that is such a masculine sport, Female Box is needed in order to recruit more women . . . here we have a safe space.

The interviewees pinpointed that the discussions at NFB gatherings had made them more aware of their vulnerable situation as "solitary swallows" and "tokens" in a male-dominated environment (Kanter, 1977). This consciousness raising had been valuable in their analyses of why they often felt second-best and marginalised in the club. Several of them said that NFB had led to a growing acknowledgment of their problems and challenges as female coaches, which implied that these were not seen as being rooted in a lack of skills and competences, but in the gendered power relationships that structured the dominant interaction patterns in the boxing gym (Acker, 1990; Hovden, 2012). This also seemed to lead to a growing awareness of the importance of women-only meeting places, such as NFB, to initiate discussions about the implications of male dominance for their career development. The interviews also touched on the importance of having female colleagues around during sparring, competitions, and participation in coaching courses; this was experienced as being safer. One of the head coaches referred to an episode in which she had felt very uncomfortable and insecure, when attending an international coaching course:

My experience of being one of the only women in the international coaching course was challenging. Firstly, the frustration that my competence and role as a coach were not taken seriously and recognised, and secondly, and more threatening, I felt chased as a woman . . . In the middle of the night, every night, some of the male coaches participating in the course would come and knock on my door. I was scared about what might happen . . . if they managed to come inside. I used a chair to block the door handle. That was the only way I could sleep and feel somewhat safe . . . I used most of my energy to cope with such unpleasant surroundings and I was always on guard. Since then I have really struggled to recommend other women coaches to travel abroad for the international coaching certificate for boxing. It's not safe to travel alone to these courses as a female boxing coach.

Based on such experiences, it is clear why women-only boxing communities, such as NFB, want to share experiences and knowledge about what it means to be a small minority in a male-dominated environment, and how the gendering of boxing affects their mastery of the sport and their challenges as boxing coaches. In this way, NFB activities empower and give new energy to better face and deal with the gendered challenges in their coaching careers. The sharing of experiences in NFB training camps aims to provide insights into how the gendering of social relationships, concrete activities and authority give women less power and freedom to define situations and develop their capacities and careers (Smith, 1987; Tjønndal & Hovden, 2016).

The Significance of Female Role Models

Several interviewees mentioned the importance of having female role models, such as the head coaches in NFB. They referred to these head coaches as women who dared to assume authority in the coaching role, show empowerment and strength, and in this way make themselves visible and respected, also to their male counterparts. One of the coaches expressed it like this:

> I think this may make a turn, people think, yes! I can also be a boxing coach . . . It becomes, in fact, a real possibility . . . It is cool somehow that women boxing coaches dare to go in new directions. It gets attention.

The power that accompanies a role model position seems to have the most impact in the first phase of the recruiting process, when it is important to show that it is also possible for women to make it to the top (Hovden, 2012). On the other hand, feminist scholars researching sports organisations (Adriaanse, 2016; Claringbould & Knoppers, 2007; Hovden, 2016; Elling et al., 2019) have concluded that few women in top positions, make women "tokens" (Kanter, 1977) because they have too little power to challenge and change the male hegemony. This leads us to a few concluding remarks about the potential and limitations of NFB as a change agent and a case of best practices.

Recommendations for Women-Centred Coaching Programmes

As well as highlighting the joys and challenges of mastering coaching, this chapter has illustrated some of the gendered challenges that women coaches face as leaders in a male-dominated sport like boxing. Furthermore, the material demonstrates how NFB responds to such challenges and create opportunities for career development by providing a women-only community and a safe space in which to share experiences and develop coaching skills. Based on the experiences of the women boxing coaches in NFB, we make five recommendations for similar programmes as follows:

1. Specific Coaching Skills

Something that is highlighted in our material is that the career development of women coaches includes a strengthening of diverse skills and competences. Thus, in order to support women coaches in male-dominated sports, it seems important for women-centred coaching programmes to focus on the development of the sport-specific skills that are relevant to coaching. In boxing, this includes being able to act as head coach for a group of athletes, learn technical and tactical strategies for sparring, being responsible for planning training sessions, and practising how to plan training programmes for specific athlete groups for longer periods of time. The NFB practices show that training women coaches in such skills gives them confidence in their coaching role. However, the experiences from the programme show that sport-specific skills need to be phased, depending on the career level and ambitions of each coach. This leads us to the second recommendation.

2. Task and Skill Development Adapted to Their Coaching Careers

In any sports context in which there are few women coaches, those who are active are likely to be at different stages in their coaching careers and thus have different ambitions and goals. Therefore, it is important that gender-segregated programmes for women coaches cater for this and allow for a diversity of activities, so that apprentice coaches and experienced coaches can both benefit from the programme. In NFB, this is done by planning a variety of training and competition activities each season. For new coaches, planning a training session for a large group of athletes and leading the session seem to be challenging enough. Established women coaches with ambitions of an elite sports coaching career need to travel with athletes to international tournaments. In the case of boxing, they need experience of leading athletes in competition, sitting at the ringside having a variety of skills, including first aid, so they are enabled to treat any minor injuries that might occur during a boxing match.

3. Community Building and Social Activities

As we have shown, the women coaches in our study highlight that the strong community ("we-feeling") in NFB plays an important role in their ambitions to continue their coaching careers. They appreciate doing things together and can share experiences with like-minded people. Similar coaching programmes should therefore give priority to the provision of different spaces where women coaches can exchange ideas and experiences and strive to create an atmosphere where they feel safe to articulate their positive and negative experiences as women coaches, especially when coaching in very male-dominated sports.

4. Discussions About Distribution of Tasks, Mansplaining, and Gendered Power Relations

If women coaches are to develop their coaching skills and assert themselves in a male-dominated environment, they need to be aware of the gendered power relations that shape their everyday coaching practices. This means initiating discussions about who does what in the boxing club and suggesting tools that challenge and question an unfair task distribution in the coaching teams and cases of mansplaining. In these discussions, it is essential to help women coaches to understand and accept that such challenges are part of the gendered structures and the uneven gendered relations in coaching.

5. Challenges and Risks That Women Coaches Face in a Male-Dominated Environment

As shown, women often face different forms of sexism and harassment in male-dominated contexts. Our interviewees indicate that this seems more likely to happen with coaches who want to develop their coaching careers. In the case of the NFB programme, the experiences of sexual harassment faced by some women coaches were especially challenging, for example, when attending international coaching courses where they were the only woman amongst older men. The sharing of such experiences at NFB has led to a general recommendation in the NBF that women coaches should travel or attend such contexts with at least another woman. From this point of departure, we recommend that educational coaching programmes and other sports initiate discussions and guidelines on how to relate to such challenges and risks.

Feminist studies of sport organisations show that women-only interventions such as NFB, are not always sustainable in the long run. When such initiatives end, the situation often returns to status quo and even to setbacks (Elling et al., 2019; Hovden, 2016). Therefore, such initiatives are not the only path to achieving gender-inclusive coaching environments in the long run. On the other hand, as the first intervention related to women's situations in boxing, NFB seems to have been an important intervention for empowering women coaches and motivating them to develop their careers. In this sense, NFB could be considered as a best practice. The point of departure has been to improve women's situation by visualising women's conditions, providing them with relevant skills, and helping them to feel empowered and supported to better face barriers and gain insights into

Figure 13.5 Norway Female Box athletes walking home together from training

what it means to be a woman amongst older and more experienced men. However, the future of NFB as a best practice will depend on how it is integrated into the NBF as part of its general activities, for example, in strategic plans and coach education programmes. Such an integration is needed to transform NFB from an initiative that is dependent on a few individual women trail blazers to an institutional practice in the boxing world.

References

Acker, J. (1990). Hierarchies, jobs, bodies: A theory of gendered organizations. *Gender & Society*, *4*(2), 139–158. https://doi.org/10.1177/089124390004002002

Acker, J. (1997). Rewriting class, race and gender. Problems in feminist rethinking. *Sosiologisk tidsskrift*, *5*(2), 93–103.

Adriaanse, J. (2016). Gender diversity in the governance of sport. The Sydney Scoreboard global index of participation. *Journal of Business Ethics*, *137*(1), 149–160. https://philpapers.org/go.pl?id=ADRGDI&proxyId=&u=http%3A%2F%2Fdx.doi.org%2F10.1007%2Fs10551-015-2550-3

Alsarve, D., & Tjønndal, A. (2019). The Nordic female fighter: Exploring women's participation in mixed martial arts in Norway and Sweden. *International Review for the Sociology of Sport*, *55*(4), 471–489. https://doi.org/10.1177%2F1012690218822307

Claringbould, I., & Knoppers, A. (2007). Findinga a 'normal' woman: Selection processes for board membership. *Sex Roles, 56*(7–8), 495–507. https://doi.org/10.1007/s11199-007-9188-2

de Haan, D., & Knoppers, A. (2019). Gendered discourses in coaching high-performance sport, *International Review for the Sociology of Sport, 55*(6), 631–646. https://doi.org/10.1177%2F1012690219829692

Elling, A., Hovden, J., & Knoppers, A. (2019). *Gender diversity in European sport governance.* Routledge.

Fasting, K., Sisjord, M. K., & Sand, T. S. (2017). Norwegian elite-level coaches: Who are they? *Scandinavian Sports Studies Forum, 8*, 29–47.

Hovden, J. (2004). *Makt, motstand og ambivalens. Betydningar av kjønn i idretten* (Doctoral disseration). Høgskolen i Finnmark, UiT Munin. https://munin.uit.no/handle/10037/6258

Hovden, J. (2012). Demokrati eller hegemoni. In J. Hvenmark (Ed.), *Är idrott nyttigt?* (pp. 164–194). SISU Idrottsbøcker.

Hovden, J. (2014). Kjønn og maktpraksisar i topptrenarverksemda. In G. von der Lippe & H. K. Hognestad (Eds.), *Kjønnsmakt i idrett og friluftsliv* (pp. 210–241). Novus forlag.

Hovden, J. (2016). The "fast track" as a future strategy for achieving gender equality and democracy in sport organizations. In Y. Auweele, E. Cook, & J. Parry (Eds.), *Ethics and governance in sport. The future of sport imagined* (pp. 35–43). Routledge.

Hovden, J., & Tjønndal, A. (2019). The gendering of coaching from an athlete perspective: The case of Norwegian boxing. *International Review for the Sociology of Sport, 54*(2), 239–255. https://doi.org/10.1177%2F1012690217715641

Kanter, R. M. (1977). *Men and women of the corporation.* Basic Books.

Kvande, E. (2007). *Doing gender in flexible organizations.* Fagbokforlaget.

Mitchell, C. (2011). *Doing visual research.* Sage.

Norman, L. (2010a). Bearing the burden of doubt: Female coaches' experiences of gender relations. *Research Quarterly for Exercise and Sport, 81*, 506–517. https://doi.org/10.1080/02701367.2010.10599712

Norman, L. (2010b). Feeling second best: Elite women coaches' experiences. *Sociology of Sport Journal, 27*(1), 89–104. https://doi.org/10.1123/ssj.27.1.89

Rana, J. (2017). Ladies-only! Empowerment and comfort in gender-segregated kickboxing in the Netherlands. In A. Ratna & S. F. Samie (Eds.), *Race, gender and sport—the politics of ethnic 'other' girls and women* (pp. 148–167). Routledge.

Rose, G. (2016). *Visual methodologies. An introduction to researching with visual materials.* Sage.

Siegele, J. L., Hardin, R., Taylor, E. A., & Smith, A. B. (2020). "She is the best female coach": Female swimming coaches' experiences of sexism. *Journal of Intercollegiate Sport, 13*(1), 93–118. https://doi.org/10.17161/jis.v13i1.11676

Smith, D. (1987). *The everyday world as problematic.* Open University Press.

Smith, M. (2014). *A history of women's boxing.* Rowman & Littlefield.

Tjønndal, A. (2019a). "Girls are not made of glass!": Barriers experienced by women in Norwegian Olympic boxing. *Sociology of Sport Journal, 36*(1), 87–96. https://doi.org/10.1123/ssj.2017-0130

Tjønndal, A. (2019b). 'I don't think they realise how good we are': Innovation, inclusion and exclusion in women's Olympic boxing. *International Review for the Sociology of Sport*, *54*(2), 131–150. https://doi.org/10.1177%2F1012690217715642

Tjønndal, A., & Hovden, J. (2016). Kjønn som sparringspartner. En kvalitativ undersøkelse av ledelse og betydninger av kjønn blant norske boksetrenere. *Tidsskrift for kjønnsforskning*, *39*(3–4), 185–202. https://doi.org/10.18261/issn.1891-1781-2016-03-04-04

Index

Note: Page numbers in *italic* indicate a figure and page numbers in **bold** indicate a table on the corresponding page.

academic studies 122–123
access 142–144
accountability measures 63–64
actionable recommendations 114–116
actions for change **56–57**, 126–132; calls to action 82–85
advocacy 59–62, 85
analysis 18–19; *see also* meta-analysis
Andrés, Ana x
Aotearoa New Zealand 159–161, 172–173; cultural safety 163–164; "fitting in" versus "finding belonging" 164–166; recommendations 167–172; representation 166–167; shared experiences and the language of "otherness" 161–163
appointment to precarious positions 21
assessing 146–147
authority 244

Barker-Ruchti, Natalie x
barriers 70–71, 86, *179–180*; to career development 75–78; marginalising effects of gender construction 73–75; methods 71–73; organisational discrimination 79–80
belonging 164–166
bespoke approach 212
best practices 148–149
biases 139–146
body, the 95–96
Boucher, Courtney J. x
Bourdieu, Pierre 90–91, 96–98
boxing 234–235, *245*; joy and mastering in 239–248; methods 237–239; Norway Female Box (NBF) 235–236; recommendations 248–251; theoretical framework 237
British Horse Society (BHS) 92–93, **92–93**, 95–97, 99
burden 166–167
Burton, Laura J. x, 73

calls to action 82–85
Canada 217–218, 229–231; ecological framework 218; organisational support in 222–224; participants and methodology 219–220; personal strategies used to stay in the sport system in 226–229; support in 218–219, 220–221; support at the interpersonal level in 224–226
capital (Bourdieu) 96–98
career, coaching as 142–143
career development 75–78, 177–178, 217–218, 229–231, 246–248; ecological framework 218; and organisational support 222–224; participants and methodology 219–220; personal strategies used to stay in the sport system 226–229; and support at the interpersonal level in 224–226; and support at the system level 218–219, 220–221
career trajectories 70–71, 86; barriers and strategies 75–78; calls to action 82–85; graduate-level coaching education 79; and marginalising effects of gender construction 73–75; methods 71–73; organisational discrimination and

Index 255

social responsibility 79–80; strategies in finding gumption within a marginalising coaching profession 80–82
Catalonia 123–124, **123**, 130
challenges 198–199, 242–246, 250–251
challenging a gendered coaching environment 98–100
change: actions for 127–132; the path forward for equality for women coaches 59–66; resistance to 125–127; signal change 15; sustainable change 1–3; transformational change 53–59
choices 15–16
Churchill Fellowship 161
clarity 209–210
Clarke, Nicola J. xi
coach certification courses **123**
coach characteristics **202**
coach education (CE) 107–109; and gendered interactions 113–114
coach educators 107–108; socialisation of 111–114; *see also* university coach educators
coaching as a career 142–143
coaching education **30**, 34–43, **35**, **123**; gendered body in 95–96; gendering 44–45; *see also* graduate-level female sports coaching students; university coach education programmes; university coach educators
coaching practices 239–248
coaching programme design 167–168
coaching programmes 168–169; recommendations for 248–251
coaching roles: access to 142–144; in football 34–38
coaching skills 249
coach–stakeholder relationships 204–205
coach students: socialisation of 111–114
coding 18–19
co-headcoaching 129–130
community 246–248
community building 249–250
competence 65–66
contextual issues 121–122
cooperation 246–248
coping 244
crisis 22
critical initiatives 55–57
cultural conduits 169–171

cultural diversity 159–161, 171–173; and cultural safety 163–164; "fitting in" versus "finding belonging" 164–166; recommendations 167–172; and representation 166–167; shared experiences and the language of "otherness" 161–163
cultural safety 163–164, 168–169, 171–172
Cunningham, George B. xi, 13, 15, 171
cutman 236, *245*

Dahlstrom, Laura xi
data analysis 72–73
data collection 18–19
data generation 72
debiasing 147–149
decision-makers 59–62
decision-making positions **57**, 61, 63–64, 124
de Haan, Donna xi, 96
Demers, Guylaine xi
demographics 72, **72**, 124, 145, 183, **202**
depersonalisation 44
design 72
developing women in sport coaching *see* lifespan career approach
development 185–186
DFB 30–31, **30**, 43–44, 46n2
dilemmas 242–246
Din, Cari xi
discrimination against men 64–65
disrupting 98–100
diversity: impact of 60–62
Dudeniene, Lolita xii
Dumbell, Lucy xii

ecological framework 218
Ecological Intersectional Model 71, *179–180*
Ecological Systems Model 71
education *see* coaching education
educational coaching environments 199–200
empowerment 246–248
Energise Stage 191–192
Engagement Stage 184–190
Entice Stage 182–184
Entry Stage 184
equality 59–66; mirage of 122–127
equestrian coaches 96–98
equestrian sport 89–90, 98–100; and Bourdieu's concept of capital 96–98; and Bourdieu's concept of field 90–91;

Index

and the habitus of coaching 92–95; and the valourisation of the gendered body 95–96
ethical considerations 238–239
evaluation 149, 209–214; challenges for women coaches 198–199; coaches' expectations of the menteeship programme 205–208; coaches' experiences of work-based placements 203–204; coaches' perceived stakeholder programme perceptions 208–209; coach-stakeholder relationships 204–205; FA elite coach mentorship programme 200–202; methodology 202–203; women's experiences of social and educational coaching environments 199–200
everyday coaching practices 239–248
Exit Stage 190–191
expectations 205–208; *see also* gendered expectations; stereotypic expectations
experiences: of coaching environments 199–200; of work-based placements 203–204

FA Elite Coach Menteeship Programme 200–201, 205–208
familial commitments 149–150
fellows of the BHS 92–93, **93**
field (Bourdieu) 90–91
finding belonging 164–166
fitting in 164–166
football 34–38, *198*; gendering coaching education programmes in 44–45; interactional situations of 40–41; organisational structures of 38–40
football clubs 44
football coaches 30–32; dealing with the effect of gender stereotypes 43–45; gender stereotypes and their social function 32–33; impact of gender stereotypes 34–43; mentoring of 45
football coaching, self-exclusion of women from 41–43
future directions 133

game officials **56**
gender 11–12, 22–24, 107–108; and the glass cliff 13–22; practice approach to 237
gender construction 73–75

gendered body 95–96
gendered career development 177–178
gendered coaching environment 98–100
gendered expectations 149–150
gendered institutions 110–111
gendered interactions 113–114
gendered power relations 250
gender equity 1–3, 89–91, 99–100
gender-equity policies: actions for change 127–132; contextual issues 121–122; future directions 133; research into suggested changes 122–127
gendering 44–45, 140; of dilemmas and challenges in everyday practices 242–246; *see also* individual gendering
gender lens training 130–132
gender stereotypes 30–32, *35*; dealing with the effect of 43–45; impact of 34–43; social function of 32–33
gender structures 104–110; actionable recommendations 114–115; individual gendering 111–114; and university coach education programmes 110–111
Germany 4, **30–31**, 57, 124, 199
girls 128–129
glass cliff 11–12, *20*, **21**, 22–24; antecedents 14–16; key tenets 13–14; meta-analysis of 18–22; outcomes of 16–17
graduate-level female sports coaching students 70–71, 79, 86; barriers and strategies 75–78; calls to action 82–85; and marginalising effects of gender construction 73–75; methods 71–73; organisational discrimination and social responsibility 79–80; strategies in finding gumption within a marginalising coaching profession 80–82

habitus 92–95
Harvey, Stephen xii
high-performance women coaches 213–214; challenges for women coaches 198–199; FA elite coach menteeship programme 200–201; methodology 202–203; programme evaluation 209–213;

research findings 203–209; research programme 201–202; women's experiences of social and educational coaching environments 199–200
Hinojosa-Alcalde, Ingrid xii, 124, 130
hiring 65–66
historical statistics 53–55
Hoeber, Larena xii
Hovden, Jorid xii

inclusion 211
individual gendering 111–114
individual-interpersonal level support 187–188
Ingwersen, Florian xiii
interactional situations 40–41
interpersonal-level support 188–190, 224–226

joy 239–248
judges **56**

LaVoi, Nicole M. xiii, 57–59, 71, 73
leadership development 148–149
leadership roles 11–16, 21–23, *131*
levels of systems support 186–190
lifespan career approach 177–180; the Energise Stage 191–192; the Engagement Stage 184–190; the Entice Stage 182–184; the Entry Stage 184; the Exit Stage 190–191; stages of career progression for women in sports coaching 180–192; utility of the SCPM 180–182
Lithuania 108–109

male-dominated sport environment 235, 239, 243, 246–251
mansplaining 244, 250
marginalising effects 73–75
mastering 239–248
mentoring 45, 227–228
mentoring programme 200–201; evaluation 209–213; key findings from the research 203–209
mentors 169–171
mentorship opportunities 83–85
meta-analysis 18–22
methodology 202–203, 219–220
methods 71–73, 237–239
monitoring progress 63–64
multilevel approach 34–43

multilevel gendered system of sport 178–180

networking 143–144, 228–229
Newton, Ajhanai Channel Inez xiii
New Zealand *see* Aotearoa New Zealand
Norman, Leanne xiii, 91–92, 166–167, 217, 219, 226, 228
Norris, Luke A. xiii
Norway Female Box 235–236, *236*, 246–248, *251*

objectives 209–210
occupational turnover 144
Olympic Games **55**
operational lessons 213
organisational culture 211
organisational discrimination 79–80
organisational inclusiveness 146–147
organisational-level support 188–190
organisational structures 38–40
organisational support 222–224
organisation-level practices 138–139, 150–151; to support women in coaching 144–150; understanding biases 139–144
organisations 140; addressing bias in 144–146; *see also* sport organisations
otherness 161–163
ownership 211–212

participants 71–72, 219–220
PASS 122–123
passion 226–227, 239
pedagogies of opportunity 82–83
peers 228–229
perceived stakeholder programme perceptions 208–209
performance 16–17, 22
personal strategies 226–229
physical education 131–132, *131*
placements 212
policies *see* gender-equity policies
policymakers 133
political levers 62–64
power 96–98
power relations 250
practice approach 237
precarious positions 21
Price, Letitia xiii–xiv
privilege 166–167
programme evaluation 209–213

promotion practices 44
Purdy, Laura xiv, 96

quality 65–66
quotas 64–66

racialisation 140
recognition 96–98, 242–243
recommendations 209–213
recruitment **146**, 147–148, 240–242; depersonalisation of 44
red flags 146–147, **146**
reinforcing 98–100
representation 166–167
researchers 133
research programme 201–202
resistance to change 125–127
respect 244
responsibility 166–167, 242–243
risks 250–251
role models 169–171; impact of 62; significance of 248

Schlesinger, Torsten xiv
seeding interest 128–129
self-exclusion 41–43, 45
Serra, Pedrona xiv
sex-integrated sport 89–90, 98–100; and Bourdieu's concept of capital 96–98; and Bourdieu's concept of field 90–91; and the habitus of coaching 92–95; and the valourisation of the gendered body 95–96
shared experiences 159–161, 172–173; and cultural safety 163–164; "fitting in" versus "finding belonging" 164–166; recommendations 167–172; and representation 166–167; and the language of "otherness" 161–163
sharing 246–248
signal change 15
skills 249
social activities 249–250
social coaching environments 199–200
social exclusion 30–32; dealing with the effect of gender stereotypes as mechanisms of 43–45; gender stereotypes and their social function 32–33; impact of gender stereotypes on 34–43
social function 32–33
social responsibility 79–80
Soler, Susanna xiv
sparring 235, 239–240, *240*, 244–245, 247, 249

sport leadership 12, 21
sport organisations 237
sport practitioners 167–172
Stages of Career Progression Model (SCPM) *179–180*; the Energise Stage 191–192; the Engagement Stage 184–190; the Entice Stage 182–184; the Entry Stage 184; the Exit Stage 190–191; utility of 180–182
stakeholders 208–209; *see also* coach–stakeholder relationships
statistics 53–55
stereotypes 14–15, 141–142; *see also* gender stereotypes
stereotypic expectations 34–38, 41–43
strategic plans 62–63
strategies 75–78
support 70–71, 144–150, *179–180*, 199–201, 208–210; advocacy opportunities 85; in the Canadian system 218–219; and career development 75–78; and graduate-level coaching education 79; at the interpersonal level 224–226; levels of systems support 186–190; mentorship opportunities 83–85; multilevel gendered system of 178–180; organisational 222–224; pedagogies of opportunity 82–83; strategies in finding gumption 80–82; at the system level 220–221
sustainable change 1–3
Sweden 108–109
Symons, Julia xiv
systemic discrimination 59–60
system level 220–221
systems support 186–190

tasks 242–243, 249, 250
textbooks 85, 107, 131, *131*
Tjønndal, Anne xiv–xv
track and field 217–218, 229–231; ecological framework 218; and organisational support 222–224; participants and methodology 219–220; personal strategies used to stay in the sport system 226–229; and support at the interpersonal level 224–226; and support and the systems level 218–219, 220–221
transformational change 53–59; the path forward for equality for women coaches 59–66
treatment discrimination 143
turnover 17, 22, 144

umpires **56**
United Kingdom (UK) 108–109, 159–161, 172–173; cultural safety 163–164; "fitting in" versus "finding belonging" 164–166; recommendations 167–172; representation 166–167; shared experiences and the language of "otherness" 161–163
United States 159–161, 172–173; cultural safety 163–164; "fitting in" versus "finding belonging" 164–166; recommendations 167–172; representation 166–167; shared experiences and the language of "otherness" 161–163
university coach education programmes 110–111

university coach educators 104–110; actionable recommendations 114–115; and gendered institutions 110–111; and individual gendering 111–114

valourisation 95–96
valuing coaching 226–227
variety 212
visual methods 238–239

Weigelt-Schlesinger, Yvonne xv
Werthner, Penny xv
women-centred coaching programmes 248–251
women's choices 15–16
Women's Football Member Association *198*
work-based placements 203–204
workplace 177–178